ADVANCE PRAISE FOR *THE RETAIL GAME: PLAYING TO WIN*

"Twenty-seven years ago we were so full of the vision of what we wanted our business to be. I wish I had read a book like this. I didn't know what I didn't know! I think there is something for all retailers in this book."

DAVID RUSSELL, PRESIDENT, SPORTING LIFE LTD.

"Written by a retailer for a retailer. Albert Plant provides real insight into successful retailing and eloquently bridges the knowledge gap between Retail 101 and the Graduate Retail degree that is, more often than not, earned on the aisles of the shop floor. This text is informative, entertaining and equally good reading for the aspiring young merchant to the seasoned retail executive."

JOHN R. BRISON, PRESIDENT, THE OLDE HIDE HOUSE
AND ACTON LEATHER CO.

"*The Retail Game* is an excellent read and is as useful for the small business owner as it is for the corporate executive. Albert Plant has an uncommon ability for plain talk, and this book is an outstanding example of what can happen when a true retailer writes about business. I want it to become recommended reading for all my franchisees."

J. GRAHAM COOKE, VICE-PRESIDENT FRANCHISE DEVELOPMENT
AND FACILITIES, A&W FOOD SERVICES OF CANADA

"Albert Plant has distilled a lifetime of retail experience and know-how into a practical guide for independent Canadian retailers of goods and services. This book is full of good advice on how retailers can make money and satisfy customers, based on proven practices that work."

LEN KUBAS, PRESIDENT, KUBAS CONSULTANTS

D1548874

"A valuable resource, packed with useful information! Any size of shop-keeper can profit from this handy reference on retailing."

LARRY ROSEN, CHAIRMAN AND CEO, HARRY ROSEN INC.

"Many sections of *The Retail Game* are great for individual executives who are in charge of a specific division. This is a practical manual for training new store executives in areas such as marketing, business planning and human resources. It is also an excellent reference guide for seasoned veterans of retail. We will be using sections of *The Retail Game* for our ongoing merchandising training courses."

KIM YOST, PRESIDENT AND CEO, THE BRICK GROUP INCOME FUND

"*The Retail Game* covers a significant number of the issues facing a small business. Retail is the most exciting place to be. Where else can you create such a multidimensional brand, with which to win the hearts and minds of your customers? Immediate feedback allows you to shape your offering to your customers, while industry trends enable you to be in the forefront."

KAREN FLAVELLE, PURDY'S CHOCOLATES LTD.

As a retailer, you are part of an exciting and dynamic industry that's constantly evolving to keep up with the demands of a global marketplace. Whether you're just starting out, or have multiple locations, your efforts to start, maintain and grow a thriving and profitable business in Canada can be challenging. But thanks to author and leading retail industry consultant Albert Plant, navigating your way to long-term success has just become a lot easier.

RBC has partnered with Mr. Plant for 13 years. During this time, he has provided valuable, in-depth insight into the retail sector, and has helped shape our product and service offerings to retail clients. Mr. Plant also regularly participates in RBC-sponsored seminars and conferences across Canada, sharing his insights on market trends and providing practical advice to retailers like you.

With almost 40 years experience in the retail sector, we are pleased that Mr. Plant has taken his extensive knowledge and unique perspective, and applied it to *The Retail Game: Playing to Win*. His book focuses on common issues facing retailers, including:

- Advice to help you achieve your short- and long-term goals for success
- Help in creating a clear vision for your business and strategies for marketing it
- Strategies for finding, hiring and keeping the right employees for your business
- Insight into the wants and needs of today's sophisticated consumer

Like Mr. Plant, RBC recognizes that to succeed in the retail industry, you need the advice of someone who truly understands the opportunities and challenges faced by retailers on a daily basis. At RBC, we take pride in our team of retail specialists whose in-depth financial expertise and industry understanding allow them to provide advice to help your business succeed.

We hope you find this book to be *your* essential reference guide to successful retailing in Canada.

Shauneen Bruder
Executive Vice President, Business & Commercial Banking
RBC Royal Bank

THE RETAIL GAME: PLAYING TO WIN

THE
RETAIL GAME

PLAYING TO
WIN

ALBERT C. PLANT, CMC

A GUIDE *to the*
PROFITABLE SALE *of*
GOODS *and* SERVICES

Douglas & McIntyre
Vancouver/Toronto

Douglas & McIntyre Ltd.
2323 Quebec Street, Suite 201
Vancouver, British Columbia
Canada v5t 4s7
www.douglas-mcintyre.com

LIBRARY AND ARCHIVES CANADA CATALOGUING IN PUBLICATION

Plant, Albert C., 1932–
The retail game : playing to win : a guide to the profitable sale
of goods and services/Albert C. Plant.

Includes index. ISBN 978-1-55365-330-1

1. Retail trade. 2. New business enterprises. I. Title.
HF5429.P54 2007 381'.1 C2007-902953-1

Editing by John Eerkes-Medrano
Cover and text design by Ingrid Paulson
Printed and bound in Canada by Friesens
Printed on acid-free paper that is forest friendly (100% post-consumer
recycled paper) and has been processed chlorine free

We gratefully acknowledge the financial support of the Canada Council for the Arts,
the British Columbia Arts Council, the Province of British Columbia through
the Book Publishing Tax Credit, and the Government of Canada through the Book
Publishing Industry Development Program (BPIDP) for our publishing activities.

To Ann

CONTENTS

ACKNOWLEDGEMENTS

To RBC Royal Bank, I extend my appreciation for their support and encouragement as I developed the concept for this book and slowly worked it through to completion. My many years as the bank's Retail Industry Advisor has given me the opportunity to meet and get to know retailers and prospects of all sizes. From coast to coast, at workshops and the bank's seminars, I have had the privilege of working with the bank's associates at many levels of management from client relations, account management, credit writing, financial analysis, industry-sector marketing, card services and electronic commerce. This has given me an insight into the ongoing and supportive relationships between the retailer and the banker throughout the life cycle of the client's business.

As I collected the background materials to support my manuscript as it grew from a series of newsletters into a book, I recognized that many of them deserved to be incorporated into the text. Following are the sources of the excerpts I have chosen and received permission to reproduce or summarize. My thanks go to:

- Tom Rubel of TNS Retail Forward (http://www.retailforward.com/), Two Easton Oval, Suite 500, Columbus, Ohio, for material summarized on pages 21, 28, 43, 45, 175–76;
- The Center for Retailing Studies in Mays Business School, Texas A&M University (http://mays.tamu.edu/), College Station, Texas, for material summarized on page 169;
- John Williams, founding partner of J.C. Williams Group (http://www.jcwg.com/), 17 Dundonald Street, Toronto, Ontario, for material reproduced on pages 49, 161;
- John Torella, author of *Whole-Being Retail Branding*, copyright © 2003, published by J.C. Williams Group, 17 Dundonald Street, Toronto, Ontario, for material reproduced on page 206;
- Tema Frank, president of Web Mystery Shoppers (http://www.webmysteryshoppers.com/), #14, 9977–178 Street, Suite 190, Edmonton, Alberta, for material summarized on pages 147–48;
- David Maister, "The Professional Service Adviser's Adviser" (http://about.davidmaister.com/), 90 Commonwealth Ave, Boston, Massachusetts, for material reproduced on pages 176–78;
- Catherine Swift, president and CEO of Canadian Federation of Independent Business (http://www.cfib.ca/), 4141 Yonge Street, Suite 401, Willowdale, Ontario, for material summarized on page 277;
- John D. McKellar, C.M., Q.C., and Lisa Borsook, L.L.B., managing partner of WeirFoulds LLP (http://www.weirfoulds.com), The Exchange Tower, Suite 1600, 130 King Street West, Toronto, Ontario, for material summarized on pages 63–65; and
- John Sotos, Founding Partner, Sotos Associates LLP, 180 Dundas Street West, Suite 1250, Toronto, Ontario, for material summarized on pages 152–53.

Special thanks go to our three children—Charles R. Plant, B.A., M.B.A., C.A., business performance improvement course director for the M.B.A. Program at the Schulich School of Business, York University, Toronto; Sara J. Plant, B.A. Hons., L.L.B., TEP, regional director of wealth services at BMO Harris Bank, Toronto; and Laura K. Plant, B.A. Hons., M.B.A., senior manager of marketing, corporate and major gifts at the Heart and Stroke Foundation of Ontario, Toronto. Each provided encouragement, ideas and insight into their own areas of expertise as they connected with different parts of the book.

INTRODUCTION

For many years, I have enjoyed playing doubles tennis. I especially enjoy winning. Retailing, like tennis, is a "zero sum" game and a team game. When someone wins, someone else has to lose. Consumers have a finite amount of disposable income available to purchase goods and services. When the customers choose one particular venue at which to spend their money, that venue's competitor loses a chance to satisfy and keep that customer or client.

Canadian businesses are often criticized in the media for being uncompetitive. Delegates at a recent retail conference in the United States heard that when Canadian retailers get up in the morning, they worry about how they will get along with the competition. When the American retailers wake up, they work on their plan to shutter their competitors.

To be successful, retailers must play to win. This includes not only beating the competition in some unique way but also meeting the challenge of retailing goods or services by growing the top line (sales) and the bottom line (profit) at the same time. Above the top line are customer satisfaction and continuing loyalty; below the bottom line are retained earnings and growing wealth. The challenge is the same for one store as it is for many: one must never forget that every great store chain began as a single store.

At its simplest, retailing is consumer fulfillment or, in layman's terms, customer satisfaction. In the world of economics the sale of goods and services is referred to as B2C—business to consumers. B2C is more than storekeeping; it is serving, servicing and satisfying. When the top line and the bottom line both expand, consumers and store-owners are satisfied at the same time.

For retailers of goods and services, when consumers enter a store or service centre, answer a telephone, open a letter or order form, visit a website, receive an email or ring a doorbell, consumers become customers, and business begins.

The principles of good retailing apply to all forms of consumer fulfillment: to spas, airlines, car repair shops, dry cleaners, landscapers, seniors' residences and any business that serves customers directly. Retailers of goods and services, regardless of their size, have the same details to consider. The bigger the retailer, the more complex the details—but those details are essentially the same. Retailers must:

·   create an awareness of the service or product offered;
·   attract customers to the store or service centre;
·   fulfill customers' wants and needs differently and better than the competition;
·   entice customers, especially the most loyal ones, to return;
·   take care of the stakeholders, especially the employees;
·   make money; and
·   accumulate wealth over time.

Satisfying customers is the art of retailing. Creating wealth is the business of retailing. Achieving the combination of talents required to accomplish both goals within a reasonable period of time is a lifetime challenge. So retailers gather around industry leaders and hope that the "best in class" will work with them to see the vision of their enterprise and to join in the challenge and the fun.

This book is not a textbook or a workbook. It is first and foremost an educational business guide for retail owner-operators who want to improve their chances for financial success and grow their bright idea and offering into something significant. Store managers and support staff also will find valuable information and suggestions here; this book includes more than four hundred "good ideas." This financially oriented book shows both retailers of merchandise and retail service providers the right steps to making money. Most importantly, it is a Canadian book for Canadian retailers—their owners, their operators, their franchisees, their company store managers and anyone else interested in what makes retailing so engaging and challenging. These retailers might recognize many of the businesses mentioned and relate to their stories, as I use them as examples to explain special concepts.

This retail book is unique in that it takes the owner-operator through the five stages of business life, from start-up to sell-out. Although each of these stages merits a book of its own the goal of this guide is to touch on many aspects of the consumer satisfaction process while covering the ownership and moneymaking process as well.

I will never forget the first management book I purchased; it dealt with five major principles of management. Those principles were plan, organize, staff, direct and control. After my fifty years of business experience, this list continues to stand the test. These five principles might have been the chapter headings of this book, but they seemed too generic for a guide focused on retailers, customers and wealth. Although these key topics are definitely covered here, this book is very much about retailing.

ONE | MARKET DYNAMICS

CONSUMER FULFILLMENT: "B2C"

> *"In the modern world of business, it is useless to be a creative original thinker unless you can sell what you create."*

DAVID M. OGILVY

We are all consumers. Many of us are shoppers. Few of us are customers—shoppers who select the store or service provider that best meets their needs and return to it again and again. The key to success for the storeowner or manager is to maximize the conversion of shoppers into customers. Some retailers of goods and services do this better than others and grow their success to great dimensions, establishing stores at many locations. Some storeowners are content to build wealth with only one store and converting shoppers into customers very well over time.

Satisfying consumers is not the same as meeting the needs of someone else's business. In the latter case, what we call B2B (business to business), the business sells goods and services to another business. In the former case, the basis of retail and what we call B2C (business to consumer), the business sells goods and services to the ultimate consumer.

Selling to another business is a process of deal making. The provider of a product or service seeks out a potential customer and attempts to secure a contract to supply or serve that business. The more customers the provider acquires, the more volume they sell, and the greater is the success of the business.

Marketing to consumers, in contrast, is not that simple. The providers of goods and services must develop and produce or acquire their offering, establish a venue where their offerings can be obtained, advertise—by word of mouth, door to door or through other media— and then wait and hope that someone learns about the offering and contacts or visits them. For storekeepers, the difference between B2B and B2C is significant.

The physical locations of B2B or B2G (business to government) providers are not important, but these businesses must invest in capital, design, marketing support, processing and production facilities, and time to develop a successful venture. The retailer (the B2C company) needs only to find something worth selling, then launch a website or rent a stall at an appropriate location and wait for customers to come by. Retailers have succeeded since humans first began to acquire food and wares that they did not produce themselves. And although over 90 per cent of retail firms employ fewer than five people, the largest company in the world, Wal-Mart, employs over 1.4 million world-wide.

THE ESSENTIALS OF B2C

The retailing of goods follows the same process as the retailing of services. Both are B2C operations—both goods and services providers handle the transaction immediately prior to final consumption. Let's look at some of the characteristics:

- The key ingredient of a goods sale is usually the product of some other provider, known as the supplier. Although more manufacturers are getting into the retail business (Sony, Nike, Levi's, etc.), the retail store continues to be the consumer's purchasing agent.
- Stores that sell goods often also sell or provide services, such as home delivery, alterations and interior design. Although these services may appear to cost the customer nothing, the cost of providing them must be covered in the sale of the goods.
- On the other hand, many service companies augment their offering with the sale of goods: lawn maintenance services may sell fertilizer, barber shops and hair salons may sell shampoos, and fitness gyms may sell athletic wear.
- Many services businesses, like goods businesses, must be concerned with location and customer attraction. Hotels, theme parks, dry cleaners, barber shops, art galleries, funeral parlours, fitness gyms and restaurants all need to be sure that their location is accessible to their customers.
- Although the balance sheets of service businesses may look substantially different from those of typical retail stores, their profit and loss statements look very similar—both have fixed and variable costs.
- Both types of businesses require a margin of profit from the sale of their goods or services in order to cover the cost of their advertising, purchases, labour, location, technology and other necessary support.
- Both also require that the contribution of their business units be sufficient to cover the cost of corporate overhead and taxes while leaving a suitable return (or bonus, or dividend) for the shareholders who made the original investment and hold the continuing risk.

CANADA'S RETAIL LANDSCAPE

From year to year, the component share of Canada's gross domestic product varies to some degree and changes slowly over time. The main components are illustrated in Figure 1.1. In this figure, consumer fulfillment is referred to as PECGS, personal expenditures of consumer goods and services—this is the B2C box. This consumer market is separated in the third line into goods and services. During a family's formative years, goods are purchased to clothe the growing family and provide the home with the usual hobby and leisure products. As the family ages, its purchasing pattern swings towards the purchase of personal and financial services, such as insurance, travel, vacations, private-school and university education, club memberships, living arrangements and retirement savings products. The services provided to each generation also change as consumers age. For example, there will be a rise in the need for services of all types for seniors as our population ages, and there will be a constant shift towards the purchase of services rather than goods.

Figure 1.1: The components of GDP, 2006

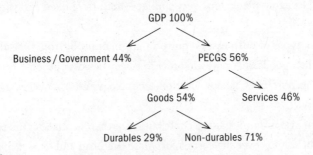

Source: Kubas Consultants and Statistics Canada

Economic analysts closely watch the PECGS box shown in Figure 1.1 for shifts in consumer confidence and its effect on gross domestic product (GDP), especially on PECGS. Consumers will increase their spending when their income increases, when they expect relief in certain fixed costs and when they notice their food and fuel costs dropping. Another significant reason for increased spending is that consumers are able to borrow against the value of their homes. Although this option buoys spending during housing price increases, when home prices fall, consumers' need to reduce debt takes top priority in their financial planning.

In the United States, consumer spending is approximately 70 per cent of GDP. The expression "the consumer drives the economy" applies there. Americans enjoy a greater disposable income from their wages and salaries than do Canadians. After all, "the pursuit of happiness," along with "life, liberty," defines the American way of life. Furthermore, whereas the government covers most health care costs in Canada, consumers in the United States must pay a significant portion of this amount themselves.

CANADIAN RETAIL ESTABLISHMENTS

As the largest participant in Canada's economy, retailing is carried out by approximately 500,000 retailers (see Figure 1.2). The vast majority of these retailers have only one store.

Figure 1.2: Canadian retail establishments, 2004

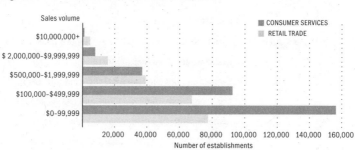

Source: Statistics Canada

The two lowest bars in Figure 1.2 describe the life's work of the more than 230,000 retailers that generate sales of less than $500,000. Since the average store in Canada has sales of around $800,000, we assume that the under-$500,000 retailers function without a store. The largest component of these "establishments" is consumer services, a category in which entrepreneurs and professionals alike do not need a store or office to serve consumers.

When we think about retailing in Canada, we naturally think about the big markets of Montreal, Toronto, Vancouver and Calgary. But, unlike retailers in the United States, Canadian retailers are more likely to be located in rural areas. Every cluster of people represents a micro-market; the bigger the cluster, the larger the potential. Look at the names of the independent retailers and service providers in small towns and reflect on how they have served this local market for sometimes generations. What do they have that is so special?

RETAIL GOODS AND SERVICES SEGMENTS

Table 1.1, which has been developed from Statistics Canada's NAICS industry classifications, outlines the eight industry subsectors that provide the bulk of Canada's retail goods and services businesses.

Table 1.1: The eight subsectors of Canadian retailing

	INDUSTRY	INDUSTRY DESCRIPTIONS
1	Auto dealers, fuel and repairs	Auto dealers (new and used), automotive repair shops, gasoline service stations, auto and home supplies, fuel
2	Home and leisure goods	Lumber and building supplies, variety stores, paint, glass, hardware, retail nurseries and garden supplies, home furnishings and appliances, radios, TVs, music and musical instruments, sporting goods, books,

		stationery, jewellery, toys, hobbies, games, cameras, photography supplies, gifts, novelty items, luggage, leather goods, sewing and needlework materials, piece goods, florists, optical goods
3	Hotel, travel and vacation services	Museums, art galleries, zoos, botanical gardens, hotels, motels, resorts, airlines, travel agencies, railways
4	Recreation and services	Camps, parks, recreational vehicles, dance halls, theatres, bowling lanes, pool halls, professional sports fitness facilities, recreation clubs, amusement parks, private membership clubs
5	Apparel and general merchandise	General merchandise and department stores, apparel, furs, accessories, footwear
6	Food and drug stores	Food stores, drug stores, news dealers and newsstands
7	Eating and drinking venues	Restaurants, caterers, fast food vendors, bars, pubs, night clubs
8	Health and personal services	Home and personal goods repairs, laundry, cleaning services, photo studios, beauty and barber shops, shoe repairs and shoeshines, funeral services, hospitals, medical services

CONSUMER FULFILLMENT GROWTH

Figure 1.3: Five-year growth, Canada, 2001–2006

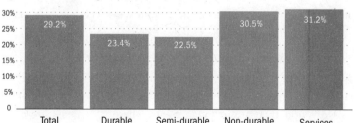

Figure 1.3 shows how consumers have increased their expenditures on different types of goods in a recent five-year period.

· Durable goods include autos, homes and big-ticket home goods.
· Semi-durables include apparel, footwear, music, books, sporting goods, gifts and other miscellaneous items.
· Non-durables include food, fuel, newspapers, health and beauty products, etc.
· Services include restaurants, theatres, travel, education, museums, hotels and personal services.

Retailing is a universal business. It has been an income earner for traders since families began living in clusters. The traders knew everyone they served and what their customers needed. Today, as then, one by one, frequent customers become recognized, and then known. If they are lucky, customers are first treated like guests and then like treasured friends. This is the process of retail loyalty.

THE CASH REGISTER

"If I had only known, I would have been a locksmith."

ALBERT EINSTEIN

Since people created a form of currency to trade for goods and services, there has been some form of cash register. The original one—the pocket or purse—is still important. From the conception of a retail venture until the day it closes its doors, its fundamental goal has always been to end the day (or the venture) with more money than it started with. The cash register—pocket, cigar box or debit/credit card slips—provides a record of this story. The day's transactions accumulate in monthly, and then annual, statements. These statements are dealt with in detail in Chapter 5.

Nothing happens in a retail business until a sale is made; retailing revolves around the cash register. Consider the following costs of doing retail business: a firm may rent its premises, lease its fixtures and technology equipment, outsource its transportation needs and purchase its goods from third parties, to whom it will owe money. For every dollar of sales revenue, the enterprise may retain a net profit of less than five cents after meeting all of its obligations. Financial success begins with keeping track of the flow of cash.

Thus the central focus of the retailer is the cash register. Thanks to the computer and the bar-coded price ticket, the cash register is an indispensable part of the cash flow. Not only does it hold cash secure, but it can also track from whence the cash came and where it went. It can become the key information tool in staff planning, managing inventory, calculating gross margin, measuring markdown effectiveness and tracking shrinkage.

Surveys show that the more efficient the cash register transaction process, the greater the sales. This efficiency includes not only the technical aspects of transaction and credit processing but also the number of registers available to handle the random surges of customer traffic. A Toronto supermarket chain with a small number of huge food stores has a cash register layout and communications system that allows it to open a new register whenever more than two customers line up to pay for their purchases.

It's not always possible, but if every employee of a business were to spend one week or just one day at the cash register, the business would be more customer friendly and perhaps more profitable. This may be the only moment in an employee's career when he or she comes face-to-face with a real live customer. Long ago, when business was simpler and store executives spent time on the floor of the store during the day, the oldtimers in the department stores would listen to the squeak of the racks in the fashion department and the sound of the cash registers on the main floor. From these observations, they could get a feel for the sales volumes of the store in the areas where the profits were made, in the fashion goods department and at the cosmetics and jewellery counters on the main floor. Depending on what they heard, they made immediate decisions to shift staff, bring out more goods or change the prices. Today's cash registers are far smarter, but are they being used wisely?

THE CASH REGISTER OF CONSUMERS DISTRIBUTING

Today's cash registers, which handle the electronic point of sale (EPOS), are today's purses or cigar boxes. Their functionality allows them to handle many tasks and to keep track of everything going on in the store. This was not always possible. For example, in 1976, Consumers Distributing Ltd. (CD) wired the store doors to its cash registers to keep track of how many times the doors opened during the day. At the end of the day, when the registers were closed, they printed out the number of transactions, the number of entries (the door total count was divided by two because customers went in and out) and the percentage of visits resulting in transactions.

CD was the only retailer that had the exact knowledge of its gross demand. Every customer filled out a request slip based on the catalogue information and took it to the sales desk. The employee went to the warehouse at the back of the store and, if he or she was lucky, found the requested item and completed the sale. Piles of unfilled order forms held the secret to CD's success. If computers had been available to record these slips, the gross demand by store and by day would be the basis for forecasting item sales, providing a better in-stock position and fulfilling a higher percentage of orders.

When the door opened and groups came in and went out, a pattern of visits and buying became a constant ratio over time. Because everyone came into the store to buy something they had seen in the catalogue, the ratio of purchases to visits was usually high. Store managers and staff were challenged to beat 80 per cent. But CD was notorious for being out of stock. Computerized inventory control and sales forecasting were in their infancy in the 1960s and '70s. The key to beating 80 per cent was the ability of the store staff to offer a substitute. The task of the company's buyers who created the catalogue was to buy and display groups of substitutable items.

This was long before the Internet, with its e-mail and the World Wide Web. For CD to capture this information, a bank of auto-dialers built into its mainframe computer spent the night dialing every store across the country, connecting to the store phone number that accessed the cash register. The sales transaction totals were extracted along with the SKU (stock keeping unit) data and the "conversion rate index" described above. The auto-dialers toiled all night to bring the information to those who needed it the next morning. A "sub-80%" conversion rate usually resulted in a phone call to the store manager. The technology has changed dramatically over the past forty years, but the management process is much the same.

TODAY'S EPOS

The EPOS becomes very important when it not only records the sale of the item but also authorizes the payment for the item to the supplier. This is known as scan-based trading (SBT). The grocery store industry (and Wal-Mart) began to adopt this practice in 2003. Although suppliers complain and refer to the practice as "consignment selling," the retail industry will embrace the concept when it has the technical capacity to handle EPOS. The cycle is simple, but its ramifications are great:

1. The customer selects the item.
2. It is scanned at the checkout.
3. A "notice of sale" is sent to the accounts payable ledger.
4. That evening, the information technology (IT) program sums all of the item sales by supplier.
5. An electronic funds notice goes to the retailer's bank.
6. The bank transfers funds electronically to the supplier's bank account.
7. A notice of replenishment goes to the distribution centre or directly to the supplier.
8. Store-direct shipments are assembled and delivered.
9. The item is replaced on the shelf.

This system reinforces the importance of supply chain management (see page 110). The better the supplier forecasts his or her production in keeping with the needs of the retailer, the faster the retailer can refill shelves with just the right amount of goods and the sooner the supplier will be paid. No longer is there a negotiation regarding payment terms or backup support. Instead of waiting thirty to sixty days for payment, the turnaround time can be rapid and payment received in days.

Finally, in a tribute to the cash register, or EPOS, it is worth examining how it compares with the cigar box. EPOS performs the following tasks. It:

· records the sale;
· stops the transaction if there is a problem with the credit card;
· calculates the taxes;
· captures and highlights unapproved or unrecognized prices;
· prints out receipts for the customer and the store;

- collects customer transaction information that can lead to customer profitability analysis;
- provides the payment to the store, whether or not the transaction is a cash transaction;
- reduces the available balance on stored-value cards and gift cards;
- reduces the recorded inventory level of the item sold;
- tells the payables department to pay the supplier if the item is on consignment or is part of a "scan and pay" program; and
- sends a signal to key suppliers to ship a replacement.

Never underestimate the value of the lowly cash register or the many support people both within and outside the enterprise who keep it running and act upon its information and commands.

TOMORROW'S CASHLESS REGISTER

Often cashiers are doing nothing one moment and at the next moment are overloaded with impatient shoppers lined up with baskets full of goods. Thus it is not surprising that self-checkout machines are replacing cash registers. Many shoppers are now using self-checkout devices because they believe this will allow them to avoid lineup delays and slow checkout clerks.

Self-checkout kiosks have been in use since 1987, but they did not enter the mainstream until around 2000. They are becoming common in large grocery stores and among mass merchants as a result of the introduction of bar codes and scanning devices. There is no reason why customers cannot scan and bag their own purchases, especially if it means not waiting in line for a busy clerk to handle the transaction. People's eagerness to use a machine rather than talk to a person doesn't mean that they don't value face-to-face encounters. Computer-savvy or not, customers understand when they need to talk to a sales clerk and when they can handle the transaction alone.

Not only is this initiative customer-friendly, but it is also a financially successful idea. The usual configuration of self-checkout registers includes one staff member for every four to six registers. This arrangement serves two purposes: it provides help when help is needed, and it deters theft.

HARD-EDGED, SOFT-SIDED

"The brain is a wonderful organ. It starts working the moment you get up in the morning, and does not stop until you get into the office."   ROBERT FROST

We are sometimes reminded of the art of retailing and the science of business. People who loved the art of merchandising led the development of the department-store era. Fashion leadership, store ambience, customer amenities and great service were the hallmarks of their trade. These features can be described as part of the art of retailing. In contrast, a more technical approach to retailing could be called the science of retailing. The art and science of retailing are equivalent to the psychology of right-brained and left-brained processing. Table 1.2 incorporates these concepts in a listing of the hard-edged and soft-sided aspects of retailing.

The theory of the structure of the brain and the mind suggests that the left side is logical, sequential and rational. It sees things as parts. The right brain is random, intuitive and holistic. It sees things as wholes. Left-brain scholastic subjects focus on logical thinking, analysis and accuracy. Right-brain subjects, on the other hand, focus on aesthetics, feeling and creativity.

As individual stores grew into chains and chains joined to form multi-bannered conglomerates, the need for structure resulted in a

Table 1.2: Hard-edged and soft-sided aspects of retailing

HARD-EDGED	SOFT-SIDED
· Performance measurements	· Branding
· Traffic counting	· Providing customer service
· Bar coding	· Employee training
· Research diagnostics	· Product advertising
· Scorekeeping	· Fashion planning
· Budgeting	· Designing floor layouts
· Financial reporting	· Colour blocking
· Keeping employment records	· Selecting suppliers
· Using technology	· Providing "greeters"
· Benchmarking	· Designing store windows
· Using AC Nielsen reports	· Providing home decor advice

need for left-brain controls, departments and processes. Throughout this expansion phase, the development of the computer and of software to keep track of customers, employees, merchandise and money meant that hard-edged approaches became the standard methods for measuring results and making decisions. Too often, left-brained people took over an enterprise because they had the numbers, while it was thought that right-brained merchants merely had vague ideas and a sense of what the customer wanted in the way of style, colour and appearance.

The customer's view of a purchase hasn't changed a great deal over time. The most popular word that describes the customer's shopping and buying decision is "value." Price is clearly a hard-edged matter: it is right or wrong, high or low in the mind of the shopper. Like store hours, delivery policies and returns guidelines, it is a predetermined, fixed issue. Quality, in contrast, is soft-sided. It rings with emotion. It speaks of many elements of the shopping experience such

as store ambience, staff friendliness, fashionability and product quality. Every shopper views it differently; the higher the perceived quality,
the higher the price. Consider the fact that most fashion magazines
advertise goods without including the price of the object. They want
acceptance to occur without regard to price.

Successful retailing needs to be run with an eye for the impact of
soft-sided issues on the business instead of a focus on numbers. What is
more important: the perceived quality of fresh food or the price of the
potatoes? The buyer's skill is in determining the freshness, not in
evaluating the imprecise choice of price.

Management tends to be hard-edged too much of the time. Meetings
need to include soft-sided matters such as staff relations, training and
customer contacts. The retail opportunity begins with the soft-sided
input—the customer—and ends with the hard-edged result—the wealth.

VALUE WEIGHTINGS
Not defined in Table 1.2 is the weight that each customer gives to each
component of transaction value. Hard-pressed, spending-controlled
wage earners put a great deal of weight on price. When members of the
general population can't maintain their purchasing power with their
disposable income, their desire for price drives them to find satisfaction
at low-priced stores. This explains the successful rise of Wal-Mart from
a family-owned variety chain to the world's largest retailer. While it per-
formed better than anyone else on the price factor, it also provided the
other elements of the transaction value well enough to build its empire.
So, although we must never forget that Wal-Mart was once a single
store, its "great idea" was greater than anyone imagined at the time.

Of the four components of the transaction value—price, quality,
ambience and experience—note that only one of them—price—is
measurable, or hard-edged. The other three components are extremely

subjective, or soft-sided. Recent research confirms the words of the original department-store merchants: "Retailing is a combination of art and science." How is that dealt with in today's highly competitive environment? Retail leadership teams need a balance of creative people and "numbers" people who respect each other's input and output.

FORMAT LIFE CYCLES

"In the business world, the rear-view mirror is always clearer than the windshield."   WARREN BUFFETT

Many decades ago, TNS Retail Forward's predecessor, Management Horizons, produced the graph in Figure 1.4 to show the phases or life cycles of the various retail formats: growth, maturity, decline and outcome. The fine dashed lines on the right side of the figure describe what happens to the model when growth is extended. How often do we read that the leader of a failing business has been replaced with a new leader? This simple chart may show why this is so. The new leader is tasked with shifting the firm from the heavy dashed line (eventual extinction) to the fine dashed line (rebirth and recovery).

Figure 1.4: Life cycles of various retail formats

Source: TNS Retail Forward

FORMAT DESCRIPTIONS

Each retail format in Figure 1.4 has a history. The oldest format, the
department store, was originated in the 1800s by "merchant princes"—
men who saw fashion merchandising as an art. Names like Neiman
Marcus, Nordstrom's and Saks in the United States and Eaton's, Simp-
son's and Woodward's in Canada held the dominant share of general
merchandising through the first half of the 1900s. Traditional department stores could be counted on for two enduring characteristics:

- They were the fashion centres of the downtown district, with the
  latest in styles and brands. Their predominant customers were
  housewives.

- They were huge and included virtually every category of merchandise imaginable that the households of the day needed or
  wanted. In their period of dominance, they included complete
  grocery stores.

The question marks in the figure indicate that there might be a
resurgence in the declining fortunes of those department stores that
remain. Without being locked into their own store-named brands,
they may be able to shift their sourcing and emphasis, especially in
fashion apparel and accessories. After many mergers, consolidations
and closures, the strong stores are getting stronger.

The first shopping mall in Canada opened in 1964. Malls were
anchored at each end by department stores, allowing customers to
continue to shop at their usual stores without going downtown, while
providing the new malls with a strong flow of loyal customers. High-
end merchants took up key locations in the malls, and many new
medium-priced operators, who provided not only fashion goods but
also all kinds of special offerings, joined them.

Power centres and their clusters of "big boxes" grew out of two
converging issues that negatively affected the traditional malls. First,

as rents and occupancy costs rose at the malls, the apparel merchants with their higher margins could afford them, and they continued to grow as their percentage of the merchandise mix across the mall increased. The lower-margined merchants, who sold toys, electronics, stationery, hardware, books, and so on, were hard-pressed to make a profit with the mall's high occupancy costs. Second, these hard-line (non-apparel) merchants saw the advantage of having extensive assortments in large stores that were freestanding and built at lower costs. They clustered their category-dominant assortments in vast plots of land beyond the malls and near the edges of the suburbs.

Restaurants, theatres, huge home-improvement stores and some-times a multi-screen theatre filled out the site. While this development was maturing, the two members-only merchants, Price Club and Costco, joined to create the Costco chain in Canada. Then Wal-Mart arrived in Canada, in 1994, and began to build its giant stores. The price and value appeal of these two businesses led them to become the leaders of the general merchandise sector of retailing in a very few years. As the big box stores mature, they find it necessary to do something different to ensure that their core customers keep coming back. Those that are male oriented, for example, are adjusting their assortments, decor and layouts to become more female friendly.

In accord with Figure 1.4, the evolution of the power centre pulled customers and sales from the malls that were in turn pulling cus-tomers and sales from the downtown department stores. In 1971, there were more than thirty department-store companies in Canada. Thirty years later, only The Bay, Sears and Zellers remained along with Wal-Mart. When Eaton's was at the height of its success in the 1960s and '70s, its share of the merchandise market in Canada was equal to the 2004 Wal-Mart's share of the general merchandise market in the United States.

Further to the left in the figure sits "High Street," a very old cluster of retail shops that is experiencing a rebirth in many inner cities. When the non-apparel merchants created their power centres, the high-end apparel merchants began to establish themselves on key city streets to provide a traditional shopping environment that still exists in many European cities. The first such street to appear in Canada was "Robsonstrasse" in Vancouver, which was soon followed by Bloor Street in Toronto. More such streets are appearing each year. They feature highly focused specialty shops, top-quality restaurants and the ubiquitous Starbucks.

The Internet is rapidly growing with its inclusion of a multitude of electronic retailers. In the United States, these retailers' sales in aggregate now surpass those of the department stores. They are climbing at approximately 40 per cent per year as more and more shoppers find the Web an efficient and secure shopping environment. Most merchants provide websites now, although a great percentage are non-selling sites that provide store, selection and product information.

THE CORNER STORE

Note that Figure 1.4 does not mention the traditional corner store or the community street of shops. Some of these stores cluster to serve the high-end consumer, but most line the main streets of familiar neighbourhoods. For the most part, the names on the facades cannot be found elsewhere. These are the independents. This retailing format has changed little over the centuries, and there is little chance that it will. Many chains have chosen to join them to be closer to the customer. The shopper is here enjoying an ancient practice—street browsing; they drop in to each unique purveyor of toys, food, coffee, clothes, cleaning services and dining experiences.

Perhaps from the best of these purveyors will grow a chain, possibly
a giant retail venture.

CATALOGUE SHOWROOMS

Off the bottom right-hand corner of Figure 1.4 was a once-thriving format: the catalogue showrooms. Three chains operated in Canada until
the 1990s, when they all closed because of the appearance of Wal-Mart
in Canada. They were a hybrid of a catalogue and a warehouse. Customers found what they wanted, went to the warehouse showroom
and wrote out their order. The clerk went into the back of the shop,
found the article (if it was in stock) and brought it to the cash register.
This format thrived by offering far lower prices than what the department stores charged. The big boxes had not appeared yet, and catalogue
showrooms might have survived if the technology had been available
to keep each showroom stocked with the high-demand items. But
when Wal-Mart came along with similar prices and plenty of stock,
the showrooms lost their reason for being and became obsolete.

THE NEXT WAVE

On the left of the figure are "lifestyle centres." Given the commentary above, you might ask: "What is going to happen to the shopping
malls?" They appear to be going through some sort of rebirth. Two
forms of change are occurring:

· The best malls, or those with the best potential, are being converted through massive capital expenditures into lifestyle centres.
   These malls will combine living quarters (condos), retirement
   homes, theatres, health and personal service outlets, recreational
   centres and space for other non-retail clubs and venues. They are
   aimed at aging baby boomers, whose interests are shifting from
   the consumption of goods to the need for services.

·   The weaker malls are moving towards "down-market" tenants by offering assortments at prices below those charged by Wal-Mart, such as the dollar stores, outlet stores, repair centres and used-goods stores.

No doubt the evolution will continue; in every shopping environment there is the potential for new and clever independent operators. Consumers seek variety while holding true to their lifestyle and income level. Clever merchants of goods and services will seek out the venue that best suits their offering and do their best to be the best.

THE STRATEGIC PROFIT MODEL

"To succeed as a team is to hold all of the members accountable for their expertise."

MITCHELL CAPLAN, CEO, E*TRADE GROUP INC.

There is always a compelling reason to improve profits:
·   to meet shareholder expectations;
·   to generate cash for refurbishing and expansion;
·   to meet the covenants of a lending agreement;
·   to provide cash for term loan repayments;
·   to harness the focus of the management team; and
·   to increase customer value without reducing gross margins.

Investors today are searching more diligently and intelligently to find maximum value. Diminishing returns are not an acceptable option to shareholders, whether they are public or family owners. Therefore, a proven approach to improving corporate financial performance is mandatory.

Working capital effectiveness and operating cost leadership require not only research and analysis to optimize the supply chain and keep the shelves full of wanted merchandise that is priced to attract buyers, but also a decrease in the investment in inventory to increase working capital. This creates a positive cycle of providing cash to further improve the profit margins of the business and support inventory levels.

The retail trade lends itself well to an organized approach to retail performance improvement (RPI). The financial and technological tools already exist; the CEO just needs to centre them in a team-oriented process of research, discovery, selection, implementation and measurement.

THE PROFIT MODEL

The DuPont Chemical Company developed the original profit model in the 1930s. Management Horizons (now TNS Retail Forward) introduced it as a retail tool during the 1960s. It provides a framework for a disciplined management improvement process with an excellent visual financial tool. At first glance, correctly filling out the model looks like an arduous task. Small chains and individual stores may not have the resources or the time to go through this process and may need outside help from the company's accountant. Regardless, the model is a great way to improve revenue generation and cost reduction through a process involving different people working on a common goal.

A simple version of the model is shown in Figure 1.5. The model positions the departmental results and combines their totals as it moves to the right until the final profit is calculated. It allows for the use of percentages to show how each component is related to total sales. This simple version can be expanded in many ways. The retail profit model combines the management organization chart and the profit and loss statement; the CEO is represented by and accountable for the profit margin on the right. The management and supervisory teams are allocated their own box, or profit performance responsibilities. As soon as a retail business grows to include more than one owner-operator, those in charge can divide the responsibilities for buying (selection and gross margin) and selling (service and costs).

Figure 1.5: The retail profit model

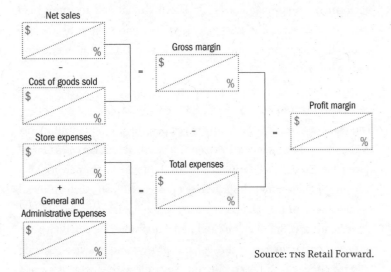

Source: TNS Retail Forward.

Profit improvement begins by looking at the right side—the profit margin box—and determining what this profit should be and what needs to be done, moving left box by box, to produce the targeted results. With present and target results set, each split box can be used to visualize the "performance gap," as shown in Figure 1.6. Supporting the items in this figure are many cost and sales components (boxes), such as price discounts, shrinkage, store labour, cash management fees, inbound freight, IT costs, and so on, of the profit model that feed into the larger elements. This figure will be expanded and broken down as its various boxes are dealt with throughout this book.

Figure 1.6: The performance gap

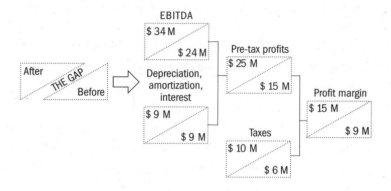

The following steps are key to improving profit model performance:

· identify the problems that hold back financial improvement in each box;

· determine, with research and IT solutions, what can be done to reduce the problems and enhance the prospects for success;

· set realistic goals for improvement and non-negotiable time frames that create a gap between today's performance and tomorrow's goals; and

· assign responsibility and accountability to specific individuals to take the necessary action to close the gap.

The five steps required to improve profit are as follows:

1. Study the details of the company's profit and loss statement, and develop a customized financial performance model. Bring into this model the key boxes of revenue, margin and expenses, where accountability resides.

2. Find good benchmarks for key performance indicators. Have the team check various sources for these benchmarks and then incorporate them into the customized base financial performance model.

3. Set performance improvement targets. Where can improvement
   be made, and how much? Using the benchmark information, have
   the team assess the gaps in performance and determine opportunities for significant improvement in performance.

4. Have the group develop an action plan to improve performance.
   This will include a timetable indicating when the group will meet
   periodically to measure progress, box by box.

5. Once gaps and opportunities have been identified, there are many
   ways to close the gaps and enhance performance, as illustrated in
   the following examples. The key is to assign accountabilities, set
   reasonable goals and time frames, and measure performance over
   time.

HOUSEHOLD EXTRAS INC.

To give greater meaning to the profit model concept of management discussed in this guide, a company has been created. Household Extras Inc.
(HEI) will be referred to throughout this book to give examples of the
business principle being applied to the financial results of a retail business. HEI is a five-store regional chain offering mid- to high-end home
interior appliances, accessories, bathroom products, tableware and home
decor. It owns its freestanding stores and leases its shopping centre
stores. Along with its retail outlets, it operates a wholesale division selling to homebuilders, renovators and decorators. HEI extends its reach
with its services division, which provides party rentals, including furniture, tableware and kitchenware, and a service business—catering.

Each of these components can be seen in the profit and loss statement in the Appendix at the back of this book. The profit model
shown there is also illustrated in Figure 1.7. HEI grew from one store
to five as it expanded its assortment and added contracting and consumer services. Customer support seems reasonable, since many

customers comment on the acceptable size of the stores and the availability of knowledgeable staff.

Figure 1.7: Profit model: Household Extras Inc., Year-end, December 31, 2005

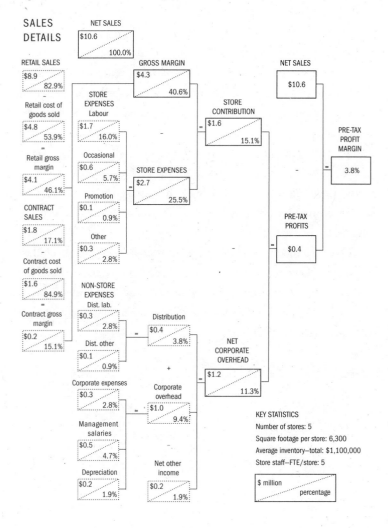

Look at the profit and loss statement in the Appendix. Note that although sales were higher in the current year than in the past year, profits were not. Furthermore, Figure 1.7 shows how little profit is earned with this level of sales. Each box must be studied to see what needs to be done to improve profit.

By studying each box, we can identify profit inhibitors. The solutions to these problems probably lie on both sides of the "people–money" axis. So both right-brained and left-brained solutions are needed. Table 1.3 is a short list of sample problems and possible solutions.

Profit modelling provides a visual, understandable and proven approach to profit improvement. It helps all levels of management feel part of overall profit goal setting and can make meaningful contributions to the business's success. Adding the balance sheet elements to the model allows us to calculate key formulas such as gross margin return on investment, inventory turnover, asset turnover, leverage and return on equity.

The profit model is a real-life organizational chart. Instead of illustrating top-down management, it shows the leader at the "front of the class" on the right, with the final profit in hand. The leader looks to the team accountable for each box and helps them collectively improve their results in an organized way.

Table 1.3: Profit inhibitors and possible solutions

PROFIT MODEL COMPONENT	PERFORMANCE INHIBITORS	IT SOLUTIONS	MANAGEMENT SOLUTIONS
Gross margin	· Is the business competitive with these high margins? · Does the contractor business interfere with the retail business? · Are prices too high generally or only in certain sections?	· Do a GM analysis of the rate of sale of each item compared with its price point. · Do an item analysis of inventory levels and comparisons of markdowns.	· Create pricing and assortment guidelines. · Concentrate price discounting on special promo days.
Store expenses	· Are labour costs inflated? –Lack of sales forecasts for setting store labour hours. –Poor balancing of full- and part-time labour.	· Demand forecasting/labour management, employee tracking and measurement systems.	· Train store managers to schedule part-time staff to match traffic forecast.
Distribution expenses	· Is there excessive storage and too little cross-docking and distribution?	· Create a more flexible purchase order management solution.	· Introduce more pre-packs and cross-docking where appropriate.
Corporate expenses	· Do excess personnel result from poor procedures and lack of automation or technology?	· Automate the capture of hours worked in stores, with automatic update to payroll.	· Migrate head office roles or outsource data management.

TWO | STRATEGY

LEADERSHIP

"Leadership is lifting a person's vision to higher sights, the raising of a person's performance to a higher standard."

PETER DRUCKER

Although team play is important, within each team a leader always seems to emerge. This individual may be the owner, the manager or a talented and ambitious member of the team. Whatever their origin, leaders are needed to generate breakthroughs in performance and produce exceptional results. In a start-up, or a small and emerging business model, leadership tends to be the role of one individual. But not long into the start-up and the early success of the business, the leader must begin hiring and developing other leaders. Good leadership does not come from the leader only; it also characterizes the team that surrounds the leader. The higher the goals of the business, the greater are the requirements for collective leadership. Leadership involves vision—the ability to see the end-result of a strategy, a new product or a service rollout or expansion. The true leader shares this vision with his or her team, captures their interest, understanding and, finally, their support. This process can begin in the first store or service location, but chances are that the team must be capable of taking the idea to a higher level, an expanded format and a more profitable venture.

LEADERSHIP PRINCIPLES

Beginning with a single sales unit, there is opportunity for leadership practices to unfold. Following are some proven leadership development ideas:

- Make sure that the strategic plan includes the answer to the question: "Who, exactly, will get this done?"
- Clearly define the new positions that will be needed as the plan unfolds. Suggest to the team the possibility that expanded roles will be theirs as they gain more experience and success in their jobs.
- Give the team leaders projects that involve unknown pitfalls and risk. Let them stickhandle their way through the hazards and pitfalls, but stand behind their efforts.
- Reward risk taking and the successful achievement of intermediate goals. Do not wait for annual reviews to do this.
- Broadcast the individual successes; make a big noise about individual breakthrough achievements.
- Reach for consensus and "buy-in." Consensus doesn't guarantee that implementation will be effective, but it does increase the likelihood that the team can work together to find the road to success.
- When conflict arises, help the group find ways to reach the right solution, rather than imposing a solution from "on high."
- As the business grows and individuals get together from different stores or the back office, work with a leadership team that includes not necessarily just the subordinates of the leader but specialists

in certain fields, such as technology and banking. Shift the members of the team periodically to prevent perceptions of permanence "at the top" and to fit the team members to the decisions that need to be made.

PETER DRUCKER

Experts in the worlds of both business and academia regard Peter Drucker as the founding father of the study of management. He wrote thirty-five books in all: fifteen deal with management, including the landmark books *The Practice of Management* and *The Effective Executive*; sixteen cover society, economics and politics; two are novels and one is a collection of autobiographical essays. His most recent book, *Managing in the Next Society*, was published in 2002, three years before he died at the age of ninety-five. Drucker had a knack for taking complicated issues and converting them into simple concepts. He considered the job of management to include five tasks:

1. *Set objectives:* Managers determine what the objectives should be, what the goals for each objective should be and what must be done to achieve those objectives.

2. *Organize:* Managers analyze the activities that need to be done, classify the work and divide it into manageable jobs. They arrange an organizational structure to carry out the work and select the people to manage those units.

3. *Motivate and communicate:* Managers make a team out of the people who are responsible for various jobs.

4. *Measure:* Managers establish yardsticks by which performance can be measured.

5. *Develop:* Managers develop people, including themselves.

Drucker explained that managers accomplish the five tasks above through four competencies:

1. listening;
2. a willingness to communicate;
3. not relying on an alibi when things aren't faring well;
4. realizing how relatively unimportant each job is compared with the overall task at hand.

CORPORATE PHILOSOPHY

Beyond being left-brained and focused on measurable results, metrics and ratios, leadership is an attitude that shows up in the way the business is run. Chapter 1 introduced the concept of hard-edged and soft-sided, and these concepts are referred to throughout this book. A defined corporate philosophy is a soft-sided description of the guiding principles of the company.

Corporate philosophies are rarely written down by small companies. They are usually in the head of the owner-operator and surface when decisions are made, when things go wrong, when a competitor steals the limelight or when someone leaves suddenly. Ideally these philosophies should be written and distributed to everyone connected with the enterprise. Following is an abbreviated corporate philosophy statement of a national retailer. It appeared in a small booklet given to all the retailer's employees.

· The mission statement: We are in the business of providing unbeatable value to the ultimate consumer.
· Corporate aims: The business plan of our company sets forth these basic objectives:
  — To increase the intrinsic value of the shareholders' investment in the company;
  — To produce planned results;
  — To increase our future after-tax earnings at a rate that clearly identifies the company as a leader in the industry.

- Marketing philosophy: We are market oriented. We begin with an assessment of consumer needs. From there, through merchandising and distribution, we design an assortment and a system to fill those needs at a profit that meets our standards.

- Management philosophy: We believe in the science of professional management. This means producing planned results by means of specific objectives, goals, priorities and strategies for both the short term and the long term. Department results are integrated to contribute to corporate objectives.

- Human resources philosophy: We want results that require highly motivated people. We believe that most people can be motivated to produce above-average results. We are interested in results, not efforts. We believe that fairness means that individuals should progress based on performance, talent and the capacity to grow.

- Business philosophy: We have a continuing relationship with six major groups of people: suppliers, customers, shareholders, employees, communities and government. We want to do everything possible to enhance those relationships to the extent that they increase the profitability of the company.

- Diversification strategy: We will choose a policy of diversification that assists us in achieving our targeted earnings growth and reduces the cyclical nature of our earnings.

This outline could be used as a model for any corporate philosophy. It is not important what type of retailer produced this statement; it is generic in its format and could have been developed by any retailer.

A true story about Wal-Mart describes the extent to which a corporate philosophy can be carried out: During a pre-Christmas toy promotion, one store (probably others too) ran out of a "hot" toy that was being promoted at a lower-than-normal price of $21.95. Rather than disappointing its customers, the store manager authorized a sales clerk to go to the nearest community toy store and buy its complete stock at that store's retail price, which happened to be $28.95. Wal-Mart then displayed—and sold out—the toy at its advertised price of $21.95. I was at the community store that day and watched this happen!

This example demonstrates how a corporate philosophy is taken to the sales staff and out to the customer. It further demonstrates that the best corporate philosophy has little value if it can't stand up to the competition. Creating wealth begins with leadership that results in top-quality customer satisfaction.

Successful leaders are able to achieve their vision of what might be possible. To achieve excellence in big things, the small things have to be handled well at all times. Leadership is not an inherited gift, nor is it learned at business school. It has nothing to do with wealth or rank. Words that go along with demonstrated leadership qualities include honesty, integrity, patience, other-centredness and, finally, a healthy sense of humour.

STRATEGIC PLANNING

"Plans are only good intentions unless they immediately degenerate into hard work."   PETER DRUCKER

It is not important how big the venture is; what is important is the need for those involved in the business to set out the vision surrounding the business, the goals that need to be achieved and the uncertainties that need to be accounted for. Strategic planning is not a big-company process; it should be part of the life of the corner store, the local cab company and the thrift shop. Real strategies are rarely determined while sitting around a conference table. They arise from engaging in conversations, interacting with customers, studying the competition, reading and researching, both formally and informally.

The concept of strategic planning and the need for carrying out this process regularly have been around for a long time. Business leaders generally agree that crafting strategy is one of the most important parts of their jobs. Top management is required to invest a good deal of time and effort into the planning process. Yet there is plenty of evidence that most of these plans do not work out as they are documented. The plans on paper often contain no new ideas and little in the way of innovation. To succeed, they require a framework.

THE PLANNING FRAMEWORK

First, agree on the need for goals—a sales target, a growth rate, a profit target, two more stores in two years, whatever. Goals stretch the business beyond its budgets and short-term targets. Although they may never be reached, they should always be striven for—

- to build prepared minds, to make sure that those who participate in running the business have a solid understanding of what makes the company tick and how people need to adapt, react to change and stretch in order to achieve measurable goals; and
- to increase the innovativeness of the enterprise, to open up the team of people to new thinking.

Strategic plans should focus on the two critical elements of the business: the business unit or operating department, such as a single store or stores division, and the company. Each store or service centre is unique and needs to be given its own life. At the same time, wherever the customer comes into contact with the retailer, the business must deliver the strategy and collect the rewards for doing it right. A workable strategy guarantees the soundness of the business.

The strategic plan of a grocery chain may have as few as four pillars:

1. cash generation;
2. a multi-banner approach;
3. a focus on freshness; and
4. a company controlled-label program, where the grocer owns the brands and dictates which suppliers will use them, establishing the grocer's exclusivity.

Strategic planning needs to set a framework to conduct the planning process, consider all of the issues, reach conclusions, set goals and involve everyone. These goals flow from the four pillars—the strategy. Following are a few questions that any storekeeper, division head or company executive should consider and ask his or her peers and subordinates to consider:

· What does the external market consist of? Who are the consumers, the customers and the competition?
· What are they doing that affects our offering?
· What would increase their interest in what we do?
· What must be done differently to improve our connection with them?

SWOT

When the research is complete and the known facts are listed, it is time to play SWOT—strengths, weaknesses, opportunities and threats. This can be done best through a group workshop that plots these findings as shown in Figure 2.1.

Figure 2.1: SWOT chart

Internal	Strengths	Weaknesses	Maximize strengths Minimize weaknesses
External	Opportunities	Threats	Exploit opportunities Avoid threats

This chart can be used to bring the leadership team together to create a retailing strategy. Groups or individuals are tasked to consider the firm's internal strengths and weaknesses while others evaluate the external threats and opportunities. When the group reaches a consensus on these key issues, the responses can be described in terms of strategies—the phrases on the right side of the table. Often, strategic planning involves choosing the alternatives that will produce the "biggest bang for the buck."

From the summary of the four central boxes that spell "SWOT," a number of key issues usually surface. When they are prioritized, an action plan can be designed to deal with them. In Figure 2.1, note the verbs used in the right-hand column. These can be applied to the key issues to define a direction and strategy.

THE BALANCED SCORECARD

Business schools suggest that the best strategic plans usually address the four perspectives of a "Balanced Scorecard," as illustrated in Figure 2.2. It is clear that the scorecard deals with intangible assets. Its four perspectives express the vision and strategy of a business entity:

- The financial perspective is where it all begins and ends. It includes considerations such as rate of growth, willingness to leverage our assets and acceptable thresholds of success.
- The customer perspective is the heart of the company's strategy. Here we identify our target customers, understand their wants and needs and develop a compelling offering of products and services that will bring them into our store instead of the competitors' stores.
- The business process perspective deals with how we will plan, deal with suppliers, maintain relations with lenders and use our systems and technology, all with the goal of creating real value.

· The learning and growth perspective deals with building an infrastructure to sustain long-term growth. The sources of learning and growth include employees, systems, suppliers, third-party providers and customers.

Figure 2.2: The balanced scorecard

FINANCIAL
"To succeed financially, how
should we appear to our
shareholders?"

CUSTOMER
"To achieve our vision, how
should we appear to our
customers?"

BUSINESS PROCESSES
"To satisfy our many stakeholders,
what business processes
must we excel at?"

LEARNING AND GROWTH
"To achieve our vision, how will
we sustain our ability to change
and improve?"

Source: TNS Retail Forward.

DEALING WITH CHANGE

Leaders have to deal with the conflict between short-term results and long-term goals. They are also bombarded with information from and about today's global environment and its impact on the local market. Technology continues to change rapidly, as do the regulations concerning any business, and as a result "coping" takes the place of "leading." What can be done to deal effectively with change?

Business leaders must also consider what is important to today's enterprise while forming an opinion regarding the consequences of external change. In resolving this conflict there should be some acceptable compromises. Leaders must embrace new technology, ensure that their employees are exposed to its possibilities and be willing to take a risk in adopting what appears to fit well with the needs of the business. They must push aside biases of the past and remain open to what's new.

Not all retailers formalize their strategic plans and set down their ideas in writing. Somewhere in the mind of the business originator and leader is the essence of what he or she believes the consumers need or want. Regardless of their format, successful retailers of goods and services tend to follow five fundamental principles of strategy:

1. They deliver a customer-driven, superior retail value proposition.
2. They are market leaders with unique assortments or services.
3. They carry out plans better than their competition.
4. They are constantly innovating and making changes.
5. Most importantly, they exhibit "leadership vision."

FAIL TO PLAN? PLAN TO FAIL

This is a warning. Planning is essential for competitiveness and business growth; when one takes risks, unpleasant surprises can result. And small businesses, just like the giants, have to think about everything. Plans can fail, but at least with a plan, there are goals to shoot for and timetables to meet. Most importantly, good plans lay out who is responsible for achieving the goals or milestones.

Plans can be strategic, dealing with the big issues of competition, growth or financial goals. They can be business plans, dealing with who should do what to meet the budget for the current year. They can be contingency plans, dealing with what to do if the plan does not work out—these are "What if...?" plans. Whatever the genre, a plan must be in writing and must be shared with the whole team.

POSITIONING

> *"Quality in a product or service is not what the supplier puts in. It is what the customer gets out and is willing to pay for."*

> PETER DRUCKER

What makes one store or service centre different from the others? Why do shoppers head down certain aisles of the mall and avoid others? Why do we see brown paper on the windows of some stores that we can't even remember noticing before they closed? Positioning is the ability to occupy a unique place in the mind of the customer. Only two rules apply to the art of being a unique retailer.

1. Customers go where they get good value.
2. Customers go where they are treated well.

When value isn't obvious and service levels drop, customers slip away. To prevent this, successful retailers of both goods and services focus their teams on finding and maintaining uniqueness. This process and attribute is often called "the retail value proposition." It is not only an act of superb creativity but also an act of superb execution.

THE RETAIL POSITIONING MODEL

Figure 2.3: The retail positioning model

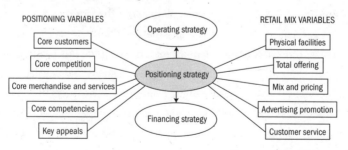

Source: TNS Retail Forward

A high-quality retail positioning model such as the one shown in Figure 2.3 will help describe each of the positioning variables and develop a retail mix variable to deal with the positioning-variable issues on the left of the figure. This model should help to clarify the resulting operating strategy and financing strategy.

SERVICE POSITIONING

Although every box in Figure 2.3 applies equally to the sale of goods and services, service companies have an advantage. Once they decide what type of service they plan to offer, the task of narrowing the offering is complete and the uniqueness is established. Service companies have a vast array of opportunities to serve their market. Their challenge is to secure a need or a want. Many service businesses grow from a disappointed consumer who has been repeatedly treated in a manner that deserves correction: "If this is all I can expect from this service provider, I will do it better myself and offer the service to others. Customers who feel like I do will rush to my door!"

This type of attitude is enough to create a new business. Whereas retailers of goods must provide a fine balance between the goods they offer and the people who serve their customers, service providers prioritize the service itself over the venue at which the service is offered. For example, consider seniors' homes—the guests usually complain about the service before they complain about the facilities.

Behind most services is a facility that provides the service, such as a cruise ship, bank branch, laundromat, fitness gym, bus, hotel, park, muffler shop or theatre. These locations are silent and useless until the service provider gives them life by enticing consumers to become customers. Behind the very special service companies are people who offer only themselves; doctors, home nurses, lawyers and accountants, for example, provide common personal services. These people are usually professionally trained and accredited and are members in good standing of a professional service organization. Businesses in this highly focused subsector of service organizations stand apart from the less-trained service businesses and are referred to as professional service companies.

When service people think about their service as a product, they can begin to position their product offering. They study their retail positioning to determine what works and what doesn't. For example, they can be more focused than a store selling clothes.

Along with the process of strategic planning, determining a best-in-class positioning strategy is best done by using a model. The model shown in Figure 2.3 first appeared in the 1970s and has reappeared in many forms and with many variations. Beginning from the centre of the figure, the positioning strategy points the way towards a supporting operating strategy (execution) and a financing strategy (flexibility).

Often, the need to position or reposition a business correctly arises from the desire to match or surpass a particular competitor. If this is the case, it is useful to create an "attributes matrix" to graphically show the competitors on a grid, as in Figure 2.4. Beyond featuring a price and fashionability dimension, this chart can also be used to position different comparative coordinates, such as:

· Income: low-to-high, up the left axis; or

· Age: young-to-old, along the left–right axis.

Figure 2.4: A sample attributes matrix

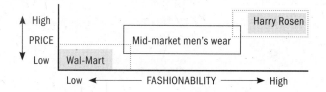

In Figure 2.4, two Canadian retailers of men's wear are shown to demonstrate what every shopper knows regarding these retailers and their offering combination of fashion and price. Such a chart is never static. At a recent turning point in the men's fashion world, a decided shift occurred from dress wear to casual wear. It began in the leisure world and migrated to the office environment. Harry Rosen adjusted its offering accordingly and broadened its positioning as indicated by the larger unshaded "box of influence." And Wal-Mart slowly expanded its fashion with a broader mix for men, enlarging its positioning. The figure shows that both Harry Rosen and Wal-Mart crept into the offering model of the many mid-market men's wear stores, which had to react with their own repositioning or lose market share.

This type of positioning lends itself well to men's and women's apparel. It provides a strong focus for buyers, designers, advertisers, store interior planners and personnel recruiters. But its positioning strength is only temporary. To maintain loyal customers, these age-focused retailers must move their core fashion statements up the age brackets over time, or they risk losing their best supporters.

Wal-Mart broadened its positioning by introducing its own men's fashion brands, expanding its fashionability and increasing its price points. This has moved it into mid-market and has forced the mid-market merchant to adjust their positioning once again.

Other retailers that exhibit successful positioning attributes include:

· Roots, with proprietary-branded casual apparel;
· Loblaws, with "President's Choice" and "No Name" branding;
· Costco, with low-priced family packs;
· Ikea, with low-cost furnishings that are prepackaged and ready to assemble; and
· Curves, with "in and out" thirty-minute fitness programs and specialized training equipment.

"E" POSITIONING

None of the above hallmarks of market success achieved success over-night. A look inside at the companies' meetings and discussions would show that they are still working on perfecting the attributes for which they are known and measuring the change in their share of market that tweaking these attributes has brought about. Another simple approach to developing a positioning statement is referred to as the "4 Es," as shown in Figure 2.5: efficiency, economy, ego and experience.

Figure 2.5: The 4 Es

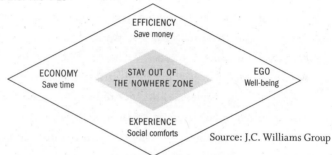

Source: J.C. Williams Group

The consumer market clearly understands statements that include words with the suffix "-est"—for example, cheapest, fastest, bright-est, biggest, best. Figure 2.5 focuses the leadership team on answering the question, "What can we be best at?" The answer might include:

·   Saving people time (Curves).

·   Helping our customers save money (Dollarama).

·   Creating a worthwhile social experience (Running Room).

·   Helping our customers feel good (Tim Hortons).

Each of these positioning techniques is a way of assisting the deci-sion makers with a framework for establishing what the consumer market refers to as the "retail value proposition" (RVP). In the book *Power Retail*, authors Lawrence N. Stevenson, Joseph C. Shlesinger and

Michael R. Pearce demonstrate through their research that retailers with an excellent RVP have superior key performance measurements.[1] These measurements include stock performance, after-tax disposable income, retail sales per square foot and cumulative growth. Their formula suggests that a superior RVP leads to a leadership position that, when properly executed, leads to an even more superior RVP.

FOOD SERVICE POSITIONING

Most customers tend to migrate towards one form of food service, depending upon their lifestyle, time availability and income level. Table 2.1 below shows three different types of food service segments broken down into their subsegments. We have all eaten at all of these venues at one time or another. We have probably settled on the one or two formats that meet our needs better than the others. All of these formats are viable; all of them can be moneymakers. They are distinguished by differences in their location, construction, menus, prices and management style. For example, fine dining restaurants are usually owned and operated by a team of two—one in the back responsible for the kitchen and food and the other in the front responsible for the bar and service. This winning strategy helps the co-owners mitigate shrinkage, which can occur from both the kitchen and the bar and is a continuing problem in the food service business.

Table 2.1: Foodservice Subsegments

FINE DINING	FAMILY DINING	CASUAL DINING
· Clubs	· Entertainment venues	· Quick-service
· Hotels	· Malls and power centres	· Take-out
· Restaurants	· Shopping streets	· Delivery

MARKET-LEVEL POSITIONING

Overriding the choices of RVP is the powerful trend of market polarization. Premium offerings and no-frills offerings are appealing to more consumers, and middle-of-the-road vendors are seeing their volumes decline over time. Certain product groups have demonstrated this high–low pull as their offerings moved away from the middle. The best example of this polarization is apparel, but appliance vendors and mobile-phone sellers also exhibit the same bipolar choices.

In the past few decades, the most powerful consumer market has been the middle market, serving the middle class. There is evidence that the middle class is shrinking; the declining importance of the department store, which originally catered to the middle class, is a telling example of the polarization of consumers.

As the baby boomers age and their consuming patterns shift accordingly, it is evident that the lower-income groups are falling behind. This has fed the growth of Wal-Mart and Costco while contributing to the demise of the T. Eaton Co. in 1998. As the middle-consumer market has migrated up or down, the specialty boutiques have succeeded at the high end of the price–quality spectrum, while the discounters, outlet stores and low-end merchants have succeeded with their big boxes by serving the low-end, or value-seeking, consumer. The lesson is that the "Nowhere Zone" in Figure 2.5 is the position to avoid.

Positioning is perhaps the most powerful influence on consumer behaviour. All kinds of firms—hotels, airlines, automobile manufacturers, retailers, car repair shops, political parties—attempt to drive home a position that calls people to "grab on." It therefore is imperative that owners and managers of consumer-fulfillment businesses spend time and money researching and developing a unique position that converts consumers to customers, and customers to loyal clients.

TRADING UP AND DOWN

The amount of money trading down in the past decade was twice the amount trading up. The automobile middle market shrank 12 per cent, and the television market shrank 40 per cent. Although the middle market is still huge, it is shrinking. This suggests that a fundamental decision in a retailer's positioning model, either in goods or services, is to choose whether to go up or down. The "down" model brings to mind Wal-Mart, Costco and the other giants. Below the value giants are many chains of community family-value stores, also known as dollar stores. In the food sector, the down-market giants and up-market specialists are both threatening the grocery store industry. The up-market, unlike the down-market, is dominated by small formats and boutiques.

Service firms may not exhibit the same strong retail format characteristics as the retailers of goods. Yet they need to recognize that it is the actions of the consumer, not the retailers that are creating the polarization. Thus, consumers who are trading down for goods will also balance their budget by trading down to lower-priced services. An obvious example is discount airlines, Web-based travel services and low-cost gymnasiums, the last of which provide an alternative to high-service fitness clubs that offer specialized equipment and personal trainers.

Differentiation is not a fixed strategy. Competitors who watch the competition quickly emulate the perceived winners. Being different is a constant challenge that involves constant change and adaptability.

GROW OR GO?

"Whoever said, 'It's not whether you win or lose that counts,' probably lost."   MARTINA NAVRATILOVA

We have often heard the retailer's cry: "We must grow or die." This has been the mantra of retailing, and it is no surprise—with rising fixed costs, new sources of sales or gross margin revenue must be found to cover them. Which brings to mind the other cry: "You can't shrink to greatness." Cutting costs for efficiency's sake is worthwhile, but if it shrinks the business, it won't succeed. Companies that are growing are creating value. They tend to exhibit the best practices of strategy, marketing, operations and money management.

Growing companies are the ones that take over those that aren't growing. Companies that are unable to increase their revenues run out of ways to stay on top of the latest information technology, innovate with confidence, attract the top talent, and generate shareholder value. They become takeover targets because the winners see that they can build value by applying their expertise. They recognize that they can grow much faster by making sensible acquisitions than by expanding from scratch.

SALES UNIT GROWTH

Sales growth takes many forms or, to put it another way, is open to many opportunities. The key measurement for analysis purposes is what is known as "comparative sales"—the sales growth rate of all stores that have been open for at least one year, a criterion that eliminates stores that have opened and closed within the years being measured. Stock market analysts watch the "top line"—revenues—while they analyze the "bottom line"—profit. Both are key indicators of positive and negative change.

Look at Figures 2.6 and 2.7, which show the sales of a twelve-store regional retail specialty chain. Figure 2.6 shows the growth of total revenues in all the chain stores. During this period (October

1998–July 2003) the number of stores increased by four. Note, as an aside, the tremendous peaks that occur during the Christmas period each year. (Managing this phenomenon, seasonal variation, will be dealt with in Chapter 3.) The chain's overall growth looks positive and steady, but is it?

Figure 2.6: Sales in all stores, monthly results, October 1998–July 2003

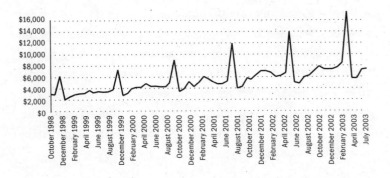

Figure 2.7: Twelve-month moving average sales-per-store growth rate, October 1999–July 2003

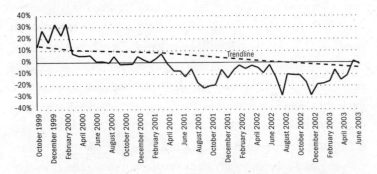

Now consider Figure 2.7, showing the same chain and the same sales, but charted as the twelve-month moving average of same-store, or overall comparative, sales. The use of a twelve-month trailing average has removed the Christmas spikes. As new stores were opened, the same-store sales declined. The additional stores appear to have drained sales away from the existing stores. Store sales growth percentage declined each time a new store opened. While revenues were climbing, productivity was falling. This is an example of market saturation, which occurs when a new store obtains some of its sales from a nearby unit that is part of the same chain.

Another explanation for the falling sales growth percentage could be the size of the newer stores. If the early stores are large and the newer stores are smaller, the graph will demonstrate the saturation effect. To better understand what is really happening, data needs to be developed to show sales per square feet. This will give a better metric for study. But the question still needs to be asked: How well are we building sales — and what works best?

INDUSTRY GROWTH

The desire to achieve constant growth is a fundamental drive throughout our economy, and it requires strategy. At its most basic level, a strategy responds to the need to increase revenues to cover increasing fixed costs. At the most public level, it strives to increase shareholder value over time.

Since the United States has so many more publicly traded retail stores than Canada does, a statistical review of its industry trends has a great deal more substance. The U.S. government plots overall retail sales growth, whereas TNS Retail Forward plots same-store sales growth. Figure 2.8 shows that as of November 2006, overall sales growth as reported by the government is climbing at a rate of 6 to 7 per cent, while the same-store sales reported by TNS Retail Forward. have slipped to a growth rate of 3 per cent. The conclusion that we can draw from this is that sales growth at this time is heavily dependent on the addition of new stores. If this trend were to continue and same-store sales growth fell to zero, it should be assumed that consumers have reduced their spending and that maybe it is time to reduce new-store growth. The key to this warning signal comes from the tracking of same-store sales growth, not overall growth.

Figure 2.8: Company vs. industry performance (percentage change year over year)

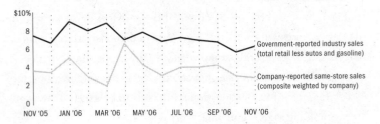

Source: U.S. Department of Commerce,
company press releases and TNS Retail Forward

Independently owned consumer businesses must set growth goals: top-line revenues, bottom-line profits and shareholder wealth. These three district goals should be connected, but retailers often forget to consider them together. Rapid growth consumes capital and often decreases wealth, defined as the return on shareholders' equity, while cutting costs to improve profits may starve the business of the essential resources needed for its growth.

OPTIONS FOR GROWTH
The retailer's options for growth must be spelled out and managed. Growth needs to be controlled; that is, it must address short- as well as long-term performance goals and measurements. Michael Treacy, in his book *Double-Digit Growth*, outlines five growth options, or disciplines[2]:

1. *Hang on to the growth already earned.* Put simply, this refers to the need to manage customer retention.

2. *Anticipate where growth will be coming from, and "be there."* For example, it may come from:

   · the opening of a new mall;

   · the introduction of a new technology (such as mobile phone features, digital photography);

   · the arrival of immigrants from countries where their needs are different;

   · changing trends, such as food choices (for example, organic, low carb, high fibre);

   · demographic changes (aging baby boomers); and

   · legislation (such as new health-club regulations).

3. *Invade adjacent markets.* These may be product, price or technology based. Ask yourself these three questions:

   · Is the new marketing promising, as indicated by credible sources and research?

   · Do I have what it takes (usually, people and cash) to win in that market?

   · Can I match the standards of competition in that market? (An example of what not to do: opening a discount store beside Wal-Mart!)

4. *Invest in new lines of business.* This is a questionable tactic for those engaged in serving consumers. But for a company that has proven its ability to be innovative and that was capable of shifting its strategic focus in the past, it might be the right growth strategy.

5. *Take business from your competitors.* This is the game of retailing. It can be fun and it can backfire, but it can be easily reversed.

   Retailers should understand the importance of beating the competition, better than other business leaders, because this is what they do every time they run an off-price ad. If successful, the lower unit prices will be offset by a greater number of transactions. But how many retailers measure these statistics? The level of customer support prior to the ad's appearance needs to be known so that the level of customer support can be calculated when the ad campaign is complete.

Then the retailer must ask, "Did the cost and complications of running that ad pay off by increasing our share of market?" If they didn't, the ad was unsuccessful and growth was not achieved. A company that truly succeeds in growing must demonstrate not only consistent sales growth but also profit growth. These companies are few and far between, but the best-in-class leaders achieve a long-term superior growth in both sales and profits. Along the way they may face extended growth periods that leave the business overextended and short of cash. At the same time, competitors may feel the impact of high-growth retailers and respond with successful campaigns. And consumers may divert their disposable income from the acquisition of goods to service offerings, dampening the growth of retail goods. Clearly, the successful growth of the business is an energy drain.

WHAT THE WINNERS KNOW

McKinsey & Co. conducted a survey of one hundred large companies in the United States to determine the relationship between growth and total returns to shareholders. It found out that management must devote as much time to growth initiatives as it does to cost control and expense reduction. McKinsey learned from the results what owner-operators know instinctively if they are on a path to financial success:

- Combine good execution with tight cost controls.
- Winning means that the bottom line regularly grows faster than the top line.

- If it's not working, drop it.
- Behind every macro strategy is the detail of each micro-strategy.
- A built-in exclusivity wins every time. (The Apple iPod is a stunning example.)
- Winners understand what makes them successful.

This section has dealt with the importance of growth. The following three sections deal with the key contributing factors to sales growth and discuss how to build sales logically.

LOCATION

"An oral contract isn't worth the paper it's printed on."

STUDENT BLOOPER

We hear it time and again: "Location, location, location." We want to believe that if our location is right, all will be well. But this cliché is a myth. What about the door-to-door salesperson, the mail-order catalogue, the direct-marketing flyer or the TV infomercial? What about the website? Clearly it's not the location that describes the successful retail venture; it is the combination of location, ease of access and the "come-on" that attracts shoppers to a store or service.

When the dot-com boom took off in the late 1990s, hundreds of website retail ventures were launched. They were referred to as "pure play," which meant that they were not connected with a retail store or chain, nor were they an extension of a print catalogue. During the year 2000, a great number of the publicly traded e-retailers became bankrupt because, generally, their marketing costs exceeded their sales volumes. Many customers could not find the sites, or when they found them, they often left before conducting any business.

TRAFFIC GENERATION

Many retailers have survived quite well regardless of their location. An excellent example of a thriving survivor is "The Olde Hide House" in Acton, Ontario. In this tiny town, a 33,000-square-foot, restored nineteenth-century brick-and-beam tannery warehouse full of quality leather goods is the main attraction. What fills the store with customers is a combination of excellent merchandise (leather apparel and furniture) and an unforgettable slogan: "It's worth the drive to Acton!" The company's owners knew that although they enjoyed extremely low rent costs, they needed to pay extremely high promotional costs to get their message out. The store draws in more than 250,000 visitors per year from all over southern Ontario, western New York and northern Michigan.

The combination of occupancy costs plus external marketing costs becomes the cost of location. Stores located in high-traffic areas, such as major shopping malls, pay extremely high rents but don't need to pay for customer attraction because they live off the mall traffic. The same is true at airport retail sites. The lower the occupancy cost, the lower the natural shopping traffic and the greater the need for store promotions, come-ons and site identification.

Over the years, the rents of suburban shopping malls have stratified such that there are now Class A, B and C malls. It may be enticing to get into a low-rent C mall, but sufficient traffic probably isn't there or the mix of retailers may be mismatched. Shopping streets have also stratified. At the top end, they are referred to as "high street" shopping. The best examples are Robson Street in Vancouver and Yonge Street north of Eglinton Avenue in Toronto.

The location decision is extremely difficult to reverse, so it's a decision worth spending some time on. Considering the cost of generating store traffic as a part of the location costs raises the question, "How do shoppers end up at or passing by my store?" Downtown department stores and malls rely on public transit to bring customers to them. Central business district retailing relies on purchases from the occupants of the office towers that populate the area, but the growth of downtown condominiums adds to the potential for downtown retailing. Suburban malls rely on major highway interchanges and the family car. Street shopping relies on the local community that lives within walking distance and sufficient nearby parking. Power centres and their big box stores rely on huge parking lots and a combination of destination stores and anchor stores such as supermarkets and giant multi-product drugstores. Kiosks rely on the mall traffic or street traffic that passes by their units. They position themselves as an obstruction to traffic to get shoppers' attention.

Leisure and travel services rely on packaged vacation promotions. Hotels rely on their reputation, established by the inherent quality of their banner, the reservation system and word of mouth. Fitness clubs rely on memberships. Sports arenas rely on winning teams and special events. For the same reason that a stadium will not attract people if the local team has a poor record, a store will be light on traffic if the merchandise or services are weak.

Statistics Canada divides retail stores into three groups: chains, franchises and independent retailers that operate fewer than four stores. Retail chains account for over 40 per cent of the retail sales in Canada. More than two thirds of these stores are located in large metropolitan centres and account for over 70 per cent of retail chain total sales.[3] Financial institutions usually divide retailing into different groups, based on ownership: proprietorships, partnerships, private companies and public companies.

LEISURE SHOPPING

The Mills Corp. is well known as the builder of giant outlet malls such as Gurnee Mills, north of Chicago, or Vaughan Mills, north of Toronto. These huge (and successful) malls are full of outlet and off-price stores that carry ends of lines, knock-offs and bargains galore and also include local independents with unique offerings. The Mills strategy is based on establishing malls near leisure entertainment parks, such as Canada's Wonderland, near Vaughan Mills, or Four Flags Park, beside Gurnee Mills, where families spend plenty of time and their spare cash on self-indulgence, both at the park and at the mall. The firm's secondary strategy capitalizes on the families that split up: the kids to the park and the parents to the mall. Either way, shopping and entertainment are blended.

TO OWN OR TO LEASE

Owning the retail location means paying no rent, but there is no such thing as free occupancy. All the other costs of occupancy (see, for example, the occupancy expenses of Household Extras Inc. in the Appendix) still apply. Ownership has the potential for capital gain as well as loss. Many great entrepreneurial success stories begin in the attic or basement of the founder's home. Unencumbered by either rent or purchase costs, the entrepreneurs worked from their home or their garage to get started and did not make the lease-or-buy decision until it was absolutely necessary. When cash is king but scarce, the better decision appears to be to lease or rent.

The decision to lease is probably the most significant decision at the time of start-up and will be for years to come. Extending for five years or more, the commitment to lease is also a commitment to run the business for at least the life of the lease. Leasing brings to the

table experts in the fields of location and of law. They know who is
doing what and where and can assist with finding the best co-location
combinations. These experts, carefully chosen, become support partners in the business.

The lease agreement is a complex and technical document. To provide expert insight into the process of leasing, the Toronto law firm
of WeirFoulds LLP offered to summarize the key issues facing owner-
operators of retail businesses. The firm has significant experience in
the areas of commercial leasing, real estate and property development.
Following is a summary of one of their news bulletins, "Don't Go It
Alone: The Top 10 Things to Know About Negotiating with Your
Landlord."[4]

1. *Know your landlord:* A good tenant's real estate agent is a source of
   invaluable information. The future relationship between you and
   your landlord may depend on how the offer or letter of intent is
   drafted, and agents often use the landlord's forms without changes
   to expedite completion. If you can, talk to other tenants of the
   landlord to discuss questions like these: Does the landlord maintain the property properly? Does it solicit input from tenants?
   Does it have a "difficult" reputation?

2. *Know your site:* There is a great deal of risk in treating every site the
   same way; it would be imprudent to treat negotiations for a location at a not-yet-built property in the same way as negotiations for
   space in an existing shopping centre. You need to know the following in virtually every case: How does the weather across Canada
   affect the traditional retail seasons? Has site plan approval been
   obtained? Is the zoning appropriate for your use? How quick is
   the municipal authority at issuing building permits? How available are the various trades to carry out tenant improvements?

What is the nature and quality of parking, signage and access? Who are the anchor tenants? How are they performing? Are there any restrictive or exclusive covenants in force that would impede or prevent you from operating your usual business?

3. *Know your minimum documentary requirements:* As a general rule, a lease is created when there is agreement over parties, property and term. Beyond the basic legal requirements, knowing your minimum corporate requirements is also essential. Knowing ahead of time, by consulting with your lawyer, about the minimum legal requirements for a deal puts you ahead of the curve when negotiating with Canadian landlords.

4. *Know your realty taxes:* In Canada, in addition to paying the basic rent, tenants must also pay taxes, utilities, operating costs, insurance and other charges—all of which, for the purposes of the document, are treated as rent. A default in paying any of these amounts gives the landlord the full array of legal remedies for the non-payment of basic rent. Probably no aspect of rent calculation is more complex than that of realty taxes. Never sign a deal until you have discussed the calculation and payment of realty taxes with your legal counsel.

5. *Know your operating costs:* You will be required to negotiate a "laundry list" of operating costs known as common area maintenance (CAM). Most landlords use a standard form of "net, net, net" lease, and every cost (including the allocation of the cost of liability) needs to be fully understood.

6. *Know your sales taxes:* Each province sets its own PST rates, and these rates vary across the country. Recognize also that along with the federally imposed GST, sales taxes are subject to political strategy and can change from time to time. Furthermore, the federal and provincial rates may or may not be blended. So be aware of

government tax announcements and be prepared to adjust the rates as needed.

7. *Know your exit strategy:* Most leases in Canada are not weighted towards tenants; they are on the landlord's form. A landlord's form provides for continuous operation and the arbitrary withholding by the landlord of consent to assign and sublease. As a tenant you may not have automatic exit strategies available to you, and you may have to rely on negotiating at the time of the proposed exit.

8. *Know your vulnerabilities and obtain protections:* At the top of the list is the exclusive use covenant. Space in good retail centres is tight, and existing centres are altered and redeveloped regularly. Correspondingly, landlords are retaining more and more control over the merchandising mix. Parking, signage, access and visibility are also factors that can seriously affect a retailer's operation; you should endeavour to obtain non-interference covenants and parking ratio minimums to preserve your rights. Your success in negotiating these types of arrangements will depend on the influence you have.

9. *Know your plan and obtain flexibility rights:* If you require special rights or flexibility, don't wait for the lease negotiation stage; it will be too late. If it is not in the offer or letter of intent, generally you are not going to get the privilege. Think ahead about whether you will need the right to expand, or a right of first offer to lease or a right of first refusal on the best space in the shopping centre. For the next few years, expect that if your business is doing well, so is the landlord's and that the landlord does not want to compete with you in leasing space at the centre!

10. *And finally:* This summary is not a substitute for proper legal advice, which you should seek from an individual qualified to practise in the province in which you plan to operate.

MARKET MATHEMATICS

"No matter how good you get, you can always get better, and that is the exciting part."   TIGER WOODS

Retail goods and services businesses must keep in mind the importance of providing sufficient store traffic for the store staff and offerings to do the rest.

Consider the mall store that pays high occupancy costs (11–18 per cent of sales) but spends very little on advertising (0–4 per cent), relying on the mall's presence and convenient location to bring in traffic. The placement cost, the combination of occupancy and attraction costs, is an average of 14–15 per cent of sales. The remote-destination store, in contrast, pays low rents but spends funds on advertising to attract customers to its sites. The combination of the two costs—occupancy and advertising—usually works out to the same total placement cost.

Conventional wisdom says that location is critical to success, and this holds true for both physical stores and online retailers that aim to be properly positioned on key search-engine websites. But overall: What is critical to retail success? Location—partly; advertising—partly; a unique offering—totally.

A typical street-located store serves a market with a population of 40,000 to 60,000. Big box retailers serve a much wider market with their larger space and assortments. But regardless of the size of the market, retailers are forever trying to maximize their share of market (SOM)—their (percentage) share of the total consumer market that the customer base of their store or chain of stores makes up. If their offering applies to groups such as women or children only, their potential market is smaller. Curiously, however, few retailers calculate and monitor their SOM.

As markets mature, the larger firms consolidate to gain SOM while increasing their buying power by extracting lower volume prices and reducing the overhead costs of running their business. Many market segments are now dominated by two or three retailers who enjoy greater than 50 per cent SOM. Yet, after all of these retailers' efforts, the rest of the market remains available to all their competitors.

In this hypothetical case study, Household Extras Inc. is interested in growing its business. With five stores averaging approximately $2 million each, including the retail and contract sales, the firm begins to collect data for one store. It then applies what it learns from this store to all of its stores. Table 2.2 illustrates the market mathematics for that store.

Table 2.2: Market mathematics for Household Extras Inc.

Market size	The consumers	80,000
Awareness	The interested ones	20,000
Visitors	The shoppers	5,000
Customers	The buyers	2,500
Spending	$270 per transaction	$675,000
Frequency	3 times per year	$2,025,000

HEI's store manager reads Table 2.2 as follows:
· if the market we are serving has 80,000 potential households;
· and 25 per cent of them are aware of us and what we offer;
· and 25 per cent of those aware of us visit our store;
· and 50 per cent of store visitors buy something;
· and the customers' average purchase (the average transaction value) is $270;

- and they visit the store three times a year, spending the same average amount;
- our annual store sales will be $2,025,000.

The mathematical formula, where

number of visitors = v

conversion rate (% of visitors who buy something) = CR

average transaction value = ATV

frequency = F, is:

- v × CR × ATV × F = Sales

Applied to the model above:

- v (5,000) × CR (50%) × ATV ($270) × F (3) = $2,025,000

The power behind this formula is the ability to measure sales by observing and counting the shoppers and their habits. This market mathematics formula is rarely used because the essential data is often lacking, yet it is a strong incentive for sales growth planning. It encourages store managers to think in the following way:

- if I can improve my advertising and awareness to get 5 per cent more visitors (5,250 instead of 5,000);
- and my staff gets an additional 2 per cent of these visitors (52 per cent instead of 50 per cent) to purchase or contract for something;
- and they each spend an additional $10 on each transaction (up-selling to $280). This could be with higher priced goods, add-ons, or impulse items;
- the revised formula will be: v (5,250) × CR (52%) × ATV ($280.00) × F (3);
- my sales will climb from $2,025,000 to $2,293,300, an increase of 11.7 per cent!

The gain in store sales came from a compounding of the improved results of each variable. There is no one key to this improvement formula. It is the combination of advertising improvements, store staff involvement, better signage, department layouts, clear aisles and an efficient checkout arrangement. Big-ticket stores like this often add an assortment of accessories or lower-priced items to bring customers in more often. Imagine the sales increase if the frequency could be increased from three to four. How does the store staff move the sales volume up 15 per cent?

- The staff can ensure that transactions are concluded quickly, purchases are made without waiting for back-office approval and price look-ups and are not hampered by over-choice.
- With the use of "shelf-talkers" that provide usage tips or care suggestions for a product, more people will feel confident in acquiring the item.
- The staff can interact with the customer, adding accessory items, extended credit features and warranties to the "buy."
- Staff suggestions or substitution selling might shift the purchasing choice to a higher-priced item.
- Placing impulse-purchase items near the cash register adds items to the purchase.
- Adding customer cards and loyalty programs might increase the frequency of visits.

An article by Marina Strauss in *The Globe and Mail Report on Business* on September 20, 2006, added credence to the formula.[5] Reporting on the decision of Indigo Books & Music Inc. to add toys to all of its stores, Strauss quoted Heather Reisman, Indigo's chair and CEO: "If Indigo can convert one more browser into a buyer—out of every 100 visitors—it would add $20 million to sales." She added: "And if each customer who made a purchase spent 50 cents more—up from the current average of $28.18—that would add yet another $10 million to sales."

Although retailers understand the importance of store traffic, they often fail to study the importance of the average transaction value and its significance in the equation. Note the extreme range of average transaction values across a number of retail categories given in Table 2.3:

Table 2.3: Average transaction values for various retail categories

RETAIL CATEGORY	AVERAGE TRANSACTION VALUE
Computer hardware	$580
Office supplies	$100
Sporting goods	$75
Home & garden	$70
Computer software	$50
Health & wellness	$45

Household Extras Inc. (HEI), with its $2 million stores, and an average transaction value of $270 and a seven-day shopping week, needs twenty-one transactions per day to meet its targets. But how many retailers know this type of statistic about their stores? Performance calculations and comparisons with industry benchmarks such as these demonstrate the need to understand what is required for each component of the market mathematics formula to convert traffic into purchases and to "trade up" each purchase.

The above example did not consider the number of households that are aware of HEI compared with those who shop there. Chances are that many of those who are aware of HEI are walking right past the store. Traffic counting could add more information to the mix: on a busy day, count the people or groups that pass by the store and compare that number with the number of those who come in. Depending on the store offering or location, the visitors could be a small percentage of the total. Apparel stores in giant malls are fully aware of this fact and spend a great deal of time enhancing the entrance, the lighting and the signage to pull customers in.

THE POWER OF CONVERSION

Retailers' focus should not be on the mere transaction value but on the process of interaction to influence browsers to buy something. Each subsector of the retail industry has its own conversion rate—the proportion of shoppers who actually purchase something. Grocery stores, for example, assume that everyone who enters the store will buy something. Their challenge is to maximize the transaction value: a full grocery cart. Apparel retailers consist of two groups: basic and fashion. They know that consumers will buy basic clothing more often than fashion clothing. It is not unusual for fashion apparel store staff to watch nine out of ten shoppers leave their stores without a purchase. This is a conversion rate of 10 per cent. If one more shopper out of a hundred can be enticed to buy something, the conversion rate jumps to 11 per cent. This is not a 1 per cent increase but a 10 per cent sales increase.

THE PROFIT MODEL REVISITED

This demonstration of the power of market mathematics can be incorporated into HEI's strategic profit model, shown in the Appendix. With the goal of increasing the store's sales as described above, the elements of the market mathematics formula can be added to the left-hand side of Figure 2.9, leading towards store sales on the right. The chart in the figure can be used to portray the situation both before and after. This exercise demonstrates the power of getting behind the financial numbers of the business (hard-edged) to get at the source of those numbers. These boxes are not just money; they are also people (soft-sided). Store managers cannot just push their staff to increase sales; they must show them what produces those sales and how staff can improve upon the elements of sales growth.

Figure 2.9: Improving the market mathematics for Household Extras Inc.

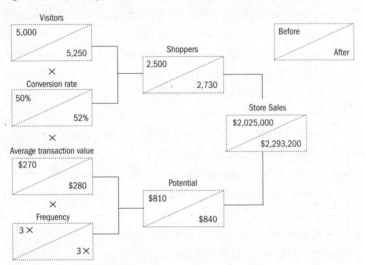

To further demonstrate the value of market mathematics, assume that HEI's customers shop at the store outlined in the figure for ten years, while they fix up their home and until they move away. Their life value is the transaction value ($270) multiplied by their frequency of visiting each year (three) multiplied by ten years: $8,100. The profit model shows that the gross margin for these stores is 40 per cent. So, over time, this customer contributes $3,240 to the profits of the store.

For a grocery store, a shopper spending $100 weekly over fifty weeks yields a total customer value per year of $5,000. Assuming that he or she shops at one store for ten years, that customer's "life value" is $50,000. This is a significant asset; a great deal must be done to keep these kinds of customers coming back. Implementing a program to accomplish this will always cost less and be more valuable than attracting one new customer to the store. Many surveys suggest that it costs five to ten times as much to attract a new customer as it does to keep one.

THREE | BUSINESS OPTIMIZATION

The titles of this and the next two chapters all include the word "optimization." According to a Google search for definitions, the word "optimization" is "Putting together a portfolio in such a way that return is maximized for a given risk level, or risk is minimized for a given expected return level."[6]

The word "portfolio" in the definition refers to a group of investments. To a magician, it refers to a group of tricks. To a retailer, portfolio represents a group of operating elements coordinated in a certain way to maximize results. "Maximization" might be a better word, but "optimization," by its definition, includes the need for a balance between risk and reward. Note that the definition describes a trade-off: returns versus risk. That sounds a lot like retailing!

EMPLOYEES: THE FIRST CUSTOMERS

"To accomplish great things, we must not only act, but also dream; not only plan, but also believe." ANATOLE FRANCE

THE SEARS STORY

In the mid-1990s, Sears USA appointed Arthur Martinez to lead a "turnaround" across its chain. Wal-Mart was finally making an impact on Sears's revenues, profits and customer support. The coffee-talk at the time suggested that Sears did not recognize Wal-Mart as a direct competitor until it was almost too late. The Target chain had successfully shifted its offering upscale to avoid competing head-on with Wal-Mart while hurting Sears as well. Kmart was going through every option at its disposal to stay alive against this competitive onslaught. Martinez conducted a great deal of research on Sears's shareholders, customers and staff. A number of task forces were created to build a fact base about the business, including its finances, innovation, core values, customer attributes and needs, and employees' attitudes and aspirations.

He concluded that an entirely new approach was needed to effect a lasting and successful turnaround. His resulting strategy was simple. He named it "The Three Cs" and announced it as follows: "If we can provide a *compelling* place to work, our customers will find us a *compelling* place to shop and our shareholders will find us a *compelling* place to invest."[7]

Martinez stated what too many retailers had forgotten along the way: the first customer was the staff. This message from the CEO of Sears, a huge company, is as applicable to the shopkeeper as it is to the big chains. It is an axiom that the staff is the first link in the chain that leads to profit. If this link is in good shape, the rest of the chain can hold the enterprise together.

First and foremost, a compelling place to work involves creating an environment that encourages the growth of people on the job and that supports their ambitions for self-enrichment. It certainly includes financial compensation and greater financial security. The word "team" seems overused, but it applies well to retailing, especially on the store floor. Although each staff member must fulfill his or her own immediate responsibilities, he or she must also be aware of what is going on elsewhere: what other staff members need assistance, what customer needs help, what backroom task needs to be completed. There can't be any rigid hierarchy in a store if the team is to win.

The importance of the employees was worked into Martinez's "Three Cs" formula to show how each individual could affect the shareholder value with improved performance. As employee attitudes improved, customer satisfaction rose and store/company revenues climbed. At the end of the cycle, rewards and better compensation lifted employee morale further and the wheel went around again.

The second C in the formula—a compelling place to shop—includes the firm's merchandise or services, the ambience and layout, as well as the customer's reaction and response. It also includes the employees once more: the service they provide, their helpfulness and product or service knowledge and their follow-through to a successful transaction.

The third C concerns ownership. Investors want to be part of a winning combination. This includes the first owner-investor as well as all those who buy in along the way. It's easy to disconnect from a public company that no longer appears to be a compelling place to invest, but it is difficult and often impossible for private investors to "pull the plug." This is all the more reason to work with the staff to attract and serve first the customers, then the investors.

The third C also deals with investment—that is, how the owners of shares feel about the prospects of their shareholdings. The better they feel, the more they will invest or the longer they will hold on to their investment. Shareholders of private business, a category that includes a high percentage of retail businesses, feel the same way. The big difference is that they can't check their morning paper and decide either to sell or to contribute more to their investment. Their commitment is a fixed, inflexible position. The private retail business owner must make the business a compelling place to invest. When the time comes to look for more equity or debt, this compelling feature will be key. We will return to the third C later in the book. Implementing the three Cs all begins with the employees.

EMPLOYEE TRAINING

The effect of training on employees has shown many positive outcomes. Well-trained employees can increase a company's overall productivity by more than 20 per cent over an untrained staff group. If a firm combines a comprehensive training program with continual mentoring, its productivity can increase by as much as 80 per cent. Employee training reduces turnover and the amount of time lost to tardiness and illness; it also improves company morale. The simple act of demonstrating an interest in the professional development of employees helps the company to achieve its sales targets.

There are three groups of employees on the job at any one time. A small minority believe they are fully engaged in their work and support the goals of the business. Over one half of employees, research suggests, report that they are just putting in time. Some actually confirmed that they were physically on the job but were actually not engaged. Marcus Buckingham, noting this trend in his book *What the Greatest Managers Do Differently*, says, "The owner's challenge is to improve the ratio of engaged to disengaged workers." As a result, the owner's responsibility for people management and improvement is never-ending. Four basic steps describe the never-ending task:

1. learn what makes employees come to work;
2. learn where the strengths of the company lie;
3. treat the challenge as soft-sided, not hard-edged; and
4. one by one, increase each employee's sense of belonging.

MERCHANDISE OPTIMIZATION

> *"The entrepreneur is essentially a visualizer and an actualizer. He can visualize something, and when he visualizes it he sees exactly how to make it happen."*   ROBERT L. SCHWARTZ

Many of the concepts of retailing goods and services are the same. They both involve the process of successfully converting an inquiry into a sale, then into a continuing relationship. Typical retail services are the establishments that look like merchandise stores but offer a wide array of personal services such as laundry, dry cleaning, car rentals, fitness gyms, ear and eye testing, and most common, banking. The big difference between goods and services retailing is this subject of merchandise optimization.

The key elements of merchandise optimization are worthy of a textbook of their own. They are summarized here with an emphasis on an overview of the task and on sound business principles. As stores grow larger and the numbers of items expand, groupings or "departments" appear. These may have been developed as part of the original strategic plan where the merchandise emphasis was laid out, or they may become more important in response to customer demand. Regardless of the reason, they become a grouping of similar products and items that need to be managed at many levels. The levels are outlined below:

1. *Category planning:* Traditionally known as "assortment planning," this involves determining the microelements of each assortment (such as source, brand, size, style, colour, package, price and store display features).

2. *Item selection:* Here the assortment plan is broken down to groupings and items, then down to brands, styles, colours and sizes.

3. *Supplier selection:* This may precede the previous step (item selection), or the buyer may search for the best supplier of the items already chosen.

4. *Supply chain management:* This involves working with each supplier to meet the demands of the consumer in the store, inventory management, distribution, demand response and evaluation.

5. *Store execution:* This step ensures that what has been planned, promoted and procured is handled in a timely and creative way at the store.

6. *Inventory management:* This involves controlling inventory levels, replenishing stock and monitoring sales levels and adjusting purchase amounts.

The staff must take care to balance the impact of planning and control. Buyers are known to fall in love with their merchandise and may overbuy. Inventory controllers are often found to be reporting to the company controller and may restrict the flow of goods for purely financial reasons. This conflict can be solved if a credible forecasting and demand-tracking environment is in place.

Merchandising is the heart and soul of a retail operation. It is here that the offering of the business is established, the look and appeal of the store is displayed, and the types of goods and prices for each item are set. In a one-store company, the owner is usually the merchant and also acts as store manager during most of the day and bookkeeper at night. Only after the owner has built profits from rising sales can some of these jobs be delegated. But the owner will hang on to the merchandising role because that is where the money originates.

THE MERCHANDISE CYCLE

Merchandising is a continuous cycle of many steps. In Figure 3.1, begin at #1 and follow the steps. Clearly, the cycle has no beginning or end. Whether the business is "buy and sell" or "sell and service," this merchandising loop represents the planning and control cycle of the offering. Learning is the catalyst to improving the offering, the sales and the profits. Feeding learning into the loop enhances it.

Figure 3.1: The merchandising cycle

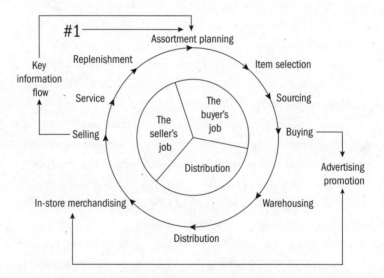

The retailer's largest expense is the cost of the goods sold. These costs must be marked up to cover all of the other costs. If the operating costs are heavy, such as those for sales service in a high-fashion shop, or there is a risk that the merchandise will not sell at the original price, the markup from the costs of the goods will have to be high. Thus the prices will be high. These costs and risks can be reduced through better merchandise planning, selection and inventory control as well as greater store productivity. This is the reason for Wal-Mart's success.

The price, range and quality of the merchandise is the reason people shop at a retail store. For service businesses, the offering is also the reason customers shop at any one service provider. The process of merchandising applies to both goods and services, but this section will deal with the merchandising of goods.

MERCHANDISE CLASSES

For the purpose of merchandise optimization all goods fall into one of three categories:

1. *Basic merchandise* is the everyday assortment of goods that are "always in, never out" of stock. Most assortments consist of up to 80 per cent basic merchandise. In the food store industry, this proportion is above 90 per cent. In a sporting goods store, it may drop to 50 per cent because of the seasonal nature of the mix, but it is always the bulk of the business.

2. *Seasonal merchandise* is, by comparison, "in and out." Back-to-school is an important season to stationers and fashion houses alike. Fashion merchants "make it or break it" on their seasonal introduction of new styles and lines of goods. Seasonal merchandise may follow the calendar, but not necessarily.

3. *Promotional merchandise* is "in—out—fast!" Promotional goods may be brought in for an advertised sale or event and then sold

out rapidly. They may be seasonal goods, highlighted for special purposes such as the launch of a season or an end-of-season sale. Basic goods on sale become promotional goods when they are sold at a lower price for a store event but return to their regular price when the event is over.

Eaton's was very successful for many years with its semi-annual "Trans Canada Sale." The rules were simple: every merchandise department submitted a few items that would sell at 15 per cent off the regular price for the length of the event, usually two weeks. The company's buyer had to guarantee that the item had a steady sales record, that the item had not been discounted recently and that there was a sufficient inventory to back up the peak in demand through the sale. Customers recognized it as a valuable time to shop at Eaton's.

Overriding the three merchandise classes above is the fundamental rule of choice—the 80/20 rule. Simply put, 80 per cent of the total sales of any assortment of goods will flow from 20 per cent of the items displayed. It has also been shown that 80 per cent of the sales will be generated by 20 per cent of the customers. An old but true story describes this well: Consumers Distributing produced an annual catalogue with 5,500 items. The 80/20 rule applied—80 per cent of the sales came from the most popular 20 per cent of the items. A Swedish catalogue chain was starting up and was frustrated with its sales results. The owner visited Consumers and studied the business. It became obvious to him that if he could just sell those "20 per cent winners," he would be much more profitable. He went home, made the adjustment to his catalogue and published his top 20 per cent—1,100 items. Guess what? 80 per cent of his sales came from 20 per cent of the items, but now the business was one fifth of its original size—and it went broke.

ASSORTMENT PLANNING

"Nobody needs anything; to make people want things, that's not easy."
CAROLE FARMER

Drop in to any independent store. What immediately jumps out as the reason for this store's existence? Does this immediate sense of "reason for being" continue as you wander through the store? Does it all "tie in"? Is there evidence of an assortment plan that falls directly out of the retail value proposition (see Figure 2.3)? This section describes how the merchandise choices are made and how the retailer's offering can be distinctive from that of the competition.

Assortment planning applies equally to the retailing of goods and services. Even department stores no longer offer all things to all people; they have refined their assortments over the decades to represent different classes of specialty stores. As a result, the department-store industry now has three classifications: value, traditional and upscale.

THE BASICS

The assortment plan lays out the product groups, subgroups and items that the store will carry, right down to the item's style, size and colour. With knowledge gained from experience or from the suppliers, trade magazines, fashion shows or trade shows, buyers choose what they want to sell and organize their choices so that suppliers can be chosen, promotion and display supports designed, and store space, including display bunks, shelving and racks, established.

Four basic decisions are made at the start of the assortment planning process:

· Merchandise or service type: basic, seasonal or promotional (see p. 81);

- Source: domestic or imported;
- Range: the offering of different price points, referred to as good, better, best; and
- Store location: West, Prairies, Central or East; or downtown, suburban or exurban.

For a service company, it is fine to decide, for example, to become the pre-eminent dry cleaner in the neighbourhood; but what will the offering assortment include? Will laundry services be provided along with dry cleaning? What about repairs and alterations? What about cleaning carpets and drapes, home pickup and delivery, early openings and late closings? The answers to these questions should be in the assortment plan. Household Extras Inc. has chosen to offer home-interior products rather than exteriors, floors, walls and ceilings. This allows it to build a service profile for installations and home repairs and replacements.

WOMEN'S APPAREL

Figure 3.2 shows the many elements and subelements of an assortment plan for women's apparel. The first breakout is the separation of apparel and accessories. A shop may carry all the assortment in the figure or concentrate on one of the two main classifications. Some of the items may be carried seasonally or for promotions only. Buyers for the shop must focus on items, sizes, colours and styles. Then they must choose brands and suppliers. Then prices are set, terms agreed to, purchase volumes committed to, delivery schedules set and returns agreements signed off. A critical part of the process is the agreement on whether the supplier produces the whole order only once, produces this item for others, or allows for reorders throughout the selling season.

Figure 3.2: An assortment plan for women's apparel

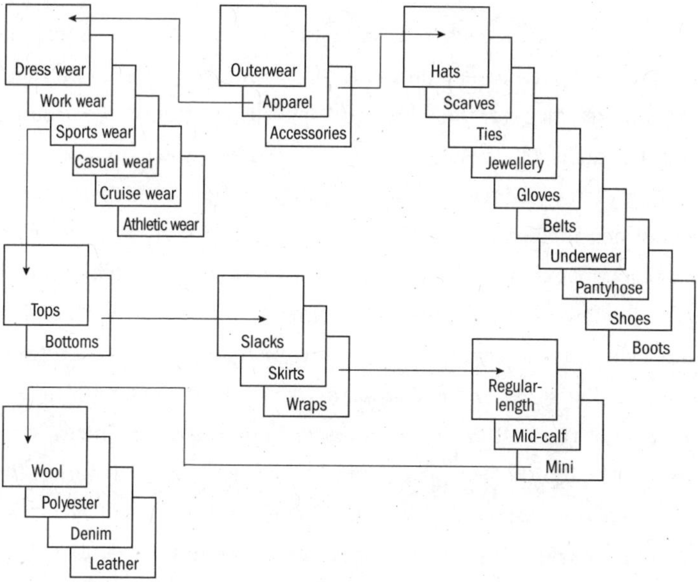

CATEGORY DIMENSIONS

A key retailing decision concerns category dominance. For example, a category-dominant store carries every type of garden tool available at various price ranges, and it is so dominant in this category that all shoppers know that if they are looking for garden tools and don't know exactly what to choose, they will find a suitable selection here. This garden-tools assortment plan is known as "narrow and deep." Specialty stores tend to be narrow and deep. But the big box stores also followed this strategy and became known as "category killers." Toys "R" Us, Indigo (books), Future Shop (home electronics) and HMV (audio-visual media) are good examples of category killers. With deep inventories, they experience few stock shortages, as goods sold are immediately replenished. Generally, customers always find what they want in stock.

At the extreme, deep and narrow assortments that are always in stock are referred to as "continuous." Customers can count on them being there whenever they shop. The opposite approach to continuous assortments is, obviously, "discontinuous." Here, the merchant seeks out "best buys" and the best prices and usually purchases them in bulk lots. When those goods are sold out, that's it. The merchant may have a category plan that sets out the type of goods to buy and sell, and he or she will maintain the category at all times while changing the brands and styles with the seasons. Outlet stores, bargain shops, used clothing stores, dollar stores and fresh food markets follow this approach.

One of the best examples of discontinuous assortments is Winners. Although the floor area is blocked out by major categories, the sources of the items and the brands are constantly shifting. The brands offered for sale one week may be different the next week, but there will always be men's dress shirts available. In the fashion industry, this creates a customer interest based on a constant search for what's new. Customers of the Goodwill Industries thrift stores are often seen waiting in the morning for the racks of goods to emerge from the processing area at the back, so that they may find something unique or fresh.

The complementary approach to narrow and deep is wide and shallow. A wide and shallow store carries a small amount of everything in a broadly related category; dollar stores would be a good example. Because the stores stock only a few of each item, customers who can't find exactly what they want will usually find a substitute.

PRIVATE LABELS

The growth of private labels can be seen on the store shelves of many retailers. Canada's retail grocery industry, dominated by a few national chains, has shifted its mix of private-label products to more than 25 per cent of its total sales. The dominant home improvement chains have also maximized the value of their own store names as their private labels. Small businesses, aware of the control feature offered by private labels, are attracted by the fact that a private label can be created at a price that can't be compared. This usually translates into higher margins.

A product or service may offer a private brand if:

- at the same price as the major national brands, the quality is better;
- with the same quality as the competing brands, the price is better; or
- with a higher quality and an exclusive trademark, it can command a higher price.

The underlying assumption is that the generic brand has costs built into it for product development and marketing that may not be necessary with a private brand. It is easier to create a private label with a lower price than one with a higher quality. In either case, the uniqueness of the offering deserves to be promoted and highlighted to demonstrate its superiority. Loblaws has been a private-label innovator for decades. Its "No Name" brand offers quality similar to that of the national brands but at a lower price. Its "President's Choice" brand offers unique qualities and combinations at the same price as the national brands. These two private-brand programs bracket the regular national-brand items by creating unique products with price points above and below the national brands.

PRICE AND SIZE PROFILES

Another key component of good merchandising is the price profile. Figure 3.3 shows the tiers of price points for a single item such as T-shirts.

Figure 3.3: Sample assortment profile for an item

$29.95	Premium
$27.95	Best
$24.95	Better
$19.95	Good
$14.95	Sale

Merchandise theory suggests that with a good–better–best price display, customers can evaluate the price–value comparisons in making their purchasing decision. The theory is that given these options, customers tend to choose the middle one. Thus the figure shows a larger inventory to support the price point at which the greatest amount of goods will be sold.

The second feature of this assortment profile is the addition of a premium price and a sale price. When planners set up an assortment of five layers, they have the opportunity to separate the prices by a meaningful distance. They also maintain a slot for temporarily bringing in low-priced promotional goods as part of the assortment or use this price point for dropping regular prices to sale price levels.

Finally, size profiling needs to be added to the price profile. A sorry sight in chain stores is the fresh new rack of jackets (or slacks, or whatever) that includes only two of each size across the rack. This is almost as silly as a rack that has two of each colour, side by side. The customer profile for each store is not equal across all sizes. Whether the store is aimed at petites, young adults or an older clientele, there will always be some sort of bell curve of the customers who shop there. So the most commonly wanted sizes sell out first, and customers who come in late may leave disappointed. In addition, different colours are popular in different regions, and assortments must reflect this preference, or stores will find themselves overstocked in one region and out of stock in another.

Grocers can respond to stock-outs quickly, but clothing retailers must order several months before the season begins, and they have little chance to replenish the hot sellers. It is at this level of detail, translated into customer satisfaction, that assortment planning "hits the road." Each store can become unique in serving its own neighbourhood.

SHIFT OF MIX

Although a "shift of mix" may result in sales growth, more often than not it is a source of sales declines. Table 3.1 shows how it works (or doesn't work): assume that for an assortment of Christmas wreaths sold at Household Extras Inc., the same prices are charged each year, but in the second year, style "A" is promoted heavily and the overall category sales climb 10 per cent.

Table 3.1: Sales comparisons of Christmas wreaths, Household Extras Inc.

STYLE	UNIT PRICE BOTH YEARS	% OF TOTAL SEASON SALES LAST YEAR	TOTAL SEASON $ SALES LAST YEAR	% OF TOTAL SEASON SALES THIS YEAR	TOTAL SEASON SEASON $ SALES THIS YEAR
A	$20	25	$5,000	35	$7,700
B	$30	50	$15,000	45	$14,850
C	$50	25	$10,000	20	$8,800
Total sales		1,000 units	$30,000	1,100 units	$31,350

While unit sales climbed 10 per cent, dollar sales climbed only 4.5 per cent. The average unit sale fell from $30.00 to $28.50. Assume the supplier maintained its prices. If gross margins were applied to the mix, it is certain that the gross margin percentage went down. This will be further explored in the next section, "Gross Margins and Pricing."

Service businesses must also develop an assortment plan for their offerings. Is the neighbourhood building contractor an interior or exterior painter, a landscaper, a plumber, a carpenter, a plasterer or all of the above? And what is he or she good at—all of these skills? Are there different tradespeople for each specialized task, or should each employee excel at all trades? Does the fitness club offer supervised and unsupervised programs? What about yoga and Pilates? Is there a daily schedule for members, as well as a weekly one? Assortment planning is the process that considers various factors—the vision, the key elements of differentiation and the target consumer group—to produce saleable items.

GROSS MARGINS AND PRICING

"Have the courage to act instead of react."

EARLENE LARSON JENKS

A great deal of attention is given to the line on a retailer's profit and loss statement referred to as "gross margin." It is fairly easy to record and show gross margin when it is based on goods purchased, but it is difficult to be exact or meaningful when dealing with retail services.

Step back to the overall concept of a retailer's "reason for being." It is to bring to the consumer market the wanted and needed products and services of the surrounding community? All of the costs in getting the store's output in front of the customer add value to the product or service. Some of them, such as supplier costs and inbound distribution costs, are included in "landed cost" and become the basis for calculating gross margin. The equivalent service costs might be the staff costs of those whose time and talent directly serves the customer.

From a financial point of view, all of the value-added product and service costs need to be known to properly price goods and services for profit. Gross margin is only part of the formula. Canadian publicly traded retailers often use the expression "cost of goods sold and expenses." This produces the key statistics "earnings from operations."

The most powerful contributor to operating profit is the price of the goods and services. From the customer's perspective, it is the basis of the key decision: "Should I buy this item or service?" To the retailer, price sets the point from which all costs will be covered, with some-thing left over called profit.

Look at the Household Extras Inc. (HEI) profit statement in the Appendix and consider a price increase of 2 per cent on the original pricing. Assuming that the transaction volume remains constant, sales will climb $214,000. This increase should flow all the way through the profit model to pre-tax profits. Given HEI's very low profit of $424,000, this is an increase of 50 per cent! In this example, the gross margin will climb from 40.5 per cent by the same $214,000 to a new level of 41.6 per cent. On the other hand, if prices remain the same and transaction volumes climb 2 per cent, the sales will again rise by $214,000 but the cost of goods sold will also rise by 2 per cent to $4,415,500 and the gross margin will remain at 40.5 per cent. Instead of the price increase flowing to profits, the margin increase of $87,000 will flow there, producing a profit increase of 20 per cent. But when the volume increases, the costs of moving that volume through the system will rise also, not by 2 per cent but maybe by half that amount. Thus the profit increase will be lower still.

This example appears complicated, but retailers of a single store or a mighty chain must understand and deal with the power of proper pricing. Pricing cannot be simplified to a formula for all items or for a brand or selection. It needs to be established at the item level, where the ultimate customer makes the buying decision.

PRICING PRINCIPLES

It is important to learn and understand the difference between markup and gross margin. Markup is the difference between the landed cost of goods and the selling price of those goods. Looking at the HEI profit statement in the Appendix again, $6,365,000 of goods at cost has been marked up to $10,692,000, or by 68 per cent. Many retailers simply double the cost price to set their selling price, an old habit known as "keystoning." The markup percentage is the amount of the markup compared with the cost. The markup provides for two types of profit: the merchandise profit that covers all other costs, and the company profit (when all goes well).

Gross margin is the markup amount's proportion of the selling price. At HEI, $4,327,000 of margin was obtained from $10,692,000 of sales, or a 40.5 per cent share.

The business of retailing must be focused on margin or gross profit generation. Using restaurants as an example, the operators mark up the cost of their ingredients and equipment costs as well as their staff costs to produce a menu price. A reasonable rule of thumb is one third food costs, one third labour and operating costs, and one third gross profit. Retailers of services also produce gross profits instead of gross margins. Instead of marking up the cost of inventory, they mark up the cost of the talent and supplies used to produce the sale of the service provided. The theory and the mathematics are the same.

The gross margin and gross profit must cover all indirect costs and provide for a final profit. The art of markup is the ability to be competitive on the one hand while providing for unknown risks on the other. The top end of high markups occur where exclusivity, high fashion and the "in thing" are being promoted. Here, customer demand for exclusivity overrides the price consideration. The sale of these goods or services is referred to as "aspirational." The low end of the markup scale is the point where price is the dominant factor, the need for the product is basic and the competition is strong. So, "basic" or "value pricing" is the opposite of "exclusive."

Figure 3.4 explains the key role of pricing. There is no fixed formula, such as the keystoning approach described above, and an individualized approach must be taken:

·   Each retail format includes elements of cost and risk that need to be covered.

·   Good pricing requires funds for markdowns and clearances.

·   Every item needs to stand up to the comparison of its price with those of its competitors.

·   The sum of the pricing decisions should produce profit over time.

Figure 3.4: Retail pricing requirements

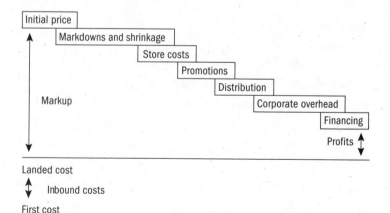

MARKUP AND RISK

Every retailer develops a unique way of operating its business, so a simple approach such as keystoning may not be the right solution for setting prices. The six boxes that set the level of the initial price in Figure 3.4 are different in size for each retailer. Each of the three types of merchandise described earlier—basic, seasonal and promotional— requires its own pricing formula. Promotional goods require a minimum markup in order to carry an attractive price and sell out quickly. The other two categories—and the third variation, imports—require different markups because of the risk associated with the product.

Table 3.2: Basic vs. seasonal pricing (preliminary)

		COMMODITY–BASIC		SEASONAL
Landed cost		$10.00		$10.00
Initial price		$18.00		$22.00
Markup	80%		120%	
Markdowns—% of price and dollar amount	10%	$1.80	30%	$6.60
Final price		$16.20		$15.40
Gross margin dollars		$6.20		$5.40
Gross margin %	38%		35%	

In Table 3.2, for example, it can be seen that:

· Specialty goods, especially high-fashion apparel, have a built-in risk attached to their price: the style may appeal to very few; weather-related goods may arrive at the wrong time; or the colours may be wrong for the fashion trends of the season. Return privileges may be restricted or unavailable. These goods therefore require a high markup, in case markdowns are needed to clear

excess goods. In Table 3.2, the fashion risk has been priced to produce a 120 per cent markup.

- Commodity goods, everyday items that are basic to household use
and acceptance, are purchased continually and thus rarely require
markdowns, except for special promotions. They usually sell well
in a self-service environment. As a result, with little need for a
markup to cover clearance markdowns or store staff costs, smaller
markups can be applied. In Table 3.2, this translates to a markup
of 80 per cent. Imported goods accumulate extra costs between
the time they leave the foreign factory and the time they arrive at
the retailer's warehouse, including the costs of freight insurance,
financing and foreign exchange. Because returning these goods
may not be possible or may be excessively costly, higher markups
are usually added to cover the risk of being left with unsold goods.

- Branded goods that are connected only to the store or chain of
stores cannot be price compared, and thus they can be priced at
whatever level the market will bear. This pricing decision will be
a quality and value decision.

Note that in Figure 3.2 the seasonal goods actually delivered a
lower margin than the basic goods. This example assumes that all
the goods will be treated in the same manner. But reality suggests
that only a portion of the goods will be marked down, depending on
many factors, including inventory levels and weather patterns. So
another two lines are needed in this example to provide more realistic results, as shown in Table 3.3.

To reiterate: the markup percentage is the difference between the
selling price and the cost, compared with the cost; the gross margin
percentage is the difference between the selling price and the cost,
compared with the selling price. In Table 3.3, the final gross margin

Table 3.3: Basic vs. seasonal pricing (revised)

	COMMODITY–BASIC		SEASONAL	
Landed cost		$10.00		$10.00
Markup	80%		120%	
Initial selling price		$18.00		$22.00
Initial gross margin %	44%		55%	
Markdowns—% of price and dollar amount	10%	$1.80	30%	$6.60
Final price		$16.20		$15.40
Gross margin dollars		$6.20		$5.40
Final gross margin %	38%		35%	
% of goods marked down	10%		30%	
Blended total price		$17.80		$20.00
Blended gross margin %	43%		50%	

after all the goods have been sold is a blended gross margin, also called a maintained margin. Some goods were sold at full price, while the rest were sold at a discounted price. The key to good merchandising is managing this blend.

Some merchants put garments on the rack for the first time with a price tag showing both the full price and the marked-down price, although this practice is illegal. Consumer laws require that merchants must demonstrate that they have sold some goods at full price for a period of time before the first markdown can be taken.

SHRINKAGE

The difference between the dollar value of the book inventory compared with that of the physical inventory is referred to as shrinkage. Inventory counting is essential to determining shrinkage. Items received are added to the opening inventory; then the items sold are

subtracted, leaving a closing inventory. The physical count is compared with the bookkeeping records, and if they are the same, there is
no shrinkage. This is rare in a retail environment, for many reasons.

Shrinkage reduces profit every day. The firm's pricing formula
must therefore ensure that it covers the ongoing shrinkage of the
business. Surveys taken over many years suggest that perhaps two
thirds of all shrinkage is caused by employees, not customers. Employees have plenty of time and access to the retail goods, and depending
on how they feel about their job and their pay, they may rationalize
their acquisition of company inventory as a bonus. They may also
make mistakes in recording receipts or transactions or sell goods to
friends at prices below those marked on the ticket. A typical source
of shrinkage occurs when store management and staff reduce prices
to move out slow-moving or distressed goods and neglect to record
the price reduction.

Shrinkage can be high in self-service arrangements, where small
goods can be easily hidden or where the sales staff can give items
away to friends or charge less than the ticket price. Depending upon
the security, staff discipline, the packaging, the checkout arrangement, the customer returns policies and the attitudes prevalent at the
firm, shrinkage generally ranges from 0.5 to 2.5 per cent of net sales.
Obviously, big-ticket appliances will not often be stolen, whereas
apparel and accessories are easier targets for store theft. The tighter
the controls on staff and merchandise, the lower the shrinkage.

PRICING ALTERNATIVES

Wal-Mart is the world's largest retailer because of its continuous
drive to reduce consumer prices and provide the best value for the
money. It does this in many ways and at every level of the organization. Most importantly, it is a master of exploiting the "productivity

loop," illustrated in Figure 3.5. This works itself out within HEI's profit model (see the Appendix) as follows:

· Record gross margin to three decimals: 0.405.
· The pre-tax profit is 0.004, or 0.4 per cent as shown.
· Thus, all the costs as a percentage of sales are 0.401.
· Now reduce all of the costs by 5 per cent to 0.381.
· The cost-to-price spread is now 0.024, or 2.4 per cent of sales.
· Now, return to the customer half of this gain, in the form of lower prices, and retain the other half as profit improvement or devote it to profit-producing elements such as improved technology. That's essentially what Wal-Mart did: "falling prices, with the familiar smiley face," has been the theme of Wal-Mart's advertising for decades. But they aren't dropping all their prices, just those they advertise to attract shoppers.

Figure 3.5: The retail productivity loop

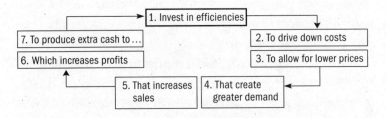

Value companies like Wal-Mart create higher demand from lower prices, and they produce higher profits. Small chains and independent stores do not have the capacity or flexibility to apply the "productivity loop" to the same extent, so they must rely on the power of a well-built pricing strategy. Using these processes, the best-in-class companies are able to grow their top line by more than 10 per cent each year while growing their bottom line by more than 15 per cent.

The Wal-Mart example has its limits. Eventually, there is no more room to lower prices, as the costs of labour, occupancy, and goods and supplies must be covered, and this limits how low prices can go. After the final settlement on supplier input costs, prices must rise or the assortment must be shifted, if profits are to rise.

Meanwhile, the market is saying, "I won't pay!" If the prices are reduced below those of the competition to attract attention, there is the possibility of failure. A smart competitor will match the reduction and go one step further. Customers are happy, but profits fall at both shops. Competitors who react by countering with further price reductions become obligated to leave the prices there, and nobody wins.

The smart move is the first move. Experience shows that the first price cut is the most effective one. It must make a statement that creates urgency in the mind of the shopper.

SERVICE PRICING

Service firms have the ability to be much more creative in their pricing. What they usually offer is unique rates or fees that can be reduced, bundled or spread out over time on certain services, or they offer membership features in which competitive rates cannot be compared.

Knowledge of customer buying habits can provide a signal to operators that will highlight just who is being adversely affected by higher prices. There is a loyal segment of every customer base that will accept higher prices if the price–value equation stays intact. There is also another segment that will switch suppliers on the basis of price only. Perhaps these clients aren't profitable to the offerer and are not worth keeping. The key to service pricing is determining who the loyal customers are, not only from a revenue point of view, but also from a knowledge of the profitability of each line of service.

EVERYDAY LOW PRICES

Although the growth of Wal-Mart has many success factors, the one most evident to its customers and competitors is its adoption of an "everyday low price" (EDLP) format. This practice is contrary to typical general merchandise practices, in which goods are marked up to introduce them, marked down to generate sales volume, and then finally marked down to clear them out.

EDLP provides a low-to-reasonable markup at the start and then leaves the price there. The goods are priced to sell without further markdowns. Customers get used to knowing that the price isn't going to change, so their value decision does not require them to wait and wonder about the possibility of a price reduction after they have made their purchase. Staple goods, such as groceries and basic wearing apparel, lend themselves to EDLP. Fashion merchandise can be sold at an EDLP price if it is part of the policy of the merchant to treat all its goods the same way. The key is ensuring that the price of the item is, first and foremost, in a consumer-acceptable range.

There are savings to be made with the policy of EDLP, the most important of which relates to advertising. Many of today's ads are created to announce a price change, so advertising costs can be dropped or used for other purposes. With EDLP, retailers are not confronted by angry customers who purchased an item at the regular price and later noticed that the price had dropped. EDLP policies usually result in lower shrinkages and reduced price-change errors at the cash register.

Retailers need the support of their suppliers when they move to an EDLP environment. The traditional method of asking the supplier for price-reduction support on an "as needed" basis takes time and is difficult to track. Although EDLP is a simple strategy and a consumer-friendly one, retailers cannot switch back and forth between EDLP and markdown pricing. The customer will not trust them if they do this.

PRICING TIPS

Here are some sensible pricing ideas for growing the business:

- Be sure to begin with a well-defined pricing philosophy. Is it value oriented or weighted towards exclusive offerings? Is it high–low or EDLP?
- Understand the types of shoppers being attracted with each chosen assortment. Are they elite? Do they demand personal service? Are they perpetual bargain seekers?
- Determine value from the point of view of the target customer, not from the markup on the cost. Is the item unique? Can its price be compared?
- Be the first to market with seasonal goods to obtain the best price.
- Add more items of higher quality and price to shift the mix to higher margins.
- Keep a reasonable spread between the good–better–best price lines across an assortment.
- Be consistent regarding item price endings and the frequency of price changes. Do not confuse customers about your prices.
- Feature the higher-priced goods in the window, using mannequins and displays in quality settings.
- Provide special shopping privileges for customers who are known to shop at the top end of the assortments.
- Make the first markdown the big one. It will get rid of the merchandise quickly and prompt the customer to spend the savings on other fully priced goods.
- Establish store brands for products where prices cannot be compared.
- Keep an eye on the competition's pricing movements and positioning.

INVENTORY AND GROSS MARGIN RETURN ON INVENTORY

*"Errors using inadequate data are much less than those using no
data at all."*   CHARLES BABBAGE

Is it too simplistic to suggest that retailers have either an inventory of
merchandise or an inventory of talent? It is here where the sale of services differs from the sale of goods. Some service businesses (such as
repair shops and dry cleaners) maintain an inventory of parts or supplies. Others (home nursing, opticians) hold an "inventory" of talent.
Yet others (fitness gyms, party rentals) acquire an inventory of equipment. Whatever the offering, service companies require an inventory
of something that is offered, used, prepared on demand or sold (or
rented) to meet the needs of their customers. Beyond all of this, the
key ingredient—one not found on the balance sheet and unique to
every service business—is talent.

The number of service establishments in Canada exceeds 800,000.
This is far greater than the number of retail goods establishments,
which is about 250,000. Although the inventories of goods for sale
can be found in every retail goods store, the variety of inventory,
equipment and talent in service companies is too varied to create a
neat business model for them. Yet, the balance sheet and profit and
loss statements for these two types of retail operations have the same
look. It's fair to say that they all have some form of inventory that
needs to be purchased, managed and replaced in a systematic way.
This section deals with the management of goods for resale, and service company operators will find common issues here that relate to
their particular business and that need to be better understood.

Usually, the retailer's largest asset is its inventory, assuming that
the premises are rented. From this asset flow the profits from its

sales. The acquisition of the inventory requires cash, and the sooner the goods can be sold, the quicker the asset is converted to cash for other uses or for buying more goods. This critical feature of retailing is known as inventory turnover. Sellers of perishable goods, such as fresh fruit and vegetable stores, need to turn over their inventory almost daily, whereas those dealing in non-perishable goods, such as furniture stores, turn over their inventory two or three times per year. Think about how long it takes a customer to decide on a bunch of bananas compared with deciding on a new dining room suite to better understand the difference in inventory turnover.

INVENTORY INVESTMENTS

Inventories are shown on the balance sheet at their cost value; this provides the right basis for determining how this investment creates margin revenues. Inventory turnover (ITO) measurements are made over a full-year time frame.

The most accurate average inventory is the value of the inventory on January 1 plus the twelve month-end values, all divided by 13. Often, the January 1 plus four quarter-end values all divided by 5, is sufficient. When only two year-end values are available, a good rule of thumb is to average these two numbers and add 10 per cent, as fall peaks are always higher than the year-end amounts.

Using the statements of Household Extras Inc. in the Appendix, an inventory calculation is possible:

- HEI's 2005 cost of goods sold (COGS) is $6,365,000.
- Its gross margin is $10,692,000 in sales less its COGS of $6,365,000, or $4,327,000.
- So, the gross margin percentage is $4,327,000 divided by $10,692,000, or 40.5 per cent.

· Assume that the average inventory throughout the year is 10 per cent higher than the year-end inventory shown on the balance sheet of $1,079,252, or $1,187,177.

· The inventory turnover is the year's COGS, $6,365,000, divided by the average inventory, $1,187,177, or 5.4 times.

· That is to say: the inventory was consumed 5.4 times over the full year. This is an excellent turnover rate. It indicates that HEI has a high-quality inventory control arrangement, an efficient distribution environment and excellent support from its suppliers.

Inventory turns are a valuable measure because they represent the result of management's assortment planning and buying skills. Better still is the determination of the yield from this inventory. This metric is known as gross margin return on inventory (GMROI). To calculate it, divide the gross margin for the year by the average inventory:

$$\frac{\$4,327,000}{\$1,837,177} = 3.64$$

To put it another way, for every $1.00 invested in inventory, $3.64 of gross margin was earned. With the reasonably high margins and rapid inventory turnover of HEI, this is a reasonable GMROI compared with industry standards.

The beauty of the GMROI formula is that it combines the inventory information from the balance sheet with the gross margin information from the profit and loss statement. Other ratios also combine the two statements; return on assets and return on net worth are two examples. GMROI deals with the key inputs and outputs of merchandising.

Step back for a moment and consider the concept of GMROI. It is an investment formula that describes the yield from inventory investing rather than stock market investing. If one invests wisely in the stock market over time, it is possible to earn a 5 to 10 per cent return on the investment (ROI). Investing in inventory that sells to a solid clientele can produce a 200 to 500 per cent ROI. Here are two extremes: one is passive investing, the other is active. The creativity of retail, its involvement with employees and customers, and its potential to earn good returns on retail investments are the driving force behind the owner-operators of the best retail businesses. The great risks of retailing have great rewards.

INVENTORY CONTROL

Just as control of the total inventory is the overall goal of making money at retail, controlling each stock-keeping unit (SKU) is the ultimate detail of retail. Items that sit in inventory and never sell are tying up cash. Items that are out of stock disappoint customers and reduce sales and profits. Sophisticated records, produced by various software programs, need to be maintained and monitored by competent analysts who can detect problems and opportunities. Inventory controllers are trained specialists, but they are not the same people who are inventory planners. Planning is part of buying; controlling is part of finance and customer satisfaction.

The previous section that dealt with merchandise optimization referred to three types of goods. Each of these types requires a different form of inventory control:

- Basic goods require a perpetual inventory with acceptable minimums, maximums, order points and economical order quantities. These measures can be fully automated and connected to the appropriate supplier or controlled by a buying office employee, with or without the assistance of the store personnel. At the most basic level, store inventories are regularly counted and orders are sent to the buying office or supplier for replenishment. This approach is referred to as a "pull" system. When non-store analysts study inventory records and unit store sales and replenish the stores by issuing instructions to suppliers or the central warehouse, the process is known as a "push" system.

The most sophisticated ordering system is known as "automatic replenishment." When an item is scanned at the cash register, the need for its replacement is signaled to a central system that combines all the replacement requests. A command is electronically sent to the appropriate supplier, which sends a shipment directly to the store or to the retailer's warehouse for redistribution to specific stores.

· Seasonal goods, or fashion assortments, require a preseason purchase arrangement plus a system that can spot the need for replenishment, the need for discounting to eliminate excess goods and the need to transfer excess items from one store to a needy store. Then the system assists in bringing the item inventory to zero as the season runs down or as the fashion item is superseded by new fashions.

· Promotional goods fall into two inventory control modes:
   — If basic or seasonal goods are to be promoted, the system must be sent a signal either to stock up for the event or to hold back replenishment if the promotion is designed to reduce inventories.
   — If the item is being introduced for a limited time, such as a weekend special, the goods should arrive, be pushed to sell out and not be replenished.

INVENTORY QUALITY

Having sufficient inventory is only one part of the merchandise program. The quality of the goods relative to customer demand is key, and the following factors must be taken into account.

1. *Shape:* Consider a pair of men's wing-tipped brogues. They are available in at least black, oxblood and brown. They are also available in every half-size from 6 to 13. High-quality brands may also carry various heel widths. So the total number of possible SKUs for this one shoe style can exceed sixty. But it is well known that most of the sales will be of black shoes of sizes 8 to 11. So the question is, what sizes and colours will be dropped to be sure the shop meets the needs of most of the shoppers? How many of the peak-demand SKUs will be kept in each store, and what sizes will be eliminated? These inventory-planning decisions determine the shape of the inventory.

2. *Rules of thumb:* Two old rules can be considered here—the bell curve and the rule of 80/20; the latter says that 20 per cent of the items for sale will produce 80 per cent of the sales. Similarly, 10 per cent of the assortment items will produce 50 to 55 per cent of the results. The best source of information regarding inventory shape rests with the supplier, who has a parallel challenge of trying to meet the ongoing requirements of all its customers.

3. *Velocity:* A true anecdote best describes this factor. A craft store carried coloured thread for cross-stitching. There were twenty-nine colours in each style. Customers were getting impatient at the cash register while the clerk scanned the product code of each packet, so it was agreed that one scan times the number of packets would record the sale. White was chosen as the product code because it was the best seller. So the reorder program automatically reordered white when the order-point was reached. Soon the storeroom was full of white thread and out of many colours.

   Velocity is the rate of sale of a SKU, not of an item. As in the shoe example, one item has many SKUs. If the total inventory turns four times per year, some SKUs will turn rapidly (bestsellers) while

others will sell slowly (slow movers) or not at all (dead stock).
Physical inventories must be taken regularly, both at the store and
in the backroom, to spot these anomalies. The best software will
be a big help in identifying these problems, but nothing matches
the keen eye of a person watching over the stock.

4. *Location:* Where are the goods that are supposed to be for sale?
   On the shelf? In a box in the backroom? In the warehouse or a
   rented trailer? At the supplier? In transit? The great challenge of
   inventory management is to maximize the shelf stock as a percentage of the total inventory by working with the suppliers and
   distributors to ensure a regular supply. This is a key function of
   supply chain management.

OPEN TO BUY

Overriding the details of controlling SKUs is the need to financially
control the total investment in inventories. Cash is consumed as
inventories rise and released as they fall. When retailers borrow
funds for the purpose of maintaining adequate inventories, the lenders usually insist on maximum levels of inventory to support seasonal
needs. Today's accepted process for controlling the total investment
is known as "open to buy" (OTB).

In this process, if the retailer's forecasted sales and purchase
receipts over the next few time periods indicate that the resulting
inventory will exceed the approved level for that time, no purchase
orders will be allowed until the forecast shows that inventory can be
bought to bring the total up to the limit. When this is the situation, the
inventory is open to buy. Once again, the importance of inventory
type must be taken into account:

1. *Basic:* Any system—manual or automatic—must allow for the continual replenishment of bestsellers and items of everyday demand.

Problems with excessive seasonal goods or fashion backups need to be kept out of this OTB segment of control.

2. *Fashion:* Two issues are prevalent here: some fashion items are really basic and need to be segregated for OTB replenishment. Other items need temporary replenishment privileges for specific time periods. Then they move to a clearance mode.

Table 3.4 shows a simple OTB calculation.

Table 3.4: A simple open-to-buy calculation

	OPEN TO BUY—AT COST	AMOUNT ($000)
1	Inventory—beginning of the month	155
2	Less—sales plan for the month (shown at cost)	30
3	Plus—expected receipts for this month	25
4	= inventory forecast for month-end	150
	Budgeted inventory for month-end	**165**
	OTB for this month	**15**
5	Less—next 2 months' sales plan	50
6	Plus—next 2 months' receipts from orders placed	30
7	= forecasted inventories—3 months out	130
	Budgeted inventory level at this point	**155**
	OTB for the full 3 months	**25**

The use of an OTB calculation guarantees that if no exceptions are allowed, variation in sales will change the OTB, change the purchase quantities and eventually produce an inventory at the budget level.

An integrated management group is key to the success of inventory control:

· The finance department must ensure that financial objectives are being met.

- The IT group must provide the best software for planning and control that fits the business model.
- The buying department must ensure that basic and seasonal plans are properly executed.
- The store staff must keep an eye on the actual goods to ensure that the right goods are in stock, that they are fresh, and that the sizes, colours and styles are balanced.

SUPPLY CHAIN MANAGEMENT (SCM)

"Great services are not canceled by one act or by one single error."

BENJAMIN DISRAELI

There was a time when suppliers sent their salespeople to the retail buyers to offer goods for resale. At the same time, buyers scanned the industry and looked for suppliers who had what they wanted or what they thought they needed. Each side kept a lid on any key information that might be valuable to the other. The deal included price, delivery terms, payment terms and volume rebates.

Consider a furniture manufacturer that made dining room tables and chairs in a number of different designs and from a variety of materials. Each style was produced at predetermined intervals. The orders on hand were "cut" (manufactured). If a retailer sent in an order for styles that had just been cut, it would have to wait until the next cutting. The same was true for seasonal fashions. The spring merchandise was produced and shipped; then the next season was planned and prepared.

That scenario has completely changed. From a "buy–sell" environment characterized as adversarial, the new approach to supplier–retail relationships is co-operative. Figure 3.6 shows how manufacturers, wholesalers and distributors act together to meet the needs of not the retailer but the retailer's customers. It is a "chain" relationship; thus the phrase "supply chain."

Figure 3.6: The merchandise supply chain

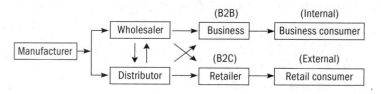

SCM SUCCESS POINTS

There are two key processes that lead to successful supply chain management (SCM):

· Integrating all the key functions or departments of the retailer with the corresponding key functions of the supplier.

· Sharing information, including information concerning:

— customer demand;

— supporting promotional and sales plans;

— supplier production planning arrangements;

— inventory levels at all points of storage; and

— excess goods, end-of-lines and the expected costs to remove them from the chain.

The shorter the chain from the point of manufacture to the retail cash register, the fewer the costs incurred and the less the risk inherent in the eventual outcome of moving out the goods. Joint decisions need to be made regarding:

1. *Shelf packs and case packs:* This will ease the work at the store or warehouse in breaking down the goods shipments into shelf-ready assortments.

2. *Backup stocks:* Will they be located at the store? At the retailer's warehouse? At a distributor? At a wholesaler? At the supplier's factory? Overseas at the source?

3. *"Push or pull":* Will the store call for replenishment? Will the retailer's inventory controller watch for reorder signals? Will the supplier or distributor have access to sales information so that it can ship goods to the appropriate location without having personal contact with the retailer?

SCM SYSTEMS MANAGEMENT

To make these choices, and to determine what information needs sharing, supply chain managers must ascertain what type of chain is needed to move the goods through to final consumption. There are four basic supply chain formats that dictate how the supply system will be managed: seasonal, specialized, basic and consumption replacement.

1. *Seasonal (or fashionable):* These goods have a short life, which is usually tied to a specific promotional campaign or to a season of the year. They must be placed on the shelf in advance of the season or event. There is often no possibility of providing follow-up orders to supplement early demand; or the relationship may be based on a seasonal order, in which 70 per cent is shipped in advance and the remaining 30 per cent is called for as required.

2. *Specialized:* The goods are made to order for a specific use or event, and 100 per cent of the order is shipped to the retailer.

3. *Basic:* Staple goods flow to the store shelf week in and week out, in response to store sales patterns and data supplied to the providers. This method is the most common one used by grocery stores, where the same goods are constantly being stocked to ensure there are no lost sales. General merchandisers know that most of their

apparel and accessories, such as underwear, shirts, shoes and socks, are basic goods.

4. *Consumption replacement:* Most service companies will need supply chain facilities for the goods they buy that are consumed as part of the service they offer; oil, parts, solvents, cleaning fluids, packaging, flour, sugar, uniforms and tickets are just a few examples.

Once it has been established what format will best serve the purpose of the end-customer, supply chain managers can design the process and determine what data will be required to meet the end needs, what technology each participant will require and how these elements will be connected, balanced and managed. Top-notch SCM can be achieved only if all parties invest in SCM software and also, depending on the level of sophistication required, enterprise resource planning (ERP) software. Although each participant takes on this obligation, all of them execute in concert with their chain partners.

SCM TOUCH-POINTS

Rarely is the finished product that is intended for eventual sale to a customer delivered directly to the store shelf. The process will always require middlemen. Today, more than ever, goods and supplies are being made offshore—anywhere in the world where the materials, labour, financing and management skills can be assembled at the lowest possible cost. From start to finish, each item has many touch-points at which manpower and support costs move it along the chain. Consider the voyage made by a case of socks manufactured in China; every step along the way to the store shelf adds costs and creates the possibility of loss, theft and damage.

For example, consider the costs of labour, vehicles, fuel, insurance, inspection, financing, security, document processing, palletization and break-bulk found at every touch-point, such as:

factory production line—factory warehouse—truck to port or
airport—air or sea transit—domestic receipt—inspection—
temporary customs and storage—truck/rail/air to import
distributor—truck/rail to retail warehouse—storage—break
bulk—staging—store delivery—store receipt—temporary
storage—unpacking—shelf arrangements.

These costs, along with a reasonable profit earned by each participant along the way, raise the factory cost to the landed cost of the
retailer or service provider.

MIDDLEMEN

Large retailers and service providers are more capable of eliminating
the middlemen; they prefer to deal directly with the producers. But
the rest of the goods and services industry needs middlemen to sim-
plify their business. The two key middleman formats are *wholesalers*
and *distributors*. Since each has specialized functions, the retailer must
define its needs to determine which format is best for its operation.

Independent and small-chain retailers that recognize the importance of SCM are few, but there is plenty of evidence that they are
rapidly developing the skills and technology to handle this process.
Too often, store people regard the supplier with suspicion, not giving
up the vital data and forecasts that will help the supplier preplan.
Suppliers, on the other hand, can miss out on the advantages of SCM
by putting restrictions on demand flexibility, not recognizing the
incentive of volume rebates, treating certain brands as superior to
others and, unfortunately, forbidding the retailer to deal with certain
competitors. Removing bad practices and opening up the sharing of
SCM requires joint planning and evaluation, not only of the sales and
flow of inventory, but also of the balance of the relationship.

The wholesaler is a supplier. It takes title to the goods it buys, adds a markup on the costs and sells at a profit. Wholesalers play an important role in gathering together a myriad of goods to create a complete assortment so that retailers need only make a one-stop shopping trip instead of visiting many suppliers to put together the desired store selection. Service providers find this method of buying especially suitable to their priorities, because each service industry tends to have its own wholesalers that are ready to serve all their needs for products and supplies.

Suppliers sell to wholesalers when they have a narrow product line and need exposure to a large industry segment. For example, consider the production of garden tools. No one supplier can manufacture the complete variety of products and supplies needed by a garden centre. Nor do retailers have time to visit every producer of every item. They are too busy with their live plants and weather-dependent store needs, so they arrange with one wholesaler to provide all of their needs for a subsidiary assortment. In this example, it is the retailer who tells the wholesaler what it wants in its seasonal assortment.

The distributor does just that: it distributes. Distributors make it unnecessary for retailers and service providers to own and operate warehouses. These operators choose their sources and then their distributors to receive their orders, hold them until required, break out the pallet loads for store delivery and then deliver as needed. They may act as the distributor for many suppliers, providing temporary storage of their goods and charging for each individual service.

Distributors do not take title to the goods they handle. They may also be wholesalers with a distinctly different process format; with the rise of imported goods, specialist distributors have appeared to handle imported goods for retailers. They provide a bonded warehouse where the goods are kept until needed by the customer. Thus distributors are service providers, mindful of their dual and simultaneous tasks of customer satisfaction and wealth creation.

One of the challenges facing the independent and small-chain operator is the task of getting the attention and continuing support of the supplier. Figure 3.7 describes the challenge. Putting this figure into words: a typical supplier of goods for sale—for example, the most popular line of jeans—has 2,000 possible retail customers available in Canada that might buy and sell its pants. The top 1 per cent of them (20) own chains across the country that make up 40 per cent of all possible stores that might sell these goods. These stores move 80 per cent of the total volume of the product. The other 99 per cent of the retailers, or all of the independent stores and chains, have 60 per cent of the outlets but sell only 20 per cent of the national volume.

Figure 3.7: The relationship between suppliers, customers, stores and volume

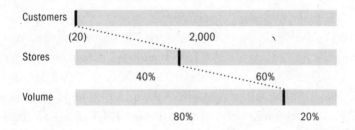

It is obvious that the jeans manufacturer will do everything it can to maximize its volume to the top 1 per cent of its customers. Its sales staff is usually structured with highly trained national account managers who build relationships with the 1 per cent group. The rest of the trade is served by catalogues and inbound/outbound call centres. So it's not hard to see that the independent must first find a niche, then find the niche suppliers and finally develop a solid relationship with them.

Two trends are evolving as a result of the capabilities of scm: scan-based payments and shared markdowns. Although both trends are based on improving customer satisfaction, both have a problem with sharing the costs of success and trouble.

Scan-based payment is a practice that takes advantage of the process of automatic replenishment whereby the supplier learns of a sale of a particular item from a signal sent by the retailer when the item is scanned at the checkout counter. The supplier assembles store packs from the constant flow of data and ships on a pre-arranged schedule. That's the good news. Now for the bad news: suppliers, instead of being paid according to pre-negotiated arrangements that set the trade terms and payment dates, are paid when the item is sold. The same signal that goes to the supplier to replenish the item also goes to the accounts payable system to electronically pay for the sold goods. Suppliers call this consignment selling, an age-old practice that leaves the supplier with full ownership of the goods until the retailer sells them. Consignment selling is still a legitimate practice today, so long as both the buyer and the seller agree to its terms.

Scan-based payments, with today's technology and high-quality scm systems, can be a better financial deal for the supplier than the older method of payment terms, which have slowly moved from "net 30 days" to 45–70 days after receipt. If the reorder arrangements are in place and the supplier can move the goods to the stores quickly, and the goods go directly to the shelves, the time from "factory" to "shipped" might be two weeks or less. Even if the cycle is one month, payment is received faster than today's 45–70 arrangement. The key to the success of scan-based trading is—once again—joint planning, collaboration and sharing, with a dedication to rapid inventory turns.

Shared markdowns are a practice that has grown in importance as the competition for business has increased in tandem with the unwillingness of consumers to pay full price for anything anymore. In addition, retailers are merchandising for more specific fashion seasons each year compared with the past. It is therefore more difficult to forecast demand and to purchase just enough goods to meet the demand for the one season. Today, retailers will take markdowns for sales events and end-of-season clearouts and ask suppliers to share in the cost of the resulting markdowns. Assuming that an agreement has been reached between them before the production and delivery of the season's goods began, a deal is a deal. The practice is abused, however, if the season works out worse than expected for the retailer and pressure is put on the supplier to provide additional financial support. The key to a shared markdown arrangement is the same as any give-and-take relationship that is built into an SCM plan: joint planning, collaboration and sharing.

SCM SUCCESS FACTORS

The business unit closest to the needs of the end-consumer usually acts as the lead. If the results of SCM are favourable or unfavourable, the lead will be the first to know. A supply chain that involves a supplier, a wholesaler or distributor, and a retailer will be most effective if it takes its leads from the retailer, where the customer can be found. There must be an environment of co-dependency: a team manages a well-run SCM process; no one is in charge; the goals are mutual.

Choosing those who will interact with the players is critical. The atmosphere must be one of sharing. Joint planning needs to be agreed to at the outset, and then the planning process must be ongoing.

Performance measurements are needed for each element of the chain so that results can be monitored and the need for corrections identified early on in the process. The success of a well-run SCM process will be evident in decreasing costs across the chain, faster inventory turnovers and an improved in-stock position.

RETAIL MARKETING

"Marketing is a fashionable term. The sales manager becomes a marketing vice-president. But a gravedigger is still a gravedigger, even when he is called a mortician; only the price of the burial goes up."   PETER DRUCKER

You might ask, isn't this whole book about marketing? Peter Drucker, the pre-eminent business guru, described marketing as:

· finding and meeting the needs and wants of a customer;
· integrating the whole company to this end; and
· making money at it.

From this perspective, Chapters 2, 3 and 4 of this book are all about marketing, or optimization. Everyone who wants to build a successful business needs to understand the basics of marketing, even if he or she doesn't like the word. Marketing doesn't require a marketing manager, it doesn't need a big budget, and it is not complicated; but it requires a bright idea and a plan to convert that idea into a profitable venture. And here, activities such as attraction, conversion and retention are key marketing concepts.

Across the big retail chains and service providers, there is someone high up in the organization chart with the title of marketing manager, vice-president or something similar. The best marketing managers of small or medium-sized businesses are the owner-operators. They have the bright ideas firmly in their sights and are constantly figuring out how to achieve their goals. Although their plan may not be written down, these owner-operators have in their minds the step-by-step approach needed to achieve success. And they are not deterred by the behaviour of their competitors, the unexpected detours they have to take or the cost fluctuations they must deal with. They press on through thick and thin, and they push and pull their staff along . with them.

Many books are written on the subject of marketing, and every company that embraces the function of marketing seems to treat it differently. To summarize the essentials of good retail marketing, the subject will be dealt with in only two steps:

· create a marketing strategy and spell it out in a plan; and
· divide the tasks, spell them out, and lead the company through the execution of the plan.

THE PLAN

The first step is to determine who will consume your bright idea, whether it is a product or a service. Determining your target customer involves casual research, such as talking to family and friends about your idea. It might lead to some research conducted alone or by a professional firm, perhaps on the Internet. Where are the people who might be your customers? Are there many of them? Do they need your bright idea? What will they pay for it? And how often?

Early on, ask yourself, "What am I trying to do?"

· Provide a better service?
· Produce a higher quality?
· Provide more variety?
· Offer a lower-cost alternative?
· Create something unique?

- Make something easy to acquire and consume?
- Save people's time and effort?
- Provide a unique skill-related service?

These questions deal with positioning, dealt with earlier in Chapter 2. Fundamentally, they deal with the "four Ps" of Marketing 101: product, placement, price and promotion. Answer the preceding questions, and the plan will begin to take shape.

Next, work out the steps required to get your product or service to the targeted consumers. Some sort of facility will be needed—a store, service centre, kiosk, catalogue, website or call centre. Or perhaps your idea requires a gymnasium, park, playhouse, hotel or helicopter? Whatever the case, spell it out in a written plan that others can understand. The plan does not need to be wordy or turned into a fancy binder of PowerPoint slides. To keep it fresh, up to date and always in the minds of the staff, it can be produced once in full and then bit by bit, as the subject of an internal weekly newsletter that includes reminders about the overall program along with comments on the details of the current week's program, the success of the previous week and a look ahead to the next few events or time frames.

A comprehensive marketing plan should cover at least the following seven subjects:

1. The product or service definition.
2. The target audience to be approached and served.
3. The public relations message and external corporate communications details. It is not enough just to advertise products and services; the company itself is a brand, and it needs to tell its story to at least the local media, especially in print. Many retailers take a supportive community role with charities, daycare, sports teams, parade participation and other activities and organizations to connect with the public.

4. The advertising program and media choices. Many experts and agencies are waiting to help and to earn income from their own service company. Make sure that no matter what program you adopt or what medium you choose, your advertising plan stands the test of assessment and measurement. Many retailers determine the cost of the ad and then determine the gross margin obtained from the promotion. This is measured by subtracting the usual sales demand from the demand through the duration of the promotion. One retailer calculates this for each selection in the ad and awards more space to the best departments on the next promotion.

5. The seasonal parameters and focal points. In-store sales promotion programs, including dates and highlights, are more successful when they are tied to customer-friendly seasonal events.

6. The training of the sales force, whether full time, part time or commissioned. Each staff category has a special purpose and needs to understand its specific roles in the overall scheme.

7. How and when the marketing program will be evaluated.

THREE MARKETING SUCCESS STORIES

One of the most talked-about retailers today is the world's largest department-store chain, Wal-Mart. Sam Walton opened his first Wal-Mart store in the summer of 1962. It so happened that F.W. Woolworth (later Woolco) opened its first store that same summer, as did Kresge's (later Kmart). Forty years later, in 2002, Woolco was gone and Kmart was struggling to survive. Wal-Mart had become the biggest retailer in the world and was on the threshold of becoming the biggest company in the world.

How did that happen? The answer is simple—Sam Walton was a variety store veteran who had a bright idea—a huge selection of basic household goods sold at everyday low prices. He then put into action the policy and procedures, the talent and the technology that would deliver his vision in a superior way. Sam spent 80 per cent of his time during the early stages of Wal-Mart's growth in and out of his competitors' stores, learning what they did and how they did it. Then he improved upon it.

Kubas Consultants of Toronto publishes its annual *Major Market Retail Report*. Now in its thirteenth year, MMRR is an informative analysis of Canadian retailers and their competitive position based on the preferences of a panel of over 6,000 shoppers in the six largest metro markets. It ranks the consumers' shopping preference of more than 130 retailers, as well as the competitive action in 32 specific product categories. The report also covers shopper attitudes, store ratings, loyalty programs, e-commerce, advertising and much more and is used by both retailers and industry suppliers.

By 2003–5, MMRR showed that Wal-Mart had the highest potential share of market across Canada in fourteen of the thirty-one merchandise categories it sold. Yet the highest share in any one category was only 30 per cent. As Wal-Mart climbed to this pinnacle of success, many competitors shut their doors and town councils tried to stop its expansion. While some retailers sulked and complained about Wal-Mart's success, other fined-tuned their bright ideas and set out to capture the rest of the market, the 70 per cent that Wal-Mart didn't own. Today, these retailers fill the malls and shopping streets of every community and give the community its own uniqueness and charm.

Another great marketing success is in the story of Whole Foods, which was built on the concept of "organic" foods. Organic foods have been around for a long time, but nobody saw the potential of putting together a complete organic food store. Shoppers knew that organic foods cost more, so many grocers offered a few organic items, but they rarely promoted them. While grocery stores were doing everything in their power to get prices down, along came Whole Foods with higher prices but high-quality organic food, attractive presentations, plenty of service and freshness promoted everywhere.

A third story is about customer-driven marketing success. Young people in China have begun to develop shopping websites based on the chat-room concept. They have organized their members to talk about goods of great interest to them, such as mobile phones, cameras and TVs. They then coordinate all of their members to arrive, at a predetermined time, at the door of a major retailer to demand reduced prices for the crowd. Team buying has turned the old practice of haggling into a form of forced discounting. Customers consider this to be a marketing success story, but retailers do not!

MANAGING THE SEASONS

> "Don't be afraid to take a big step. You can't cross a chasm in two
> small jumps."   DAVID LLOYD GEORGE

Many of us are energized by the change of the seasons. The best goods and service providers recognize this and build a large part of their offerings around this annual cycle. Each new season presents an opportunity for them to bring some new product or service to the market. For the customers, it offers a new opportunity to shift their interests and habits. Think about the yard-service truck on the neighbourhood street each day. In spring, its operator cleans the garden beds of the households, then he or she mows lawns, prunes hedges, washes windows, cleans gardens for winter, cleans eavestroughs and finally shovels snow.

SEASONAL PLANNING

Seasonal planning begins with the determination of the number of seasons worthy of special merchandising and promotion. When retailing was less competitive and customer choices were fewer, retailers planned around two basic seasons: spring/summer and fall/winter. A host of goods and services promotions highlighted the advent of both of them. The first sign of spring and fall was the Eaton's catalogue. This "wish book" was supplemented with special smaller publications for summer and Christmas. Today, customers expect to be bombarded by a greater number of seasonal promotions, depending upon the offering. Consider the cycle illustrated in Figure 3.8.

Figure 3.8: The seasonal retail cycle

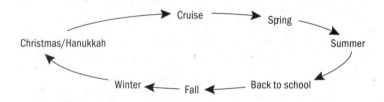

Note that some of these seasons are calendar related while others are weather related. Key promotional days can be found within some of them, including Valentine's Day, Mother's Day, Father's Day, June weddings, school starts, Thanksgiving, Hanukkah, Christmas and New Year's. No day of the year, however, matches the hype of Boxing Day, or Boxing week. It has become the time of year when the biggest clearance sales are held and maximum sales volumes are achieved.

Seasonality at a retail store creates a sense of newness. Many service businesses can exploit the changing seasons with changes to their service packages and promotions to bring the customer back to the service provider. Remember the age-old expression "spring cleaning"? The change of seasons represents a key shift in what one wears (a personal consumption pattern involving both goods and services) and what one does, especially with leisure time. For retailers, key events— for example, ones that highlight the act of giving—offer opportunities for promotion. For instance:

· Mother's Day is the number one day for flowers.
· Christmas is the peak time for chocolates, with Valentine's Day and Mother's Day not far behind.
· Halloween is all about candy and costumes.
· Easter is also a candy event, as well as a "new clothes" time of the year.

Preparing for these key dates requires plenty of advanced planning and carefully designed store presentations. Research shows that women plan and buy for these dates much earlier than men do—men are infamous for last-minute purchasing. This requires the retailer to maintain a full in-stock position right up to the day itself.

Figure 3.9 lays out many of the steps of seasonal planning. It shows how planning for each retail season begins long before the season is launched. The purchase of imported goods, for example, requires long lead times. Before placing the order, the marketing and merchandising themes of the upcoming season need to be settled, and the colour and style and the assortment plan must be prepared, at least to the category level. A study of the previous years' results will provide many clues as to what worked and what didn't, what was unsold and what sold out.

Seasons tend to fall into specific time periods that match the periods or months of the financial statements. A study of the periodic operating results of the previous year will also highlight the departments that grew and met their objectives and those that didn't.

Figure 3.9: Seasonal planning time chart

To ensure that this practice becomes a regular event, the figure includes a postmortem process after the quarter or season ends.

SEASONAL PRICING

Figure 3.10 shows how the pricing of seasonal goods can be played out over the length of a season. Maximum markups are used at the start of the season, when the styles are new and consumers are waiting to get at "the latest and greatest." Markdowns are then used to bring customers back to the store and, at the same time, to move out the remaining merchandise. The gross margins of seasonal goods are the composite of the different prices and the amount of goods sold at each price.

Figure 3.10: Seasonal pricing

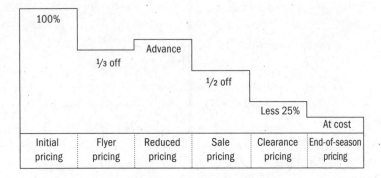

The figure shows that a price increase was imposed after the "⅓ Off Sale." This was the result of a decision to return the goods to a better margin level because they were selling well and the inventory was depleting according to plan. Seasonal planning is a critical part of financial planning, as this illustration demonstrates.

SEASONAL FINANCING

Seasonality creates peaks and valleys in sales results, inventory levels, staffing requirements and lending needs. Consider some of these examples of extremes:

· Independent garden centres sell up to 50 per cent of their annual volume in the months of May and June.

· Toy stores live for Christmas and spend the rest of the year preparing for it.

· Ski resorts rely on good snow conditions from Christmas to New Year's Day for the bulk of their annual traffic.

- Golf courses need a sunny summer to make money.
- When the catalogue showroom chains were at their peak in the 1970s and '80s, they were so heavily reliant on pre-Christmas business that they sold over 25 per cent of their annual volume in the ten days prior to Christmas. They operated at a financial loss up to that period, thus earning all of their annual profits in that ten-day period.

If inventories need to be built up in anticipation of a high season, they will be purchased using cash that probably isn't in the bank, as the preceding low season is encumbered with high fixed expenses and poor cash flow. It thus becomes necessary to borrow the funds. The security for these loans is the inventory value being accumulated. If all goes well, the loan will be paid off by the end of the peak selling season. Banks need to follow this loan and the subsequent inventory movement, so they arrange for a cash management connection to the retailers, feeding the funds as the supplier cheques are written and withdrawing the funds from the retailer as the merchandise sells and the inventory drops.

CHRISTMAS

The Christmas season has the double peak of gift merchandise sales prior to Christmas and Boxing week sales. When the retailer's sales peak settles down in the early weeks of January, the retailer is pleased to be "out of the bank." If all of that activity leaves the retailer with a loan balance, then something is wrong with the business plan in relation to the actual results, and it needs to be investigated.

There was a period in the 1960s and '70s when Eaton's dominated the retail scene, especially in Toronto. Jack Eaton, the man responsible for all store operations across the country, insisted that no markdowns or discounted sales be held between the Santa Claus

Parade day in mid-November (always held on the Saturday after Remembrance Day) and Christmas: "Customers have to shop at that time for clothes and gifts, so there is no need to entice them with wasted discounts."

How times have changed. In those years the Boxing Day sale was held to clear out goods that were considered dead stock at the end of the Christmas season. The first item to be purchased specifically for Boxing Day sales was Christmas cards, believe it or not. Slowly, other goods were bought to beef up the day's sale volume. Then the sale became the Boxing week sale. Now that this event begins in early December and continues right through the month, discounting has become the key seasonal strategy.

Because of this end-of-December sales crunch and the ensuing cleanup following the heavy inventory movements, most retailers set their year-end at January 31. The annual financial statements will probably show the inventory levels at their lowest then. If the borrowing from the bank to cover inventory purchases was well planned, there would be no operating bank loan. Each quarter thereafter has its own peaks. Q1 includes Easter in either March or April, whereas Q2 is usually the weakest quarter because it is the run-up to summer. Q3 includes the back-to-school peak, and Q4 includes Christmas and Boxing Day.

A January 31 year-end means that the bulk of the business comes in the fourth quarter. If there is a problem at this time due to weather or competition, there is no further time to correct for poor results. Thus every operator must study the seasonal sales trends for possible problems and correct for them as soon as possible—it is essential not to wait for Christmas. The key to each seasonal success is the advance planning process and the creation of a weekly budget, combined with a weekly comparison of the budgeted and actual results for the same week the previous year.

LEASEHOLD IMPROVEMENTS

"Never take the advice of someone who has not had your kind of trouble." SIDNEY J. HARRIS

As part of the "perception" element of the retail offering, the retail unit's interior and exterior must be maintained to a high standard of excellence. The premises need to be changed and upgraded regularly, a process known to the operator as "refurbishing." The landlord who rents the store refers to it as "leasehold improvements."

The barrier-to-entry for purveyors of goods and services is very low. Little capital is needed, but competition is fierce. Extensive research has demonstrated that the first thirty seconds of a consumer's time in the shop and the perception of the first sixty square feet of floor space surrounding the opening are critical to establishing a distinctive ambience. Dealing with these perceptions is a key aspect of refurbishing. Clever retailers know that upgrading has tremendous value. The capital spent on the process actually enhances the value of the asset, both tangible and intangible. Potential lenders need to consider the benefits of refurbishing when providing loans for upgrades. When refurbishing is properly executed, increased cash flow should cover the cost of the refurbishing.

The requirement for the operator to upgrade is embedded in many leases, especially in those of the "A" class malls. It is usually tied to lease renewals. Thus a five-year lease requires the retailer to refurbish, in the hope of producing improved results in the form of additional sales. There do not appear to be any software programs to collect such information and monitor the results, so it is left to CFOs to conduct an analysis of the "before" and "after" benchmarks as well as the cost and benefits of refurbishing. But it's worth emphasizing that refurbishing should not be treated as a landlord's requirement; it should be regarded as part of maintaining a sales unit that is up to date, appealing and welcoming.

THE NEED TO UPGRADE
Leasehold improvements or upgrades may be either simple or extensive. Many elements of change need to be considered:
· exterior signage and structure;
· receiving and warehousing improvements, including vehicles and shelving;
· window, flooring and wall treatments;
· ceilings, including lighting and A/C improvements;
· energy-saving upgrades;
· fixtures, change rooms, wall units and cupboards;
· improved security measures;
· interior departmental signage and directional signs;
· kitchens, bathrooms and restrooms;
· refrigeration units, backroom kitchens; and
· cash register kiosks, EPOS systems and card transaction devices.

Most retailers agree that refurbishing is necessary at least every five to seven years, depending upon the nature or quality of the structure, the nature of the goods or services for sale or rent and the need for a new upscale "cachet" or a downscale "economy" look. Refurbishing costs vary greatly, for the above reasons. Typical costs range from $30 to $250 per square foot for interior work. The cost of external and internal signage can vary widely, depending on the street location, mall management policies and the appearance and condition of nearby stores. Thus a typical mall store of 1,500 square feet, refurbished for $80 per square foot will cost $120,000 to upgrade.

Just as every home needs to be kept up to date, so does every sales unit. When separated into its two components—the surfaces (floors, walls and ceilings) and the interior—the task of refurbishing can be planned and carried out on a continuing basis rather than all at the same time. Refurbishing surfaces involves structural changes, capital costs and, usually, landlord approval. The interior—shelving, racks, change rooms, display stands and checkout areas—can be upgraded regularly with little discomfort to customers. Suppliers can be called upon to assist with their own fixtures or cost support for their selling space improvements. The costs of the interior adjustments can be built into the ongoing store expenses instead of being treated as a capital investment.

When a retailer secures a loan for inventory swings, it should also specify the need for cash for refurbishing in the loan agreement. If retailers do not have free cash for these extraordinary expenses when it is needed, they may ask the bank for support. The handling of the accounting for all of these upgrades is important to a lender, who will want to see that the expenditure resulted in some form of increased performance. Some of the costs of upgrading are capitalized; others are expensed. This decision depends on the attitude of the chief accountant. Maximizing the upgrade costs as expenses reduces taxes, while capitalizing them requires amortizing the cost over time.

REFURBISHING ACCOUNTING

Leasehold improvement programs are mini-strategies. The answer to the following questions will determine the success expected from this important form of capital spending:

· Is there an annual capital plan as well as a financial plan?
· Is the store staff involved in the planning and execution?
· Is there a forecast of future capital expenditures over three years?
· Does each capital project require a written and approved plan?
· Are goals set to limit expenditures to a pre-approved amount?

- Does a steering committee monitor large refurbishing projects?
- Is a goal set for a return on the invested capital (ROIC) by project?
- Is a report prepared after the project is completed, to show the actual ROIC achieved?
- Is there an effort made to complete the refurbishing during low-demand periods for cash for inventory building?

CHANNEL MARKETING

"I don't look to jump over seven-foot bars; I look around for one-foot bars that I can step over."   WARREN BUFFETT

Retailing began in the ancient village marketplaces. This clustered form of activity has survived the ages and still functions around the world, including in the developed nations. Later, the door-to-door salesman began to call on the town's homes. He would leave a small catalogue on the doorstep if nobody answered the door. Then, permanent stores were built side by side on the main streets. These choices of retail marketing are still viable. While the formats of the clusters of stores in malls, in power centres and on the street may have changed, the only truly new concept is the Internet.

The major department stores have practised multi-channel marketing for more than a hundred years. In the early days, the catalogue was the only retail operation available to rural populations that didn't have time to go to the nearest town to shop. Each new catalogue heralded the beginning of each season and was the "wish book" of every child who searched for his or her favourite choices for Christmas gifts. Eaton's built its local markets with its catalogue until the total volume of business in a town could sustain a local store.

The telephone became the third retail channel or banner or format, added to the store and the catalogue. It was first used to receive calls from customers who were ordering from their catalogue or from the sales piece left by the salesperson. It didn't take long for the manager of the inbound call centre (although it was not known by that name then) to realize that when the switchboard was quiet, its time could be better used to phone and sell something to known customers. In the early stages, they were customers who agreed to be called if there was a special item or deal of interest to them.

This quick trip through a history of retailing demonstrates that nothing is new. The store, the catalogue, the door-to-door salesperson and the phone are still the four main choices for multi-banner marketing today. Now add to this the Internet.

CHANNEL BREAKOUTS

Different retailers build their many banners with various factors in mind. These include price, sizing, styling, offering and location.

Price: The first channel breakout was the development of the budget store. The key criterion was price. Low-priced goods were purchased to appeal to economy-minded customers. Later, goods that needed to be cleared were marked down and delivered to the budget store. This tactic allowed the parent store to keep its price image intact. Budget departments in many stores serve the same purpose today.

As power centres developed, retailers created the ultimate budget store and named it the outlet store. It is an outlet for getting rid of ends-of-lines, end-of-season leftovers, excess inventories and goods purchased from suppliers who are anxious to move out similar inventory problems. When supply chain management (SCM) programs are working well (see pages 110 to 119), both the supplier and the retailer are winners. Pardon the pun—Winners is an excellent example of an outlet store. Few people associate it with its parent company's home-decor banner, Homesense.

Sizing: To streamline the assortment and offer a focused mix of goods, store chains now offer different store formats for different apparel sizes—for example, The Gap, Gap Kids and Baby Gap. Customers appreciate the difference and do not have to be bothered by having the different groups of children all in the same store. Sizing breakouts are the basis for petite, maternity and plus-sized stores.

Styling: Unknown to many customers, retail chains offer different styles in stores with different names that have no obvious relationship to the parent. Specialty apparel companies can add new banners without creating a brand trade-off from the original. Technology for one banner can be adapted for the additional banners. Central financing and personnel programs can serve each of them as the need arises. Not many consumers know, for example, that Aldo Group Inc. operates a variety of shoe stores including Transit, Pegabo, Aldo and Globo. The Gap Inc. operates Gap, Banana Republic and Old Navy—three distinctly different formats.

Offering: There is no reason why successful retailers cannot add different banners offering different merchandise or services. Companies who recognize that they excel at a certain aspect of retailing, such as store size or small-market special interest, are able to open new chains with different products and services that have no connection to one other.

For this array of output to be profitable, three key factors must be kept in mind:

1. Each banner must present a similar quality of consumer-centred experience, regardless of the merchandise mix and the location.

2. The practice of decentralization has to be followed. The central office must provide the background of essential services that are common to each banner but at the same time stay out of those matters that are banner-unique.

3. The store or service-centre owner, franchisee or manager must take ownership of the distinctive offering of the brand.

Location: Today's retailers have found that sticking to one location format leaves them vulnerable to consumer shifts of preference. The best mall merchants are now on the best retail streets and in the best power centres. Customers choose these different venues for different reasons.

THE CATALOGUE

Until the Internet takes over as the primary choice for non-store shopping, the catalogue will be the non-store retail alternative. Long before the retail scene became what it is today, the catalogue brought the full merchandise selection to homes. Catalogues are appearing with the delivered newspaper in ever-increasing numbers; they have some great advantages over a visit to the store:

· Customers don't have to leave the comfort of their homes to shop.

· Decisions can be postponed until the time is right.

· The price in the book lasts as long as the book does.

· Product descriptions that support the photography are usually more complete and understandable than those provided by salespeople, especially of technical products.

· The goods can be delivered to the home, the office or a nearby store.

· The catalogue has a shelf life based on the retailer's seasonal plan.

Multi-channel marketing creates a multi-touch environment. Customers become used to the differences in each banner and use the banners in the way that suits them best. Time-starved workers can shop at home in their leisure moments. Catalogues become research vehicles that hang around the house for months as a reminder of the retailer.

INTERNET MARKETING

The introduction of the World Wide Web to the Internet brought to the consumer market an entirely new channel for retailing. Because of its importance to the future of the retailing of goods and services, it is dealt with in the next major section, "E-retailing."

CHANNEL MIGRATION

The benefits of having additional marketing channels are obvious. New market subsegments can expand the customer base of any retailer; customers who haven't the time to visit a store can buy their goods online or from the catalogue. Many surveys have compared the buying behaviour of customers of single-channel outlets with those of multi-channel enterprises. It has been found that individuals who used more than one channel to satisfy their needs usually spent 20 to 30 per cent more money with the providing retailer.

Migrating customers to new channels has its risks. The cost to serve customers may rise, and problems not evident in the traditional channel might become a bother in the new channel. The best example is on the Internet, where start-up websites have "turned off" or ended countless customer connections with the stores. Store-based services have a much easier job of controlling the service environment than do home-based services of the same company. Where the services are not supervised and standards are not maintained, traditional customers are lost.

But migrating customers to different channels also has its benefits. The financial aspects of each channel are very different. The store has real estate costs to contend with, whereas the Internet has technology and marketing costs to cover. Catalogues can be very efficient, but delivery and returns costs can wipe out the operating profit. It is therefore wise to put the financial details of each approach on a side-by-side chart similar to the HEI operating statement shown in Table 5.2. Using promotional techniques and "cross-selling," sales can be moved to the channel that produces the highest margin of contribution.

GEOGRAPHIC EXPANSION

There is no law or magic formula demonstrating that bigger is better. Many great examples of brilliant retailing, of both goods and services, can be found in a single venue or a local cluster. Also, building a bigger store may be more profitable than building another store. The challenge is to remind the staff what made them what they are, which is probably something very local and worthwhile in that little market.

When the time comes to expand, find a location formula that makes sense. A great comment from a great retailer comes to mind. When Irving Gerstein, founder of Peoples Jewellers, received the "Retailer of the Year" award from the Retail Council of Canada many years ago, his "thank you" address to the convention included some useful advice to the effect that "I should not accept this award; it should go to Eaton's instead. I never needed a real estate department because I always located within five hundred feet of an Eaton's store." Eventually Eaton's disappeared, and sadly Peoples Jewellers, after many years of financial difficulty, was sold to Zales, the U.S. jewellery chain. The connection between the two events may not be accidental.

International exposure begins with exposure in a neighbourhood, then in a city, in a region, in a province, throughout the country, then finally in a foreign country. There are enough examples to suggest that those who build a chain of retail stores finally become satisfied by reaching one of these spans of influence. Somewhere along the path to greatness, retailers may face a personal control matter, a financial constraint or a competitive barrier. In dealing with the question of expansion, three simple guidelines can be applied:

· Never lose sight of the value of the local touch. Many retail businesses are an extension of their owners' personality. This may make it impossible to grow beyond that personal touch between the customer and the provider.

· Make sure that the timing is right and the personnel situation is ready. Nothing hurts a business more that overextending its key people.

· Understand your strengths and weaknesses. The issues of foreign languages, local regulations, different forms of competition and local and regional cultures must all be understood and embraced by whoever takes the business to other venues.

CHANNEL ECONOMICS

Why does Dell sell personal computers only on the Internet, while Hewlett-Packard sells them in stores as well? The answer lies in two places: customer preference and channel economics. The Internet has no store costs, whereas the store has low technology costs. Finding the "bricks," depending upon their location, may be easier than finding the "clicks" on the Internet. There is no single formula for multi-channel success; what is important is the willingness to develop accurate operating costs for each banner or channel while researching customer preferences.

THE PERIPHERAL MARKETING CHANNELS ·

Gone are the days when marketing outreach merely meant advertising in the daily papers, on radio or on TV. Thanks to the growth of digital media, there are many marketing opportunities to take your message to and interact with the public. The marketing opportunities listed in Figure 3.11 may not be complete, but they do illustrate the many new ways of reaching out to the consumer.

Following are descriptions of the choices numbered 4 to 10 in Figure 3.11—ways beyond the store, the catalogue and the website to reach the retail market.

Figure 3.11: Ten ways to reach the retail market

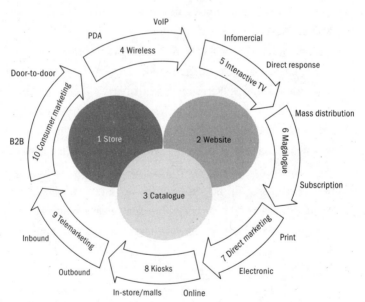

4. *Wireless:* This includes the personal digital accessories (PDA) such as the cellphone and BlackBerry and related products. It also includes

VoIP, voice over Internet protocol. As this technique is adopted, it widens the market for calls out and in by reducing costs and connecting the call to choice no. 2, the Internet. It also assists with lowering the costs related to choice no. 9, telemarketing.

5. *Interactive TV*: This choice will grow in importance as the personal computer becomes integrated with television and Internet companies use this new tool to offer and sell products, take orders and complete the transaction payment. For now, the common technique among infomercials and direct-response TV is the use of call-centre phone numbers and website referrals.

6. *Magalogues*: This combination of magazine and catalogue, a "classy" approach to advertising and product promotion, is becoming more common in the slick magazines that arrive with the daily newspaper. Magalogues may be the product of one retailer or a mix of fashion or home products from many retailers or suppliers.

7. *Direct marketing*: Our doorsteps and mailboxes attest to the effectiveness of the little pieces of paper that arrive there daily. If they didn't work, they would have been stopped long ago. They are cheap to produce and easy to distribute, and they work well in supporting a neighbourhood store or service. Websites and search engines add direct marketing promotions to their pages and directories, hoping that consumers will click on them and become customers.

8. *Kiosks*: These are the carts and interactive electronic stands that provide products and services at convenient locations both in and outside of the store.

9. *Telemarketing*: This technique began when call centres that received orders from shoppers started to use the downtime of the call-centre staff to phone out to promote products and services. In the beginning, the retailer obtained permission from customers to call them when a promotion or product placement might

be of interest to them, based on their purchase patterns and their use of the phone for purchasing. This practice is referred to as permission marketing. But it has now become abusive and interruptive by relying on computer-generated phone calls.

A historical anecdote highlights the importance of call centres. The T. Eaton Co. supported its catalogue operations during the 1960s and early '70s with Canada's largest telephone call centre. There were no computers; each operator had a wall-box full of sales forms and an out basket that was cleared regularly by a "runner." The operators also kept a list of customers who agreed to receive a call from the operator if certain products came up for sale at discounted prices, such as TVs, washers, dryers and stoves. Following any national "White Goods Sale," the prizewinner for selling the most stoves or refrigerators was often the call-centre operator. E-retailing and e-mail have taken this "permission marketing" to a high science, but the principles are exactly the same: get the customers' approval first, establish their interests second, and then advise them of buying opportunities.

10. *Commercial marketing:* Many retailers have found new markets for their products and services by offering them to institutions and commercial businesses on a supply-contract basis at reduced prices. This expands the retailer from B2C to B2B, and even to B2G (government). For example, Henry's Camera, Ontario's premier camera store, operates a large commercial business staffed with salespeople who call on clients such as trade associations, real estate and insurance companies and schoolboards.

The message should be clear: explore every possible and economical way to reach out to existing and potential customers. Determine the plan and purpose; work out the costs and technology; take a trial run; find a profitable niche.

Henry Mintzberg, a management professor at McGill University, suggests that when we plan, we often get too serious. We fill the pages with predictable, uninspiring results. We avoid novelty, and we fear chance taking. Usually, our strategies are too long; they fill binders and sit on shelves. So, to avoid this trap, keep it simple, especially at the start.

E-RETAILING

"What makes the difference in the functioning of a business is not what you do in a single encounter but what you do over a period of time in dealing with the customer."   LEONARD LEE

The e-retail website is the ultimate retail store. It has an infinite amount of shelf space. The store is open 24/7. There is no need to restrict the size and shape of any assortment because of physical constraints. The further restriction of serving only the local market is gone; the consumer market is worldwide. The costs of cash, cheques and cheque fraud are gone also. The product and service information is easy to read and complete. No store or service representative will "get it wrong" or misrepresent the offering.

E-retailing began to work for some major corporations and other entrepreneurs as early as 1997, when Dell reported that multi-million-dollar computer sales orders were taken at its website. The success of Amazon.com and eBay—the two rare pure-play e-retailers (no "bricks," only "clicks")—overshadowed the many failures of the many unknown neophytes. Concerns about secure order taking kept most buyers off the Web until technology caught up with the need to handle millions of transactions with credit card security. Coincidentally, 1997 was also the year in which the first auto site sold its millionth car over the Web.

By the start of twenty-first century e-retailing had become a craze, as hundreds of companies started up to sell products and services on the Internet. Most of them failed, because their marketing costs to attract customers often exceeded their total sales.

WHY A WEBSITE?

E-retailing is growing rapidly, as more sites are always being developed and the ease with which one can browse, shop, pay for and receive goods proves to satisfy customers. In 2005, Canadians spent $39.2 billion on the Web, up 38 per cent from the year before.

A knowledgeable retailer of goods and services that does not have a website is rare today. It is a pleasure to find a great site that offers worthwhile product and service information, multiple choices, delivery costs and a secure and convenient way to close the transaction. The Internet offers a number of features that set it apart from traditional retailing:

- It is the ultimate shop-at-home opportunity for just about everything.
- It provides a convenient form of education for those seeking information about a product or service.
- It provides information about the provider, not only "what and where," but "who."
- It can show new goods and services and bring them to market faster than any conventional way.
- It can offer an electronic catalogue.
- It can provide comparisons of price and features with those of other merchants who offer similar goods.
- It can handle transactions in an efficient and secure manner.

BRICKS AND CLICKS

The greatest advantage to e-retailing in conjunction with "bricks and mortar" retailing is the ability to get the customer interested in and knowledgeable about the product's benefits and price and then closing the sale quickly when the customer comes into the store. Commissioned salespeople often refer a customer to their website to help them reach a decision regarding choice. This frees up the salesperson to spend time with more customers on the floor.

Bricks and mortar retailers have the advantage of possessing a name that consumers already recognize. A strong brand name provides powerful benefits of credibility for establishing a Web presence. Bricks and mortar retailers can use their various print, radio and TV media outreach to get the word out about their online shopping venues. They can include their Web addresses in advertising campaigns as well as print their Web addresses in store catalogues and on store receipts. Moreover, they can also tie their store loyalty cards and catalogue circulation lists to their mailing lists to increase public awareness and usage of the online channel. The other advantage of "bricks and clicks" retailing is the ability to close the order online but have the customer pick up the purchase at the store. This also opens up the possibility for impulse shopping when the customers come into the store to pick up their goods.

E-mail offers another banner for marketing. In the strictest sense, it is part of the practice of permission marketing. Today, it is referred to as e-tailing. The merchant obtains the potential buyer's address from one of a number of sources and gets the customer's permission to send messages regarding sales and services that might interest the e-mail recipient. This practice is well developed by subscription information centres that give the receiver the opportunity to fill in a questionnaire indicating items of interest for which "push e-mails" would be accepted.

Search engine marketing is a rapidly growing marketing channel. Retailers buy pop-up advertising or "right-column" advertising that appears as searchers work their way to their chosen website. By clicking on the ad, viewers are linked to the seller's site.

TEN TIPS FOR WEB-BASED SALES

Businesses believe that their business is healthier—that it has a competitive advantage or stronger economic footing—when they have a website. Tema Frank, of *webmysteryshoppers.com,* has developed a Web-based mystery shopping service that operates similarly to store mystery shoppers. Her "shoppers" study the websites of retail clients and report back on the ease with which buyers can find what they want, get the information they need and then conduct business with the e-retailer in a secure and efficient manner. As a result of her work to date, she offers ten tips for building Web-based sales:

1. *Make your home page shine.* It must clearly state what you do, why people would want to deal with you and what makes you different from your competitors.

2. *Look professional.* Avoid animated cartoon figures or scrolling words; those are sure signs of amateurs. If your site looks amateurish, visitors will assume your company is too.

3. *Introduce yourself.* Put a picture of your president on the website, even if the president is the only employee. (Shoppers don't need to know that!) Put an e-mail link right below it.

4. *Give complete contact information.* Make it as easy as possible for people to get in touch with you, in any way that works for them.

That means providing an e-mail address, your phone number, a toll-free number and your complete physical address.

5. *Be brave about pricing.* Let's face it—people need to know your prices before they decide whether or not to buy. Price isn't the only factor in the buying decision, but it is information that inquirers will be looking for early in their search.

6. *Include taxes.* This can be tricky if you sell in a number of provinces, states or countries. If you cannot provide the exact tax amount in advance, at least state clearly that the pricing does not include tax.

7. *State the currency that you accept.* Currency accuracy is critical; there are, for example, twenty-two different world currencies that are called "dollar," and Internet shoppers exist worldwide.

8. *Avoid premature registration.* Don't ask potential customers to register until after they've decided to buy and have placed the order.

9. *Check your spelling.* This seems obvious, but it is a detail some folks forget; and spelling errors kill your credibility.

10. *Test your website.* Have your website tested by independent outsiders, preferably by someone or some firm that is expert at website design and function.

Everyone shops differently, according to his or her needs. Sometimes shoppers prefer to browse in order to obtain information or make comparisons. At other times, they may be very decisive and go to a store for a specific item; their minds will be made up. These two distinct modes of shopping behaviour can be described as "hunting" and "gathering." Both modes are common to bricks and clicks shopping, and your website needs to keep this in mind. It must not be an order form for the gatherers or an artistic wonder for the hunters, but it must make it easy for customers to close the sale (hard-edged) while providing information and even entertainment for browsers (soft-sided).

FRANCHISING

"Handshakes are just the beginning."   LLOYD SHEARS

Optimizing a business by means of franchising can produce the best of business partnerships. The owner of the franchise concentrates on developing the product or service concept in a starting location. When the concept, products or services and sales format are developed to the point where other locations can be introduced, new owners are invited to "buy in," open their own location and market the concept in accordance with the rules and guidelines set by the owner, or franchisor. Each new location, owned and operated by a franchisee, benefits from the owner's proven formula for success by using the company name, operating characteristics and control systems. Thus the franchisor is the business builder and the franchisee is the customer developer.

BENEFITS OF FRANCHISING

The financial benefits of franchising are significant. The creator or franchisor focuses the capital expenditures on product and service development while the franchisees focus their capital on the local real estate and working capital. For the privilege of using the franchisor's format and marketing materials, franchisees pay a royalty that is usually some percentage of their sales. Thus, the more units franchised, the more wealth is created for the franchisor. At the same time, the more successful the franchisee is in developing its site and local market, the more wealth is created at the unit level.

The best-known franchise systems are the fast-food companies that sell coffee, hamburgers, pizza and chicken meals. Many service businesses expand and succeed through franchising—for example, hotel chains, printing and delivery, dry cleaners and hair salons, and rental and vending businesses. These chains may be local, regional, national or global. Often, a franchisor opens up in a new country by entering into a master franchise agreement with an individual who has the right to create subfranchises across that country. Locally or internationally, franchisors maintain the right to own more than one store. They may also use this privilege to expand and later ally themselves with a local entrepreneur who takes over the unit as a franchisee. On the other hand, franchisors must often buy back a failed franchised unit and operate it until a new franchisee takes over.

GIVE AND TAKE

Essentially, franchisors agree to carry out certain obligations for the franchisee, and the franchisee agrees to follow the franchise program and rules of the deal. For the privilege of carrying the business name and offering the business's products and services, franchisees pay the franchisor certain fees:

- The first fee is usually the initial fee or setup fee. This is a non-refundable lump-sum payment made when the agreement between the two parties is signed. It covers the cost of setting up the facility or store, the first supply of fixtures, furniture, training materials and other pre-opening expenses.

- The ongoing fee, or royalty payment, most often a percentage of the sales volume of the franchisee's unit, is the key revenue source for the franchisor. The more units opened, the greater the franchise revenue; the greater the sales success of each unit, the higher the volume of franchise funds. To the franchisee, the key is making sure that the financial model proves that this fee will leave the unit operator with sufficient opportunities to make a reasonable continuing profit after the start-up period has passed.

- Two other support fees are usually charged as well. The first provides for the training of personnel as new employees are hired at the sales unit. The second goes towards a marketing fund to cover the advertising costs of the franchisor, which is responsible for overall advertising of the market area on behalf of all unit holders. The franchisee runs a local advertising program to supplement the franchisor's national program.

Although the agreement is critical to the success formula, an equally critical aspect of the partnership is the franchise concept. Joining into an existing franchise network allows the newcomer to determine whether the concept is viable and whether the brand has long-term value that is sustainable. For example, does the concept have a uniqueness that is recognizable in the marketplace? Are people talking about it in a favourable way?

The "four Ps" of marketing can be applied when reviewing the potential of a franchise program:

- Product or service: Is it differentiated in the opinion of consumers, and is it attractive to them? Do copyrights, patents or, more importantly, barriers to entry and imitation protect it?
- Price: Is it priced with a view to consumer value? Is it a price that can be beaten easily? How does the price–value relationship compare with that of the competition?
- Place: Are the products and services sold from the best venue and in the best possible location, considering the consumer marketplace? Is there a suitable role for Internet sales and a workable consumer interface?
- Promotion: Are promotions at the franchisee's place of business effective? Are they supported by the franchisor, or is the franchisee restricted to its own resources in this regard?

THE FRANCHISE AGREEMENT

Franchised arrangements require a formal franchise agreement that is as important as a lease agreement, because it is the framework for growth and financial success over an extended period of time. Since the critical business documents need to be created by experts, the best advice on franchise agreements should come from the best franchising experts. For example, Sotos LLP, a Toronto law firm, is dedicated to helping entrepreneurs develop, grow and protect their business in franchising, licensing and distribution. The following list summarizes important franchise-agreement elements that Sotos has prepared for prospective franchisees and franchisors:

1. A "proven system" needs to be worked out before undertaking a franchise program. This means that the design and operating features of the retail unit or service formula must be duplicable elsewhere.

2. A distinctive trade name and identity must exist that includes trademark registration as well as a uniform trade appearance, signage and trade dress.

3. Proven methods of operation and management must be stipulated. These should be written in a comprehensive operations manual and enforced through objective quality-control standards.

4. A capable and proven management team, consisting of founders and senior officers in addition to qualified consultants (where appropriate), must understand the industry and have an overview of the legal and business aspects of franchising as a method of expansion.

5. A training program for franchisees must impart all the basic components of operating and managing the proposed franchise. In addition, the training program must be supplemented by updates to deal with problems or issues not covered by basic pre-takeover training.

6. If the proposed franchise concept is a business format, the franchisor must have consistent site-selection criteria and architectural standards for premises that can be secured affordably in a competitive real estate marketplace.

7. The franchisor must have positive relationships with suppliers, lenders and real estate people in order to launch an effective franchise program.

8. Each franchisor must create a typical "franchisee profile" that takes into account the nature of the franchised business, both in terms of the franchisee's personal qualities and the kind of financial investment required (although this should not be the final consideration).

9. The prospective franchisor must have an effective accounting and reporting system. This is necessary as a management tool as well as to ensure that franchisees report and remit royalties and other dues accurately and faithfully, as and when required under the system.

10. Finally, the franchisor must have a comprehensive set of legal documents in place that reflect the peculiar needs of the specific franchise format as well as the operating style of a given management team.

THE PERSONAL SIDE OF FRANCHISING

Written agreements, rules and regulations are undoubtedly important, but the franchise's key to success is the personal relationship between franchisees and the franchisor. The "zees" are placing their life's savings and capital from friends and relatives into the business. This feature is referred to as "buying a job." The "zor" has a dream of creating an expanded chain of customer-friendly units and, hopefully, amassing a personal fortune. The success stories of Kentucky Fried Chicken, Tim Hortons, and McDonald's demonstrate that with

the right idea, giant franchise chains can provide lifetime opportunities for wealth-creation for thousands of franchised operators.

Franchisor and franchisee should be compatible and open in their
business relationship. This good working relationship must be established at the outset, even before the deal is signed and sealed. The
parties must take the time to get to know each other and learn about
each other's strengths and weaknesses. Third-party recruiters are
often used by franchisors to find and investigate new candidates, but
nothing replaces the "getting to know you" phase of one-on-one meetings between the principals.

The franchisee should take the time and effort to get to know the
other franchisees operating under the same terms. This source of
information can help answer some key questions: What was the other
franchisees' total investment, and over what period of time? Have the
working relationships been cordial and professional? How long did it
take to receive a reasonable income on a steady basis? Is the training
program adequate? Does the marketing program drive customers to
the site? Is communicating with the franchisor a help or a burden?
What about the reporting requirements and paperwork?

The prospective franchisee has an equally important obligation to
get to know who is behind this enterprise. Have the franchisors put
their own money into it? With whom are they associated in govern-
ing the business? For how many years have they operated the system?
Who makes the key decision on site selection? Have any units failed?
How were they handled?

The key word describing this process is disclosure. Not only is this
a personal investigation, it is also a legal requirement. Legislation in
most jurisdictions requires that a franchisor disclose his or her success story in such a way that the prospective franchisee is satisfied
that it is possible to make good money at this business. Thus a pro

forma financial statement of a typical franchisee is produced for the newcomer to investigate.

Another key element covered by disclosure laws is the possibility that legal actions are under way between other unit holders and the franchisor. Situations can arise where a dispute between the franchisor and franchisee cannot be settled amicably. Maybe the two of them didn't spend enough time getting to know each other, or perhaps they interpreted the agreement differently. These situations are important for anyone else contemplating a deal to be aware of. Perhaps the dispute is deep-rooted, or perhaps it might form the basis of a conflict that might negatively affect all the other franchisees. Whatever the reason, it is incumbent on the franchisor to disclose these issues.

FRANCHISING AND MONEY

Because of the division of responsibilities in a franchise agreement, the combination of the talents and drive of both parties enhance customer satisfaction as well as wealth creation. One party concentrates on concept origination and uniqueness, while the other concentrates on customer service. If this combination works, both create wealth.

For the franchisee, creating wealth takes time. The start-up phase of one to two years is the time for capital input, physical construction and installation, staff acquisition and training. It should be possible to break even financially by the end of the second year. As the sales unit becomes more profitable, the early providers of capital can be paid off. Now the franchisee may want to open a second or third unit. Time goes by, and by the end of the fifth year, financial success should be the rule, the banking arrangements should be solid and the associated investors should be satisfied.

The reason for this commentary here is to demonstrate the importance of an initial franchise agreement that has a long enough time frame to allow the franchisee not only to make a living, but also to create wealth. The agreement may include an initial trial period or introductory period, but it should provide at least five years for the business to unfold and become financially successful. A five-to-ten-year agreement is preferable. This is written up as a five-year agreement with a five-year extension. If existing franchises have a successful record of five years or more, new franchise candidates can quickly learn whether or not this five-year commitment is worthwhile financially. This arrangement is beneficial for both sides: the franchisor relies on long-term relationships, whereas franchisees need long-term employment opportunities.

FRANCHISE FINANCING

Financing a franchise can be much easier than financing a brand-new venture because the franchisor will have a track record that includes the stability and success of the existing units. Lending institutions that have already provided financing to existing franchisees are aware of the system's successes and have insight into the problems that may have occurred elsewhere in the system. Often, the lending institutions have an agreement with the franchisor as well as some of the franchisees; this "triangle of support" provides an incentive for all parties to succeed with the venture.

Strong franchisors often provide a "comfort letter" to the bank stating that if a franchisee fails, the franchisor will take over the business, continue to honour the loan agreement and find another candidate to take over the unit. This greatly reduces the risk to the lender and eases the task of obtaining financing.

The rules of business financing (see pages 244 to 253) apply equally to franchising, because the franchisee is a business owner in all respects. The same steps are required to successfully finance the business at the start: obtaining initial capital from personal resources, additional capital as needed from friends and associates, and bank financing for inventories and receivables if applicable.

It is wise at the outset to consider the various forms of financing available:

- Long-term financing brings in the capital that underpins the whole venture.
- Medium-term financing covers the costs of certain permanent features of the franchise, such as the initial franchise fees, the fixed assets, fixtures and the technology platform.
- Short-term financing is needed for the purchase of resalable goods and supplies.

Many new franchisees have little or no experience with business financing. The franchisor can make a big difference by opening doors, making introductions and providing letters of reference. The introductions apply to the acquisition of private capital as well as corporate lending.

In summary, the expansion of a successful business concept by means of a franchised network is a proven formula for success. The franchisor can concentrate on business concept and market development while the franchisee concentrates on customer service and sales unit productivity. Feedback from the franchisees can improve the sales and service formula of the franchisor. As a result, when it is well run and backed by a solid offering, it is a win-win combination.

FRANCHISE SUPPORT

A wide variety of newsletters, Internet sources, trade associations, books and manuals can be accessed for background information on franchising. Many franchise companies hold annual conventions at which franchisees can get to know their compatriots. These gatherings usually include training sessions, guest speakers and the presentation of awards to franchisees in many categories of excellence.

The franchise industry is well represented by trade associations. The most recognized association in Canada, the Canadian Franchise Association, is headquartered in Toronto, where it holds an annual convention and trade fair. Individuals interested in a franchise can view the latest entries and meet the key people behind the venture.

TECHNOLOGY

"Not even computers will replace committees, because commit-tees buy computers."   EDWARD SHEPHERD MEAD

Technology is the technical means people use to improve their sur-roundings. It is also the knowledge of using tools, machines and systems to perform tasks efficiently and make people's lives easier and better. People use technology to improve their ability to do work. Through technology, people communicate better.

Flowing from the technology of the cash register, the card trans-action device, the payroll ledger, invoices, receipts and all other forms of "input" is the creation of *data*. In isolation data is relatively useless, but in concert with other data it is essential to the health and wealth of the enterprise.

To make sense of data, computer software packages manipulate it and summarize it so that an end product—*information*—is created. Now it is possible to view summaries, see totals, compare different sets of data and reach conclusions regarding the status of the operation.

Information without analysis is little more than merely "nice to have." What does it mean? What can be learned from it? On the basis of the information provided, what actions or reactions should be considered? These questions are now being answered with sophisticated software that meets the many needs for understanding what the components of the enterprise are, how they react with one another and what outcomes can be expected with certain inputs. Information is upgraded by technology to become *knowledge*.

Now the brains of the business are brought into the situation. Through teamwork, dialogue, supporting presentation materials and expert advice, management acquires *insight*. Now the chain of input to output is complete, as illustrated in Figure 3.12. With insight, the owner-operators can make decisions based on facts instead of hunches.

Figure 3.12: From data to insight

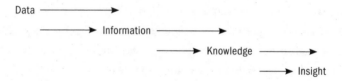

It is no longer acceptable to make decisions "by the seat of our pants" or "by guess and by God." Every retailer who wants to compete successfully in the world of retail, satisfy customers and create wealth needs to make technology a high priority. The best retailers know this and shift technology to a top-tier business function.

THE ROI OF TECHNOLOGY

Independent and small chain retailers lag far behind their larger competitors in implementing specialized programs that provide key information about assortment planning, inventory control, automated replenishment, sales staff planning and pricing analysis, or profit optimization. It appears that small and medium-sized retailers of goods and services do not recognize that properly chosen IT solution software has a return on the investment that makes it well worth installing. There is a tendency for independents to use their older technology for as long as possible and to buy as little new technology as necessary. Without having an idea of what or how much technology would be right, they are reluctant to take risks when they aren't comfortable with technology and how it works.

The best return on investment (ROI) on technology is at the point of sale (POS) and the point of receipt (POR). POS systems pay for themselves by properly monitoring and controlling each transaction at the correct price, with the appropriate taxes and automatic electronic payment, thanks to the debit and credit card, thus avoiding accounts receivables. What is less appreciated is the usefulness and need for similar technology at the point of receipt. What is ordered is not necessarily what is received, not only with regard to quantity (overs and shorts), but also with regard to pack size, store location, accuracy, date of promised receipt, brand switching and theft.

The right technology can reduce costs and improve margins. Tracking both hourly sales and part-time labour costs will reveal a pattern of customer visits and allow the retailer to accommodate customer surges with sufficient staff. At the POS, "price-giving" (selling the item at a price below the ticket price) is eliminated with the use of scanning devices while inventory records are automatically adjusted.

TECHNOLOGY AND THE PROFIT MODEL

A number of key factors can negatively affect the potential sales of a store:

· lack of sales help;
· lack of stock;
· excessive checkout waiting times;

Table 3.5: Profit model elements and IT tools

PROFIT MODEL COMPONENTS	PERFORMANCE INHIBITORS	IT TOOLS	MANAGEMENT SOLUTIONS
Stock-outs	End of season, poor replenishment, lost goods.	Assortment planning, open-to-buy, in-store perpetual inventory control, automated replenishment.	Responsibility tied to each element of the process, collaboration between IT people and store staff.
Price reductions	Unauthorized markdowns, excess of seasonal goods, wrong size mix.	POS analysis by SKU and supplier, store and buyer.	Improved authorization controls, tighter controls on store transfers.
Store expenses	Lack of sales forecasts for staff planning, lack of demand forecasting for suppliers.	Demand forecasts, labour by hour, by employee and by sales volume comparisons.	Management and staff training, proper training of full-time and part-time staff levels.
Distribution expenses	Excessive inventory requiring excess of labour, unnecessary warehousing, wrong store packs.	Open-to-buy, supply chain management reports, auto-replenishment, store-specific pre-packs.	Specific controls for inventory buying, planning and allocation.

· wrong size and colour; and

· customer returns.

Because the profit and loss statement begins at the top with "net sales," these "pre-net sales" factors are excluded and often go unnoticed. Imagine the lift in overall results if each of these sales-erosion elements were analyzed and steps were taken to reduce them. As a result, software solutions are available that collect the necessary data, organize it into meaningful files, analyze it and produce reports that can be acted upon.

Across the complete profit model, technology tools are available that highlight problematic results and provide solutions for management. The J.C. Williams Group Ltd. developed a retail profit improvement (RPI) program that both combined the profit model with IT tools and suggested management solutions. Table 3.5 describes some of the profit model elements and IT tools that move data to the information and knowledge stages, where appropriate action can be taken.

WHO'S IN CHARGE HERE?

One of the main reasons that IT investment programs are often too small or misplaced is that retailers fail to recognize their importance and fail to delegate the management of the IT function to the right person at the right level. Historically, in small businesses, the accountant or controller managed IT, because it was used primarily for accounting, payroll, taxes and sales audits. As the functionality of IT programs grew, they became the control mechanism and information tool of the merchant (inventory control), the store manager (staffing costs), buyers (supply chain management) and the marketer (advertising effectiveness, customer purchase records). This widening of interest created competition for various IT investments and solutions.

If the leader of the IT function has the ear of top management and is capable of proposing appropriate implementation programs, the question of who is in charge of the function is not a critical one. What is important is that the decision maker is made aware of how investments in IT benefit the management of each function. This is where management, acting as a team, must meet to prioritize the opportunities in relation to the results—the potential ROI.

Certain IT requirements, such as payroll taxes, paycheques, GST remittances, payables control and utilities payments, are mandatory. Setting these requirements aside, owner-operators must learn about the cost–benefit relationships of possible IT solutions. To bring these innovations about, the business leaders of each function of the enterprise must investigate the possible benefits, the cost and timing implications and the possible results of implementing these IT solutions. Many service businesses exist to provide retailers with technical assistance and training in these areas.

PERFORMANCE IMPROVEMENT TECHNOLOGY

For too long, the technology of a goods and services retailer was focused on process and product and was designed to handle payroll, receivables and payables, along with elements of sales, returns and expenses. But thanks to technology, retailing of all forms of goods and services is shifting to a customer orientation. The expenditures of consumers, as well as their retail habits and attitudes, can now be tracked, analyzed and configured to allow sophisticated retailers to determine who bought what, where and when. With the shift away from mass merchandising, the higher-end specialists are able to produce narrowly defined product, service and marketing initiatives aimed at special client groups. Complete stores may now focus on a very select group of customers, and multi-banner offerings can be finely tuned.

The specialized technology shown in Table 3.5 can analyze lost sales and provide solutions that assist merchants to recapture those sales while turning inventories faster, with higher margins and, at the same time, reducing aged and dead stock. The shift in management priorities that has allowed all of this to come about is the development and acceptance of "off the shelf" software packages designed for specific applications such as those described above.

Gone is the attitude that company IT departments must develop their own IT solutions because each company is unique or because their data is secret and outsiders must not be allowed to help with matters such as programming or analysis. Even after these commercial applications were developed, IT people still modified them to suit their individual needs. But problems developed with staffing and overhead costs: it became difficult to attract and retain IT talent when each company's systems environment was complicated and unique. With today's programming languages and specialized end-use purposes, knowledgeable people familiar with inventory applications can be hired to manage the IT department to the benefit of the various users throughout the company. Some interesting IT applications now on the market allow for:

- store staff forecasting so that deployment of part-time staff can be correlated with variations in customer traffic;
- analysis of inventory movement, with automatic signals to reduce prices when goods move out at less than planned velocity;
- individual customer segmentation based on customers' purchasing habits related to product groupings or brand preferences;
- identification of repeat customers for the purpose of offering specially designed loyalty programs;
- measurement of the success of advertisements, sales promotions and in-store product and service signage;
- website traffic metrics to improve customers' online shopping experience;
- analysis of census and postal code information to help determine store locations and refine assortment features.

For technology to play its rightful part in a company's performance enhancement, three strategies must be adopted:

1. The technology leader or chief information officer (CIO) must have access to the company leader so that he or she can educate the management team about the potential of IT solution software while acting as the gatekeeper for a balanced IT program improvement program.

2. Technology must be treated as an investment, not an expense. Every application needs to be measured against its ROI.

3. IT departmental budgets need to be grouped by department and project so that the right leadership team can prioritize the projects and commitments to staff, software and hardware.

The more detailed the profit model breakdown into its components, the more subelements of the model show up that need an IT package and solution.

TECHNOLOGY MIGRATION

In a small business life begins with little more than an electronic point of sale (EPOS) device and a PC in the back office or the home. The initial cost of the technology seems to take precedence over functionality, connectivity, redundancy, interaction and capacity. But soon each of these issues becomes more important, and a connected backed-up computer environment becomes essential. The single PC becomes one of a number of workstations; servers are added to provide a secure backup as well as common software and file management for each user connection. Card transaction devices are introduced. Wired and wireless connections are made between the store and the back office. A local area network (LAN) is added. Payroll and banking software improves the financial processing and control. Each of these steps is usually taken only if and when it becomes necessary.

Get to know a computer service provider who is knowledgeable about start-ups and small-business growth. Such a company will have a proven pathway for IT growth and will provide informed suggestions about the right hardware and software to add, and when to do so. The most knowledgeable service provider will also be able to advise the business operator regarding the need for in-house and outsourced services.

FOUR | CUSTOMER OPTIMIZATION

UNDERSTANDING THE CUSTOMER

"In the factory we make cosmetics. In the store we sell dreams."

CHARLES REVSON, OF REVLON

All forms of retailing, of both goods and services, are very personal, serving one customer at a time. Thus, success as measured by growth and profit begins with satisfied customers, and meeting the customers' needs and solving their problems must be the goal of the personal service business. There is a big difference between customer service and customer satisfaction. Customer service is the moment when a store or service transaction is concluded. A transaction may or may not leave a lasting impression. This impression is customer satisfaction (or the lack of it).

CUSTOMER DIFFERENTIATION

It is critical for goods and services providers to understand the customer. Most of the details of planning must be aimed at the things customers are concerned about: merchandise, price, location, and so

on. But review the simple model in Figure 4.1. All retailers know who is
in the "bull's eye," but how many keep track of the outer three rings?
Most know how many visitors made a purchase, but few know how
many visited the store and left empty-handed, and why. There is a big
difference between visitors and shoppers. As for the outside ring, market research is required to learn about these uninvolved consumers
who don't know or don't care about the retailer's existence.

Figure 4.1: Consumers vs. customers

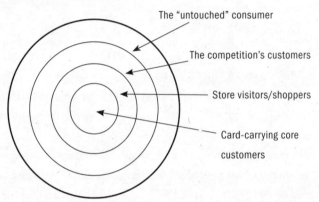

The "untouched" consumer

The competition's customers

Store visitors/shoppers

Card-carrying core
customers

Consumers fundamentally focus on place, price and product:

Price has always been an important factor: it relates to one's disposable income, it is the easiest factor on which to make a decision to
buy and it sets the tone for the store or service provider's profile—high-priced or low-priced? It must never be forgotten that what
is considered low-priced to a few is high-priced to many.

Product carries many attributes, including the little-understood
word—value. The product can be tangible, hence the term "retail
goods," or intangible, thus "retail services." Regardless, the product
has value as perceived by the customer, the final judge.

Place might be the store location, the athletic club, the website address, the catalogue page or even one's front door. To appreciate the variety of "place," consider the many ways in which you have answered the question, "Where did you get that?"

THE VALUE PROPOSITION

Now more than ever, the customer faces increasing complexity. With over-choice and less time available for shopping, the "offering" (price, product, place) must be balanced with the "exchange." Figure 4.2 details the key elements of the consumer's perception of value. Price and quality are the foundations of value. Ambience is an environmental attribute, whereas experience involves the staff members who interact with the customers—the salespeople and checkout clerks. Once again, retailing is a combination of "hard-edged" and "soft-sided."

Extensive research conducted by the Center for Retailing Studies in Mays Business School at Texas A&M University uncovered an equation for customer satisfaction that consists of more than just price and quality: shoppers were also influenced by everything they could absorb of the shopping situation—the "exchange."

Figure 4.2: The consumer's perception of value

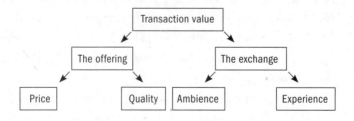

Understanding the consumer as a potential customer requires an understanding of consumer trends and forecasts. Consumerism became

an "industry" after World War II. As the veterans returned home, society sought to find gainful employment for them. So women were
enticed to become homemakers, vacate their wartime jobs, create
families and fill their homes with appliances, furniture and clothing.
The rise of television created an ideal venue for promoting consumption, and to this day TV continues to entice viewers to consume.

CONSUMER DYNAMICS

Consumer society has changed tremendously since the 1950s and
'60s. It is sobering to note that The T. Eaton Co., during its best years,
from 1965 to 1975, enjoyed the same share of market in Canada that
Wal-Mart held in the United States in 2004. Consider the following
trends, and think about the potential of continued change in each of
them. What will they mean to retailers? Some retailers will adapt,
while those that do not will fade away.

- Immigration: Canada's population growth results from immigration, not births. This is a continuing and an accelerating trend
  that flows from a decline in Canada's birth rate since the baby
  boom of the 1950s and the government's policy of sustaining a
  growing GDP through population growth.
- Diversity: Immigration is increasing from China and India and
  many other non-English-speaking nations. In 2004, nearly 20
  per cent of Canada's population were immigrants. Many of these
  immigrants choose to live in Toronto and Vancouver, increasing
  the proportion of immigrants in these metropolitan markets to
  one in three.
- Family composition: After World War II, nearly 70 per cent of
  Canada's households included a traditional family: a working dad,
  a stay-at-home mom, plus the children. Two-income families rep-

resented less than 10 per cent of household units. By 2000, the traditional family had dropped to less than 20 per cent of the total number of families, whereas two-income families had increased to greater than 40 per cent. The balance of household units consists of a variety of combinations, including multiple families and single-parent families.

· Aging population: As the baby boomers age, their impact on consumer fulfillment is dramatic. They are responsible for the great rise in consumption of housing, cottages, home decor, and leisure and sports equipment. By 2000, they had moved into their forties and fifties. It is estimated that from 2000 to 2015, this age segment will be the only one of the Canadian population to grow. It is also evident that this group's needs will shift from goods towards services.

· Disposable income: In the year 2000, the top 1 per cent of Canadian earners shared 14 per cent of all income, up from 9 per cent in 1980. In the United States, the top 1 per cent shared 20 per cent of all income earned, up from 12.8 per cent.

Table 4.1: Average personal income (in $ thousands), by quintile, Canada, 1970–2000

	1970	1975	1980	1985	1990	1995	2000
Quintile 1	81	83	87	95	104	111	124
Quintile 2	45	46	50	52	55	55	60
Quintile 3	34	33	34	35	37	38	39
Quintile 4	21	20	20	20	21	21	23
Quintile 5	8	9	9	9	9	9	10

Source: Statistics Canada

The Bank of Canada's inflation calculator demonstrates that, as of Fall 2006, a basket of goods and services costing $45,000 in 1970 would have risen to $214,000 by the year 2000 as a result of an average rate of inflation of 5.34 per cent for that thirty-year period. Note that the $45,000 income measurement of 1970, shown as the second line from the top in Table 4.1, has risen to only $60,000 for the same period. It is evident that with typical wage and salary increases, very few personal incomes have kept up with the rate of inflation. Far more consumers have had to trade down than trade up. This trend has resulted in the explosion of low-priced retail formats, in which Wal-Mart leads the industry with its huge selections and the image it projects that its prices are constantly being reduced.

Companies hoping to take advantage of this trend must develop a keener understanding of the changing needs of the consumer. Equally important, they must focus on their competitors:

· What drives the competitor?
· How is the competitor's business currently faring?
· Is the competitor satisfied with its current position?
· What moves is the competitor likely to make?
· Where is the competitor vulnerable?
· What will provoke the greatest and most effective retaliation by the competitor?

The answers to these questions will form an important part of the retailer's strategic planning.

SERVICE LEVELS

Another important but often overlooked feature of customer satisfaction is service levels. Consumer fulfillment businesses must define and demonstrate that they understand the differences between three distinct levels of service: full service, self-service, and customer-sensitive service.

- *Full service*: The personal interaction and dialogue between the "servicer" and the customer helps the client come to the decision to buy. This factor of selling brings to mind what the farmer knows best: "You can't milk a cow if you don't sit beside her." With many product categories, such as certain lines of apparel and footwear, full service is essential for completing the sale.

  A full-service engagement usually begins with the ancient question: "May I help you?" (A contest was once held to find a better introduction, but no better replacement surfaced.) The sensitive salesperson who sees the customer searching for something is better positioned for a sale by stating: "Let me know if I can help."

- *Self-service*: Increasingly, discounters and bargain stores staff their stores sparingly because they believe they have done such a good job of merchandising and display that customers can complete their shopping experience without interacting with a service representative. Banks have successfully created a service-free environment with automatic banking machines and Web-based banking services while continuing to meet the needs of customers who need or demand full service at their retail branches.

  The supermarket is based on self-service. But what if a certain item can't be found? Or what if it is out of reach, or a shopper can't decide between two similar products? Where is the staff member to help solve these problems? Obviously the self-service model needs some enhancements.

- *Customer-sensitive service*: In between full and self-service are many different forms of service profiles. As technology improves, perhaps voice-activated, interactive screens will appear on store shelves and in shopping baskets to assist those who need help in deciding what to buy. These customers may choose self-service but may also want to know how to get assistance when they need it.

SHOPPING HABITS

One interesting section of Kubas Consultants' *Major Market Retail Report* (see page 123) tracks what is known as cross shopping. It compares where shoppers prefer to shop to where they also shop; the report lists all of the large chains and shows how the shoppers spread their visits across many different competitors. Using the example of children's wear in its 2006 report, for every hundred shoppers who say their first choice is Wal-Mart, 56 per cent of them also shop at Zellers, 48 per cent also shop at Sears and 33 per cent also shop at Winners. The report also notes that for every hundred shoppers who choose Zellers as their no. 1 choice, 71 per cent of them also shop at Wal-Mart. This small sample shows the power of Wal-Mart—their shoppers are less likely to shop at its competitors.

In the *Toronto Star* Dana Flavelle published an interview with Shelley Balanko, an ethnographer and consultant with the Hartman Group.[8] Balanko offered the following advice to retailers: "Consumers' pickiness supersedes their sense of time famine. You should concentrate on what you do best. As you add more things, consumers will continue to shop your store, but every consumer will shop your store for different reasons."

CUSTOMER DEMANDS

There was a time when the pundits forecast that the average work week would get shorter and that families would have more time to shop and relax. It never happened. The double-income earners, bogged down with their personal digital assistants, cellphones and laptops, work more hours each week than they did before the digital age. This factor has led to fewer visits to the mall, less time spent in the mall and fewer stores visited. So the providers of goods and services must cater to consumer needs with a more focused approach.

TNS Retail Forward, in a report titled *Retail Innovation: Ten Opportunities for 2010*, identified customers' demands for help.[9] Following are a few of those requests:

- "Solve my problem" by adding services, information and support;
- "Do it for me" by offering installation and home-setup services, and in-home technical help;
- "Help me choose" by offering a Web-based product selection, samples and in-store information kiosks;
- "Come to me" by way of design services, home delivery, simplified tools;
- "Speed it up" by making the trip through the store, the checkout counter and the call-centre response more efficient.

These demands lead to three key opportunities for retailers:

1. Clearly define store formats or specialized services that meet the particular wants and needs of each market in which the sales units are located. It is no longer acceptable to create store plans using a cookie-cutter approach, which lays them all out in exactly the same way.

2. Find a way to build an emotional connection that brings customers back while encouraging them to tell others about their favourite features, such as the private brand, the high-quality change rooms, the store record of past purchases, or that special salesperson who greets the returning customers by name.

3. Use technology that collects data about store visits, transactions, special sales results, gift-card purchases, frequency of visits to the store or website and any other customer connection to better

understand the customers' preferences and provide a personal service over time.

RELATIONSHIPS VS. TRANSACTIONS

The cash register rings up the sale; the customer leaves the store—does anything else happen? Is this a transaction or part of a positive, ongoing relationship? This key to customer satisfaction and wealth creation is like distinguishing the difference between a one-night stand and a romance. A business built on transactions is doomed in the long term, but a business built on good relationships is guaranteed to succeed. Rather than talk, the business listens, and rather than seeing the customers as "them," the business considers them part of "us." Suspicion is replaced with trust; business-centricity is replaced with customer-centricity.

At a Toronto seminar in May 2006, David Maister, acknowledged as one of the world's leading authorities on the management of professional service firms, spoke about the difference between transactions and relationships:

> Relationships, by their very nature, are not as clear-cut as the negotiated contract terms of a transaction. On both commercial and psychological grounds, it is easy to see why some individuals might prefer the clarity (and short-term gratification) of a 'propose, get hired, deliver, get paid' transaction. Transaction skills are very 'scalable': expertise at winning and delivering transactions can be codified and disseminated quickly across an organization. It is less clear that the interpersonal skill of relationship building can be developed as quickly in a business that wants to grow rapidly. Transactions are also very appealing to those who find comfort in the ratio-

Table 4.2: Transactions vs. relationships

TRANSACTIONS	RELATIONSHIPS
One-night stand	Romance
Them	Us
Opponents	On the same side
Short-term benefit	Long-term benefit
Suspicion	Trust
Goal is to make yourself look attractive	Goal is to understand the other party
Negotiate and bargain	Give and be helpful
Preserve options, avoid obligations	Make a commitment
Focus on the present	Focus on the future
Develop a detailed contract	Be comfortable with ambiguous understandings about future reciprocity
Main goal is to prevail	Main goal is to preserve the relationship
Style can be impersonal, detached	Style must be personal, engaged, intimate
Preparation and rehearsal of what we're going to say and do	Adaptability and flexibility to the responses of the other party
Listen to what they're saying	Listen to what they're feeling, why they're saying it
Usual feeling during the interaction is tense	Usual feeling is relaxed, comfortable
Interactive style is defensive, protective	Interactive style is open, inquisitive

Source: David Maister, *www.davidmaister.com*

nal, the logical, or the analytical approach, which description covers people in most professional and technical businesses.

Little in professional training prepares one for the psychological complexities of dealing with clients (or liking it). An analysis of just how different transactions and relationships can be (and their relative appeals) is given in [Table 4.2].

A relationship attitude is born at the top and fed down through the staff at every level. Programs are built around giving something to the client before expecting to receive something in return. Service providers, by the very nature of their work, are more prone to developing relationships than are providers of goods. Yet, for both types of retailers, it is through the careful and lengthy process of establishing a positive relationship that wealth can be created over time. Unlike a transaction-based business, a relationship-based business involves consultation, give and take, collaboration and positive results on both sides. Simple methods of developing a long-term relationship include club memberships, client cards, rewards, informational subscriptions, e-mail-based promotions and special events for special groups.

THE MOMENT OF TRUTH

Somewhere along the path of search and fulfillment, there is often a "moment of truth." It either elevates or lowers the customer's opinion of the provider. What is key from a psychological point of view is the finding that any negative impression is always stronger and longer-lasting than a positive one.

The negative moment of truth is easy to identify and shows up in many ways: a call centre with a too-long waiting time, a promised delivery date that is missed, parts missing from a toy that must be assembled, a store closed when it is usually open, unexplained extra charges on the invoice, a "no returns" policy—and so on. These moments all have to do with the retailer's response to the customer. Positive moments of truth are more elusive (and more soft-sided)—the friendly welcome and assistance in the apparel store, the cabbie who steps out to load your bags into the trunk, the dry cleaning that has been specially wrapped for rain protection, and so on.

The higher the client's investment of emotional energy in the transaction, the greater the impact of a moment of truth. There is no equal to a completely satisfying store visit involving helpful staff and a painless checkout. Moments of truth are remembered and research has shown that negative moments talked about among friends and neighbours far more often than positive moments are.

Service organizations are particularly susceptible to negative moments of truth. Yet these providers have a great opportunity to turn a bad situation into a good one by the way they empathize with the client and deal with a problem. Customers who come into a service centre grumpy and leave happy become loyal customers and unpaid promoters of the provider.

WHY DO SALES GROW?

"Growth companies take ownership of great ideas and act on them."   TNS RETAIL FORWARD

A statistician met his friend, an economist, on the subway platform one day. "How's your wife?" he asked. "Compared with what?" was the reply.

Too often, company spokespeople give only one or two reasons for their growth or decline. But it is never that simple. A brainstorming session at the head office of a national retailer identified 74 contributors to growth. The following is a list of 24 of the best.

MAIN REASONS FOR BUSINESS GROWTH

· Consumer confidence	· Better advertising	· Add-on selling	· Bigger inventories
· Longer business hours	· Larger stores	· Price inflation	· Rising incomes
· Shift of mix	· New products	· More	· Lower prices
· Increased population	and services	promotions	· Branding success
· Lower taxes	· Loyalty rewards	· Failing	· "Scratch and
· More stores	· Sudden weather	competition	save"
	changes	· Customer	· Pleasant staff
	· New fads	rebates	
		· Gift cards	

GROWTH COMPONENTS

Some of the reasons given in the above list are retailer driven, others
not. When retailers blame lost sales on poor weather, it's easy to
check the records to see if this is a reasonable explanation. But what
was the real reason for declining consumer satisfaction? Store owners and operators should know the answers. Certain factors deserve
a further review:

·   Inflation: General inflation is the result of price increases, which
    can emanate from supply sources or from retailer action. For
    many years, in Canada, inflation has risen 2.5–3 per cent each
    year. So store sales should rise at this level unless pricing and
    assortment decisions add to or subtract from the inflation rate.

·   Rising disposable income: Personal incomes have recently risen
    approximately 3 per cent each year. People tend to spend more when
    they earn more, so sales should also rise at this rate each year. But
    there are many factors indicating that rising consumption and spend-
    ing are greatly affected by how consumers save and borrow money.
    Furthermore, a discernible rise in price can bring about a "trade-

down" reaction by the customer and result in the purchase of a lower-priced article. Carried to the extreme, instead of buying a lower-priced item, the customer may shift to a lower-priced store. Without going into a full economic analysis, it is safe to suggest that the long-term growth rate of retail sales should be a combination of inflation and personal income growth—4 to 5 per cent.

- Increased consumer confidence: We spend more when our fears about the future are reduced and we aren't worried about coming events or trends.

- Increased population: As the population of a market climbs, its sales are expected to rise as the new consumers share in the spending.

- Changes in competition: Nearby store closures or negative reaction to a retailer's service or assortments can quickly drive sales to other retailers.

- Improved promotional tactics: Advertising can be gentle ("Trust us!") or dramatic ("everything half off!"). The problem with successful promotions and suddenly rising sales becomes apparent the next year at the same time, when the same type of incentive must be given to grow sales over those of the previous year. Successful retailers keep this in mind when building their promotional calendar.

- "Shift of mix": All mixes of merchandise are priced at various levels, unless the merchant is a dollar store. By carefully adjusting the assortment, the percentage of "good" merchandise can be decreased while the percentage of "better" merchandise can be increased, and so on. The key to success is to make these shifts slowly over time, or at the change of a season, so as to avoid a negative customer reaction. Reducing the amount of goods "on sale" accomplishes the same thing.

- Overall customer satisfaction: As customers become more satisfied, they become more loyal, they shop at their favourite store more often, they stay longer in the store and they buy more. Customer satisfaction is a measurable factor that can be tracked over time.
- Weather: This is a favourite reason given when sales differ from those of the previous year—usually when sales are down. I was reminded recently by a successful retailer of sporting goods that retail is as weather-dependent as farming!

Many other factors contribute to sales growth. Some are the result of management action; some are the result of happenstance. Just as one element may result in growth, if it is mishandled or accompanied by bad luck, it can easily become a contributor to decline. The topic of why sales decline is the subject of the next section.

CLUSTERING

Adding stores has its share of risks and rewards. Once a successful store is opened in a definable market, in time it becomes evident that the customer potential exceeds the size of the store. So, another store is opened in the same market. This phenomenon is referred to as "clustering." Stores that are close together can trade merchandise and supplies, and they are easily supervised. They benefit from the print and electronic media that are already in place to serve the local market. This principle applies to service offerings as well as merchandise stores.

The key here is to make sure that sales don't slip from the first to the second store. Eventually, success will have extracted enough share of market from this cluster to allow the company to consider new territories, where the same formula applies. And although the easy approach of opening a new store in a number of unrelated markets looks appealing, it is dangerous. Radio and flyer coverage become efficient as a cluster of stores in a "media market" increases. A new store in a new media market has to bear all of the advertising costs. Supervision is expensive, and monitoring the new stores can become difficult. Instead, choose the best second market, cluster it until the maximum market mathematics are at work, and then consider a third cluster. In short: grow locally, then regionally, then nationally.

GROWTH MINING

TNS Retail Forward tracks what it refers to as "growth miners"—publicly traded retailers that sustain above-average rates of both sales growth and profit growth over a five-year period. In 2005, only fifty-one of two hundred companies met this criteria, growing revenues at more than twice the rate of all publicly traded retailers while growing profits at an even greater rate.

Table 4.3: Compound annual growth rate of growth miners, 1998–2003 (%)

	1998–2003 REVENUE	1998–2003 PROFIT
All U.S. public retailers	8.6	0.7
Retail "growth miners"	17.6	21.5

The retail "growth miners" shown in Table 4.3 would provide a great composite profit model. This top group demonstrated that their growth strategies matched the key consumer trends of that time:
· They focused on the home-related categories.
· They exhibited a strong value orientation.
· In the apparel sector, they focused on the youth market.
· The upscale retailers focused on high-fashion clothing and accessories or on the drug and health-food interests of the aging baby boomers.

Why do sales grow? A true story: In the locker room at the club one morning a few years ago, I spoke to a friend who runs a chain of well-known sporting goods stores. I asked: "How's business?" He replied: "It's only November 20, and we've had the earliest and the longest snowfall I can remember. I'm a genius!"

WHY DO SALES DECLINE?

"We count on winning. And if we lose, don't beef. And the best way to prevent beefing is—don't lose."   KNUTE ROCKNE

The list of reasons for sales growth on page 180 could easily be converted into a list of reasons for sales decline. To be a retailer one must be a perpetual optimist, so negative charts are unacceptable. To stay in the game and remain calm, many retailers of goods and services are quick to take credit for their sales growth while blaming someone or something else for a decline.

From the 1960s to the mid-1990s, Consumers Distributing Ltd. grew from one store in Toronto to more than two hundred outlets across Canada. Consumers was a catalogue warehouse store: shoppers filled out a slip with the catalogue number on it and presented it to a clerk at the counter, who went into the warehouse to find the item and bring it forward.

The concept was brilliant: costs and gross margins were extremely low, and the prices couldn't be beat. This now-antiquated process gave the retailers a complete list of everything anyone ordered, regardless of whether the item was in stock. It was a classic case of knowing what very few retailers know today—their gross demand. No other retailer had a record of the name and address of everyone who filled out the form, how often they came in, what they wanted and what they actually bought. Mail-order catalogue companies have always collected gross demand statistics and forecast their future sales and inventory requirements.

Unfortunately, the computers available during Consumers' growth period couldn't deal with this mass of paper-based input. The sales order slips filled many rooms, waiting for the day when customer records could be created. Without a knowledge of gross demand, the company could not forecast demand well enough or pull inventory from its suppliers quickly enough, nor could it distribute to its stores regularly enough to maintain a satisfactory "in-stock" position. The "stock-out" problem is one of the most important issues facing retailers today. It is interesting to note that today's e-retailers have the same process for customer purchases, but now all the data is filed and analyzed electronically.

It has been estimated that 40 per cent of all intended purchases are never completed. Why do more than 90 per cent of those who enter a shoe store leave without buying something? Why would couples leave a restaurant before they ordered? Why would anyone go into a convenience store and leave empty-handed? Why would hotel guests leave without checking in?

One large part of the loss of sales is due to the impatience of customers; they will not wait in line with goods to buy when they see other unmanned cash register stations.

THE PROFIT MODEL APPROACH

The partial profit model of Household Extras Inc. can be expanded to show the impact of lost sales, as illustrated in Figure 4.3. While HEI's profit and loss statement in the Appendix shows $10.7 million of sales, the unrecorded sales losses, for a number of reasons, add up to a potential gross demand of almost 50 per cent more than the resulting

sales. The four reasons in the second column are the result of decisions made by the customer that are similar to the goods-returned
decision. A quick study of Figure 4.3 shows that the solution to the
problem of lost sales is in the hands of the two most important groups
of people in the business: the buyers and the sellers. One is responsible for *what* sells, the other for *who* sells.

Figure 4.3: Household Extras Inc., impact of lost sales

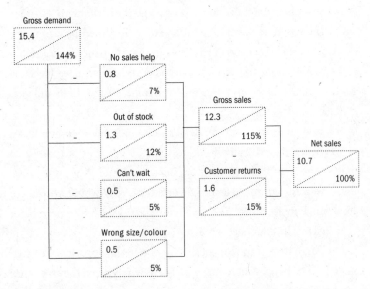

LOST-SALES SURVEYS

A regional chain of home-improvement stores decided to find out
how many visitors left the store without buying. This is easy to do:
compare the number of shoppers or shopping groups, such as families, who enter the store with the number who leave the store without
a shopping bag. The first year, the study covered only one store; the
results were so revealing that the next year all of the stores were studied.

It became evident that there was a pattern of "leakage" that was related to the known competence (experience, training, capacity, insight, and so on) of the store managers. So the study was conducted on the same day, a Saturday, for all of the stores. The results became the outline for a management-training program as well as a contest-based rewards program, as each manager strived to stay out of the bottom of the list and rise to the top. Here are some of the highlights of that study:

· 30 per cent of visitors left the store without buying anything (the market math formula calls this a 70 per cent conversion rate).
· Of that group, 17 per cent said they were "just looking."
· The rest, 83 per cent, gave as their reasons those shown in Figure 4.4.

Figure 4.4: Store visitors' reasons for not buying

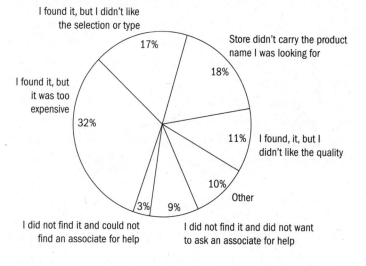

It was not a surprise to management to find out that the greatest reason for walkouts was price. This retailer had positioned itself towards the mid- to upper level of quality, service, assortments and after-sales service. What did surprise them, though, was the dominance of this factor—almost one third of the responses. So they attacked each key reason for walkouts with specific initiatives to reduce the lost sales. This research is now conducted at different times of the year and at every store, and prizes are given to the best stores and the most improved staff.

In 2002, the IBM Institute for Advanced Commerce published a survey on the relative importance of key drivers of customer satisfaction. It developed a point system that indicated the importance of certain store attributes in relation to the customer's level of satisfaction. The five attributes measured were person-to-person experience, store experience, prices and value, marketing and communications, and data integrity. The institute noted that a score above 110 indicated a high level of customer satisfaction. The first attribute, person-to-person experience, scored the highest, by a large margin, followed by the store experience. These two most important attributes are "people issues." Once again, in a retail experience, the soft-sided factors trump the hard-edged ones.

Table 4.4 provides a more comprehensive list of reasons for lost sales. No doubt a brainstorming session similar to the one described earlier in this chapter would generate a much longer list. This list is more informative; it includes information about who is responsible for improving the situation and what might be done.

All across the retail landscape, group meetings are held weekly to review the previous week's sales and other available operating statistics. Inevitably, the group ruminates about what went wrong when sales fell. What needs to be discussed is what can be done to recover those lost sales and move forward.

Table 4.4: Reasons for lost sales, and solutions

	REASONS	MANAGEMENT FOCUS	SOLUTIONS
1	Store hours not convenient	Store management	Competitive research Meet or surpass the competition
2	Parking lot closed, too expensive, full	Store management	"Carry-to-car" service Stamped parking tickets
3	No sales help available	Store management	Traffic counting and profiles Reduce non-selling activities
4	Sales staff not suitable or helpful	Store management	Recruiting, training Focused supervision
5	Stock-outs (as explained above)	Merchandising	Inventory management Supply chain management
6	Stock-outs (advertised items)	Marketing, distribution	More detailed advertising planning Closer distribution coordination
7	"Can't find it"	Store management	Organized rack and bunk displays Signage, ticketing and sales help
8	Items not as advertised	Merchandising	Quality control In-store receipt checks
9	Wrong sizes, styles and colours	Merchandising	Detailed receiving sampling In-store inspection
10	Product quality appears to be poor	Merchandising	Pre-ship sampling Factory visits or guarantees
11	Items or packaging damaged	Merchandising	Receipt inspection Further in-store checks
12	Poor fit or product construction	Merchandising	Supplier selection Quality control
13	Prices too high	Merchandising Supplier choices	Competitive price checks
14	No lay-away plan for customers	Store management	Credit function support Store backroom controls
15	Better prices found elsewhere	Merchandising	"Lowest price" guarantees Constant monitoring of competition
16	Waiting lines at the register too long	Store management Supervisory direction	Store staff planning

CUSTOMER FULFILLMENT

> *"I wish shoppers demanded more respect. If they don't get what*
> *satisfies them or what they think is coming to them, I hope they*
> *have the sense to spend their money somewhere else."*
>
> PACO UNDERHILL

Chapter 1 of this guide dealt with consumer fulfillment. Customer fulfillment is quite different: now, the consumers have found their way
into the store and must be converted into buyers. Customer fulfillment
can mean a number of things:

· maximizing the number of customers;
· maximizing the transaction value of every customer;
· maximizing the frequency of shoppers' visits;
· maximizing the percentage of profitable customers; and
· maximizing the "life-value" of customers.

Growing a business in an orderly way requires the retailer to consider the various approaches to growth. Working from the simplest
approach to the most difficult, the steps are as follows:

1. Sell existing products and services to existing customers.
2. Sell new products and services to existing customers.
3. Pause, review, adjust and clarify the results to date.
4. Sell expanded products and services to new customers.

It's easy to become distracted by steps 2, 3 and 4, but the foundation of any goods or services business is its existing customers. Much
can be done to maximize their support and contribution. The step-by-
step approach shown in Figure 4.5 moves the organization from the
simplest ideas to the most complex. If no more is accomplished than
steps 1 and 2, continuous growth will be ensured. The effort and com-
plication created while exploiting steps 3 and 4, however, may alienate
customers. They may even sink the business.

Figure 4.5: Four steps to retail growth

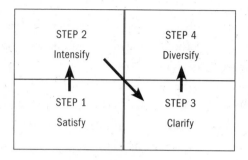

STEP 1: SATISFY

Turn to Chapter 2 and review the discussion of market mathematics on pages 66–73. This model demonstrates the power of satisfying those customers who are already in the store. By reducing the number who walk out without making a purchase, by convincing those who buy to buy a little more or something else, and by treating them so well that they return more often, customers are being satisfied. Satisfying customers is more art than science, but applying a scientific approach to the process helps a great deal. For example, it is important to develop a method of measuring the sales gained or lost during a specific period:

· Measure the entry traffic.

· Ask the non-shoppers about their reasons for leaving.

· Focus on an appropriate age and income group, not on everybody.

· Conduct customer focus groups.

· Hold research and review meetings with the associates.

· Provide incentives for increasing transactions, reducing cash-register lineups and increasing the average transaction amount.

· Study your competitors' habits, layouts and presentation features.

· Provide a greeter who is more than a greeter—one who communicates and interacts with the customers, both coming and going.

- Read everything about your industry sector, and go where the market is hottest.
- Find out what is missing from your mix, and fill the void.
- Learn what forms of advertising increase traffic and what types of advertising increase sales volumes.
- Consider going "narrow and deep" in the parts of your assortment of goods or services that seem to be the customers' favourites.
- Promote sales with surprises such as "lucky customer" discounts, especially when traffic is high; they are much less costly per customer at these times.
- Add new units, call centres, hours of service, home delivery, after-sales service, and so on.
- Maintain some form of regular market research.

This is, at best, only a partial list. Brainstorming and further research will add to it and put it into a better context of priorities. Keep in mind, and make others aware, that growth is essential to the success of the business as well as that of its employees and shareholders.

The importance of growth flows from the old adage that all strategies eventually fail: this is the catalyst for innovation, and it holds true across the retail industry now more than ever. Those who do not innovate will not survive. Consider the growth of e-retailing and the success of firms such as Amazon, eBay and Google. Consider also the decline of the department store and the struggle of regional malls to reinvent their reason for being.

Customer satisfaction is a standard component of every retailer's success metrics, but just because something seems measurable doesn't make it meaningful. Many retailers are adopting some form of survey to learn about their customer acceptance. A simple measurement is the "top box." Phone surveys are conducted to get the response to various questions such as "Do you shop at ...?" and "When you shop at X, are you satisfied with your visit?" The results are collected in a four-box chart shown in Figure 4.6.

Figure 4.6: A sample "top box" chart

Always	Often	Sometimes	Rarely

This type of survey is referred to as a "forced choice" survey. Respondents are prevented from being neutral because a "don't know" response is not possible. The responses are either positive or negative. The percentage of replies in the "always" box represents the "top box" score. Suppose the responses of 177 customers are broken down as 27–86–55–9. The top box score is 27 of 177 responses, or 15 per cent. While 63 per cent of the responses were positive, only 15 per cent were superlative. This would be considered a weak rating, so something needs to done to improve it.

The top box score, by itself, has little meaning until it is compared:

· One store's score should be compared with those of other stores in the chain or departments of the company.

· The retailer's score should be compared with those of competitors named in the survey (the same survey can be taken by naming another retailer).

· The score of the current year should be compared with that of the previous year.

· The scores of the periods before and after a major promotion should be compared.

· Scores should be compared quarter after quarter.

Smart retailers of both goods and services are using the results from surveys like these to improve everyday management and coaching. They set goals for top box percentages by store, division or grouping. Such comparisons can be great incentives for improvement when they are tied to recognition, prizes or even financial rewards for the team with the best score or most improvement. Stores or departments can be compared, and contests can be established or prizes and bonuses paid for the best results over time.

STEP 2: INTENSIFY

The intensification phase of growth can consume the whole organization if intensification isn't treated as a planned process occurring in tandem with the core activity of Step 1. Yet, it is the phase in which a retailer faces the test of "grow or go." Intensification adds products, services and customers to the enterprise in many ways:

1. Products:
   · additional sizes, styles, colours;
   · new brands;
   · new suppliers;
   · expanded product lines;
   · additional floor space for selling.
2. Services:
   · home delivery;
   · provision of expertise for renovations, landscaping, decorating;
   · drive-through, pickup and drop-off stations;
   · alterations;
   · product repairs;
   · item rentals;
   · in-home setup;

- mall kiosks and carts;
- e-retail;
- extended warranties;
- longer hours;
- increased promotional incentives;
- expanded stores;
- new store locations;
- mall and street kiosks and carts.

The profit statement of Household Extras Inc. in the Appendix shows (see Other Income) that the company is growing with Step 2 strategies. It has entered the equipment rental business, it has doubled its catering business and it is growing its party rentals. As a new sales division, these three businesses have grown 70 per cent while the traditional business has grown 4.5 per cent.

STEP 3: CLARIFY

Clarification is often ignored or given little priority in the overall thrust for growth. Yet no growth plan can be executed without some troubling outcomes, disappointing results or competitive retaliation. The results of trouble always show up in the financial statements or performance metrics.

Market research and customer feedback may signal the need for further change. Recognizing when changes must be made needs to be part of the management function. Furthermore, management should encourage an environment that accepts criticism and nurtures introspection.

Clarification may include many small or large changes, including:
- closing of unproductive stores;
- replacing non-performing assortments;
- redirecting advertising funds from one medium to another;

- outsourcing certain technical operations;
- creating special incentives to move out non-selling goods;
- creating exit programs for non-performing individuals.

Often, the original retail value proposition needs to be reviewed (see pages 45–52). It is relatively easy for competitors to see the direction a company is taking and to replicate it in a "me too" format. While this may be a form of flattery, it diminishes the unique thrust of the one who developed the proposition in the first place. So it is wise to be constantly in the competition's stores, surveying customers, watching who walks out of the store with what and gauging the success or failure of the other side's promotional programs. Armed with solid facts, you may need to rewrite strategies and implement changes to put your venture onto a new course.

The first step in clarification is to make sure that the key retail responsibilities focus on the needs of the customer, not the functions of the business, such as financing, operations and marketing. Customer strategy trumps the company functions and focuses on:

- attraction: the job of marketing;
- conversion: the challenge of store operations and merchandising;
- retention: the joint responsibility marketing and store operations; and
- profitability: the financial summary of everyone's output.

STEP 4: DIVERSIFY

Diversification is a significant departure for the business. It is much more than intensification; it usually means finding a new way to do business, new forms of businesses or customers, new geographies or new and unrelated products and services. This leap requires the adoption of new talent, new processes, new technology and new organizational groups.

Some of the typical routes of diversification and some well-known examples of their implementation are as follows:

1. *Complementary banners:* Women's-wear merchants are adding store formats that allow them to cater to various age groups with different styles and sizes in highly focused stores. The Gap has added Gap Kids and Baby Gap.

2. *Competing banners:* Different styles or price points are created within a merchandise category and with a disconnected banner name and look. Reitmans (Canada) Ltd. operates Reitmans, Penningtons, Addition Elle, RW & CO., Smart Set and Thyme Maternity. Consumers may settle on just one of these formats because of the differences in their assortments. The Aldo Group Inc. operates many banners, and consumers may visit a number of Aldo formats while shopping for shoes.

3. *Country-wide expansion:* The first task in a retail expansion strategy is to saturate the local market where the business began. This is usually where the head office is located and where early successes and experimentation can be watched closely. Any of the retailer's media expenditures are more efficient when each new store can draw customers off the initial media purchase at no additional cost. When the first cluster of stores proves to be financially successful, another cluster can be built nearby. Expansion then moves to a new city or another province until the company has locations in all its chosen markets. As the breadth of the company's expansion increases, the timing for seasonal inventory building and promotional selling must be fine-tuned, because its key spring and winter seasons occur at different times in different parts of the country.

4. *Foreign expansion:* Canada has seen a dramatic influx of American operators who have exhausted the locations for their stores

across the United States and have chosen to expand into Canada, where the market is similar. Canadian retailers have not had the same success in expanding south because of their lack of preparedness, the intensity of the competition and the lack of U.S.-related executive experience.

5. *Channel blurring:* Since Wal-Mart's arrival in Canada, there has been a significant mixing of traditional merchandise formats. Canadian Tire integrated its Mark's Work Warehouse into newly formatted Canadian Tire stores. Loblaws has added general merchandise and expanded its Real Canadian Superstore concept. Shoppers Drug Mart is selling fresh and frozen food. Each of these moves is an attempt to extract more dollars from visiting customers and to bring them back to the stores more often.

6. B2B: When retailers sell to contractors or installers, they are selling B2B—business to business. This customer base is often made up of independent operators who run a specialty service in a local neighbourhood. Unlike typical store customers, they are usually served at a special sales desk, order in bulk quantities, truck away their goods and pay on delayed terms. Another example of B2B diversification is the establishment of a contract in which an institution will buy a retailer's goods or services at commercial prices for local pickup at the nearby stores.

7. *Embedding services with products:* Long ago, clothing stores included the cost of alterations in the cost of the garment. Today, some do and some don't. Obviously, there is a customer-satisfaction advantage to the clothier who provides the service free of charge. Other examples of embedded services are home installation and setup, trade-ins on new products, home delivery, customer-only sales events, free seasonal catalogues and fashion shows for selected clients.

8. *E-retailing:* Building a successful retail site on the Internet is just as difficult as creating a first store. Here, customer attraction is not a visual-location matter; it is an electronic-location challenge. But adding "clicks" to "bricks" provides an excellent new opportunity for diversification. Why build stores and sales units in another country when e-retailing can reach the same markets with no new fixed assets?

CUSTOMER RETENTION

> *"Loyalty is caught, not bought."* CAROLE FARMER

Every retailer of goods and services suffers from "churning," the constant loss of regular customers and the resulting need to replace them with new ones. It is far cheaper to keep a customer than to acquire a new one; the common expressions to describe this key management process are "customer retention" and "loyalty management." Survey after survey shows that behind the customer's motivation to stay with a provider is his or her satisfaction with what the company does in comparison with the competition. This satisfaction is rooted in the management strategy of differentiation.

Loyal, long-term customers are the backbone of every business. But good customers are hard to win and easy to lose. Some guidelines:

-   10 to 15 per cent of the customers of typical retail goods and services businesses leave and go elsewhere each year.
-   They move or die, they discover competitive advantages elsewhere, they experience product or service dissatisfaction, or they feel the lack of a customer contact strategy.
-   It takes five to ten times more money to capture a new customer than it does to keep the existing customers.

- It is accepted that 80 per cent of the revenue of a business is derived from 20 per cent of its customers. When one of these "20 per cent" customers leave, it usually takes a number of new customers— and a long period of time—to replace the lost volume.
- Another study that looked at loyalty programs found that 87 per cent of the customers contacted said that they would purchase from a company even if it didn't have a loyalty program.

The churn rate differs among various industries. The wireless phone industry has a churn rate of over 30 per cent, which explains why it provides big rebates for signing on and long-term contracts to trap customers into staying. Banks report that the top 30 per cent of their customers (when ranked by profitability) make up 100 to 150 per cent of total customer profits. The rest of them either produce no profit or cause a loss just by being on the books. Banks know the profitability of every client and always have some clients who don't make money. Like every diligent retailer, they attempt to shift their products and services to create profit where it is nonexistent.

Every customer relationship is a tangible asset in that each has an economic value. Assume that a typical family spends $200 per week at a grocery store and shops there for five years. This amounts to $200 × 52 weeks × 5 years = $52,000. This example of one family clearly demonstrates the value of customer retention.

CUSTOMER LOYALTY

Before developing a customer-relationship management program, it is important to understand what is meant by loyalty. Business leaders have come to accept that the key to loyalty is the customer's repeat buying at a provider over a long period of time. In addition, they recognize that a sign of loyalty is the willingness of repeat customers to recommend this provider to their friends. These factors are more emotional (soft-sided) than practical (hard-edged).

Until recently, shopkeepers generally knew their best customers because they spent time "on the floor" and were usually stationed where the cash was kept: the shopkeeper handled the sale and usually knew the key customers by name. Today, the staff operate a centralized cash register and the owner or manager is buried under administrative details in the back office. And the chain store has moved management to the corporate office. How often have we heard the question, "Who's minding the store?"

Large companies with the resources to track loyalty and relate it to their financial results generally report that comprehensive loyalty programs produce higher profits and revenue growth. And when they measure their share of market, they see it rising. Their advertising and sales promotion programs are more productive.

CUSTOMER RELATIONSHIP MANAGEMENT

Customer retention programs are not the same as customer relationship management (CRM) programs. CRM is a systematic business approach using information to build long-lasting and mutually beneficial customer relationships.

CRM integrates marketing and communications data, technology, analysis and retention processes across all customer touch-points. In CRM, the customer is the building block for data management, reporting, measurement and goal setting. Because CRM is a data-based approach to customer management, it is IT-based and may be costly for small and medium-sized companies to install and operate. But the process itself, with or without the technology, is as old as retailing.

A retailer of any size can pursue a CRM strategy by adopting either a personal-touch or a program approach—preferably both. Surveying customers is where the measurement begins. Third-party research firms provide a variety of techniques to capture customer reactions and opinions. The simplest study they carry out is the exit survey. Non-employees are posted at the store's door to intercept shoppers and ask them a few questions about their visit. On a grander scale, customers willing to participate in a survey provide their phone numbers or e-mail addresses and agree to respond to the questionnaires.

CRM software programs provide the key customer information from their tracking of customer shopping habits. The information includes frequency of shopping, choices of goods or services, and the amount of money spent over time. A deeper search of this data can indicate if a particular customer is profitable or unprofitable. This is where CRM has its greatest benefit: now the loyal customer can be defined not only in terms of "business bought" but also in terms of the profitability of the purchases. Using these findings, retailers can focus on their key supporters in many ways.

THE PERSONAL TOUCH

The website *www.retailindustry.about.com* published a series of articles on loyalty retailing. Part 5 in the series was titled, "The Value of Interaction."[10] The provider of the material, Melody Vargas, commented: "Friendship is the most effective branding a store can ever use. It isn't loyalty programs that set retailers apart form their competition, it is friendships."

Friendship is built up over time from the many services provided that pleases the customer, as well as the personal contact that is made along the way. Ms. Vargas comments further: "Just because a retailer is based online doesn't mean they can't create one on one contact too."

As friendships develop, so does loyalty. Supporters of a business, especially a service business, like to talk about their good relationship with their service provider. This brings friends into the store, and new business opportunities are opened.

The most universally known personal retention program anywhere is the one involving the Wal-Mart greeter. These individuals give Wal-Mart an immediate positive image by making people feel good on their way into the store. And the sole-store shopkeeper can provide the same advantage. Interesting, isn't it? The largest and smallest retailers do this best. What's the difference between this greeter and the reception desk at the entry point of most service establishments? It keeps track of those who enter and directs them to the right place or, alternatively, directs the right service representative to them.

Chain store managers have the same opportunity to meet customers as they arrive. But corporate bureaucracy seems to keep them busy in their office or in the backroom stocking shelves. So they must delegate someone to be the greeter. The Gap learned that an individual at the front of the store acting as a greeter could also act as a security inspector, simultaneously watching for stolen goods going out the door. People who are given the task of greeting have another opportunity to help the store: they are able to estimate the traffic count against which the transactions can be compared.

If customers begin to feel ignored or neglected, look out! Personal programs are a way to prevent this; their strategies for retaining customers include many simple approaches, including:
- thank-you notes;
- birthday cards;
- e-mail announcements;
- newsletters;
- personal invitations to special events;

- regular promotional events such as "seniors shopping days";
- free delivery for special customers;
- phone calls to indicate the arrival of new goods; and
- membership rosters with periodic discount periods.

Many retailers refer to their customers as guests, but having a guest is a once-only experience. If the visit is satisfactory, the guest may become a guest again. A level above "guest" is "friend," and the true retention of a customer involves the development of a friendship. Friends are always welcome, both during busy, crowded times and in an empty store. Friends take an interest in the success of the store or service; they get to know the key servers by name; they take time to talk about their lives while they learn about how the business is going. Best of all, when something goes wrong, friends forgive and forget.

THE PROGRAM APPROACH

CRM programs have been packaged and automated, and now a number of techniques are available, depending on the interests of the operator and on his or her willingness to give something away in order to acquire a long-standing customer or client:

- Discount programs: The customer receives a price cut on repeat purchases or combo purchases. Insurance companies apply this program for long-standing clients—for example, purchase home insurance and receive a discount on car insurance.
- Loyalty programs: Prime examples are AirMiles and Aeroplan, with their free air travel points. Many retailers have their own card-based programs in which a member's card is swiped at the time of purchase; often instant discounts are also available.

CRM software is a crucial part of these programs. The best of them gather data about customers and store it in an easily accessible format so that it can be analyzed. Then decisions are made regarding the identification of high-value customers, "losers" (customers that are not profitable), customer communication opportunities, retention program decisions, events, seasonal pricing choices and a variety of other features.

The cost of running and managing a CRM software program can be high. Many firms outsource their program needs to specialists. But the retail provider of goods and services must first become and then remain customer-centric. Customer-retention metrics must become the subject of regular meetings. Here are some ideas to think about when considering a formal customer retention program:

- Begin with pilot projects.
- Test new programs and communications.
- Hold customer focus groups.
- Interview top supporters.
- Involve store staff who get to know the top clients.
- Avoid contacting customers too often.
- Find a way to separate the profit-takers from the profit-makers.

Whoever is responsible for the marketing program of the business is also the leader of any CRM program. This person must be able to work with the IT people as well as with the store staff and customers, where the moment of truth resides.

BRANDING

"You can't build a reputation on what you are going to do."

HENRY FORD

All providers of goods and services have some sort of brand. Just ask their customers to describe the business in a few words, and out comes their personal understanding of the retailer's brand statement. But does the customer's understanding of what the company stands for and how it behaves match with what the company sets out to do?

WHOLE BRANDING

John Torella, a senior partner at J.C. Williams Group, has written a book titled *Whole-Being Retail Branding*, a concept he defines as follows:

> Think about a company as a living being, a person:
> · How it is born;
> · How it grows, develops and matures;
> · How it is refreshed, revitalized and in some cases, reinvented;
> · How it goes from one generation to another.

Torella goes on to say:

> Developing a brand is not just about 'every day in every way, just a little bit better' but also about taking giant steps which leapfrog ahead of the competition. Retailers need to understand who they are, what they stand for or what their innermost substance is.[11]

Every good business plan or strategic plan has a section on branding. This is more than an image statement or a promise to customers; a good brand strategy spells out many elements of the company's approach to its market, such as:
· the product or service concentration;
· the ways in which these attributes are different from those of the competition;

- a delivery promise regarding quality, responsiveness, service levels, assortment depth and breadth;
- the image of the product line, the store or service location, the advertising and promotional materials;
- the level of staffing and support;
- the class of customer identified for the purpose of focus and concentration. For example, is it a high-end aspirational offering or a low-end "quick and cheap" offering?

Branding is not just the packaging of the products or services. It involves all the ways the company interacts with the marketplace, especially the customers. It includes the level and quality of the staff and support personnel, the policies regarding hours of operation, rebates and returns, loyal customer benefits, the advertising image, the social responsiveness to community needs, support for the industry standards of excellence and the partnership stance with the suppliers. There are many good books on the subject of branding. In keeping with the theme of wealth creation, this section deals with the potential for a financial return on the investment (ROI) in branding.

BRAND EQUITY

A Google search produced a list of seventeen definitions of brand equity. The most appropriate one for the purpose of this book is: "The marketing and financial value associated with a brand's strength in a market."[12] There is increasing evidence that brand equity drives business value and financial success. While B2B organizations can measure their client support and the shipment of goods over time, B2C companies need to be able to measure productivity, retention and loyalty as these factors relate to customer support. They need to gain insight regarding this support in terms of financial performance.

There is plenty of debate about whether or not the value of brand equity can be found on the balance sheet. In public companies, it is possible to place a measurable value on brand equity: the difference between the market cap of a public company and the purchase price is a reasonable example of what a buyer considers the brand equity of the business. Lenders need to recognize brand equity as part of the value of the business when lending funds for growth and expansion.

Brand equity is both hard-edged and soft-sided. It is possible to measure both the financial results—the economic impact on the performance and finances of the business—and the consumer results—the impact of perception and experience on the customer. See Table 4.5 for an illustration of how brand equity can be charted. Every item in the table is measurable, but some aspects are easier to measure than others. Obviously, the financial results are the easiest to track, but without tracking the customer, a true expression of brand equity is not possible. A simple way of calculating the return on the investment of branding is to compare the costs of the key business inputs with the key business output—the cash flowing from operations.

Table 4.5: Impact of brand equity on financial and consumer results

IMPACT ON FINANCIAL RESULTS		IMPACT ON CONSUMER RESULTS	
PERFORMANCE	FINANCES	PERCEPTION	EXPERIENCE
Sales per square foot	Sales	Awareness	Satisfaction
Same-store sales growth	EBITDA	Credibility	Frequency (retention)
Share of market	Net profit	Differentiation	Loyalty
Gross margin	Market cap	Perceived quality	Likelihood to recommend
Inventory turnover	Net worth	Brand recognition	Price premium

To measure output as a percentage of sales, use the value of the earnings before interest, taxes, depreciation and amortization (EBITDA). To measure input as a percentage of sales, use the key inputs of:

- M—marketing costs (including advertising, promotion, special client card costs);
- L—store or service-centre labour and management costs; and
- C—direct costs of operating these units, such as supplies, store technology, advertising and sales promotion, transaction costs and delivery.

As an example of the calculation of branding ROI, assume that EBITDA is 18 per cent of sales—a reasonable amount. Assume that $M =$ 5 per cent, $L = 12$ per cent and $C = 5$ per cent, for a total of 22 per cent. Branding ROI = 18 per cent divided by 22 per cent or 82 per cent. This translates as follows: 82 per cent of the total costs of the key elements of this company's brand image are returned in the form of cash flow. By itself, the number is of little use, but when compared across a number of stores or year by year, the number becomes meaningful. Setting a target of 100 per cent from the above example will result in new programs to improve the effectiveness of marketing, staffing and support costs. The thinking is as follows: assume that the collective efforts of the business produce exceptional customer spending that results in high levels of productivity and profits. Some of the inputs that produced the excellent output are non-financial. Even though they are intangible, they have a monetary value.

There is a need to understand how the key drivers of consumer perception lead to the customer experience that affects the retailer's financial performance. Marketers today focus on this course of action and refer to it as "value creation." Market analysts and financiers must move beyond the pure numbers and recognize that there is a "balanced scorecard," the structure of which varies with the industry subsegment under review, the maturity of the segment, the size of the market and the purpose of the company. Is it to sell goods? Is it to provide services? Or is it to offer embedded services—activities that extend the product mix into non-store activities such as a twenty-four-hour drive-through, home delivery and installation, or the removal of replaced articles?

BRAND EQUITY DEMONSTRATED

A recognizable grocery business with high brand equity is Whole Foods, a publicly traded U.S. chain of more than 175 stores of organic foods, with sales in excess of $5 billion. Table 4.6 compares Whole Foods with more than twenty-five other public supermarket chains to show how the perception of consumers becomes the satisfaction of customers, which leads to superior financial results.

Table 4.6: Whole Foods compared with the supermarket industry in 2005*

	INDUSTRY MEDIAN	WHOLE FOODS
Year-over-year growth rate	5.5%	22.8%
Same-store sales growth	5.4%	14.9%
Gross margin	28%	34.7%
Inventory turnover	10.7 x	14.8 x
Net profit percentage	1.4%	3.4%

*Reported company results, compiled by TNS Retail Forward

While the U.S. grocery industry has struggled with the arrival of Wal-Mart, Whole Foods seems oblivious to the retail giant. Whole Foods' customers do not compare the two chains; the organic food retailer's brand equity sets it apart from the competition. This is due to Whole Foods' unique positioning. Its customers may shop for certain

basics at Wal-Mart or the neighbourhood grocer, but they will purchase their fresh food from Whole Foods. Starbucks possesses the same
attributes of setting itself above and apart from the competition.
Similarly, in the service segment, Curves is rapidly establishing itself
as a neighbourhood fitness centre unlike any other. Supportive customers talk about the simplicity of the arrangement and the ability to
get in and out of the premises quickly, feeling great.

Finally, "brand equity" speaks to the future potential of a retailer
of goods and services, whereas the financials speak to the results of the
past. The financial ratios that describe a successful retailer, if traced
to brand equity values and a demonstration of customer loyalty, provide confidence to the lender that the borrower will be able both to
service the loan and someday retire it. Retailers, including the service
companies that have little or no inventory, need to be evaluated according to their ability to generate cash from their operations in the
future. This will help the lender establish the retailer's "appetite for
risk," for the purpose of providing funds for operations, upgrades
and expansion.

Other retailers appear to have a high degree of brand equity.
Lululemon, for example, has a rapidly growing customer base. Canadian Tire has a tremendous following among male customers and a
growing loyalty with women. Brands belong to products; brand equity
is the goal of retailers. Perhaps the greatest statement about brand
equity in Canadian retailing was uttered more than one hundred years
ago by Timothy Eaton: "Goods satisfactory or money refunded."

FIVE | FINANCIAL OPTIMIZATION

Throughout this book, I have referred to Household Extras Inc (HEI). This chapter will rely on this hypothetical company and its financial statements in the Appendix at the back of this book to demonstrate a number of financial metrics and formulas that can be used to better understand the dynamics of the money of retailing. Although the company name is fictitious, the numbers are plausible. This chapter explores the details of making money at retailing—the activity in which the fun of wowing the customers pays off.

FINANCIAL STATEMENTS

"Slump? I ain't in no slump ... I just ain't hitting."   YOGI BERRA

No matter how small or big the business, there are financial statements to describe its profitability and value. Three standard financial statements describe the overall financial situation of the company: the balance sheet, the profit and loss statement and the cash flow statement. Operating statements, unlike the corporate financial statements, vary with the type of business, the size of the company and the degree of departmentalism.

THE BALANCE SHEET

Figure 5.1: The balance sheet items

	What is owned	What is owed	
	CURRENT ASSETS	CURRENT LIABILITIES	
Can cash	Cash	To staff	Must pay
in now	Receivables	To suppliers	for now
	Inventories	To banks	
	Prepaid expenses	To governments	
	FIXED ASSETS	LONG-TERM DEBT	Must pay
	Land	To banks	for later
Might cash	Buildings	To financial companies	
in someday	Fixtures	etc.	
	Equipment	NET WORTH	Should
	Vehicles	Owner's capital	pay off
		Retained earnings	someday

The balance sheet is the ultimate financial document. The word "health" best describes the balance sheet. (It rhymes with "wealth.") It is similar to the comprehensive report of an individual who has just completed an annual medical check-up. Many tests are taken and questions asked. Healthy people may see their doctor only once a year, and the comparisons of the same tests taken one year earlier are the most important determinants of health: "Did my weight go up? My blood pressure? My cholesterol levels?"

All financial balance sheets balance: what the company owns is equal to what it owes. Figure 5.1 describes the key parts of the balance sheet and prioritizes them in terms of their ultimate conversion to cash. After all, when the business is wound up voluntarily or shut down successfully, all that remains is cash. This is the ultimate source of wealth; if anything is left, it belongs to the shareholders.

The key parts of the balance sheet are as follows:

1. *Working capital:* the net of current liabilities subtracted from current assets. This ratio explains a lot regarding the day-to-day liquidity of the business. The word "current" means that, with a reasonable effort, these assets can be converted into cash in a reasonable amount of time to pay off the current liabilities with cash left over; the implication is that this will be done within the fiscal year. With current assets exceeding current liabilities, the company is considered "liquid." HEI's working capital ($1,691,828 less $1,870,222) is negative, but it has improved in comparison with the previous year. The bank will like this improvement, but it will want to know what steps HEI plans to take to get to a reasonable level of working capital—a ratio of 2:1. This requires that the value of the current assets be double that of the current liabilities. The bank sees sales climbing and profits static, and it must judge whether this is a warning signal. HEI must control costs better and stay away from capital spending for a while. Also, if the company avoids paying dividends for two or three years, more cash will be available for paying down the bank debt somewhat,

2. *Fixed assets:* the permanence of the enterprise lies in these physical assets. Working capital is being created and reduced daily, and financial institutions recognize this impermanent characteristic when they value the business. Fixed assets, on the other hand, are just that—fixed. They were purchased originally with shareholders' capital and financed later with one of many forms of debt. The B2C sector tends to avoid incurring the heavy cost of fixed assets

by renting its stores, offices, trucks and computer hardware. This frees up cash for working capital but ties it up to cover rental payments. HEI should look at ways to convert some of its property and equipment into cash by selling and leasing it back.

3. *Net worth:* total assets less current and long-term total liabilities. This is where is the original and subsequent investments are placed and where the continuing net profits and losses are accumulated. As profits grow, the net worth climbs, and the value of the shares or equity in the business climbs also. This assumes that dividend payments are controlled to allow this sum to grow steadily, keeping the company liquid. Net worth is where the satisfied customers' contributions should eventually wind up—creating wealth. HEI's statement refers to net worth as "shareholders' equity." Its net worth ($4,525,378 less $2,022,222 = $2,503,156) appears strong as its assets are more than double its liabilities, but it slipped from the previous year as the net worth–to-liabilities ratio declined slightly from 1:1.32 to 1:1.24.

THE PROFIT AND LOSS STATEMENT

For some unexplained reason, business owners carefully scrutinize their profit and loss statements, briefly scan their balance sheets and pay little attention to their cash flow statements. But the fundamentals of making money suggest that the opposite should be the case. The profit and loss statement shows what has happened in the past time period; the balance sheet shows how well the company is financially balanced over time; but the cash flow statement shows where the cash is coming from, how it being used up and what is left over for wealth creation.

Figure 5.2 shows how the profit and loss statement feeds the balance sheet.

Figure 5.2: How the profit and loss statement feeds the balance sheet

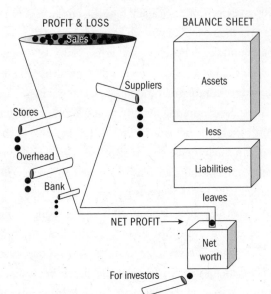

For every dollar that flows in at the top of HEI ($10,692,000), only 2.5 cents ($267,300) makes its way into the owners' net worth after taxes. It's not hard to recognize that if HEI's net income after taxes can be raised to a more acceptable benchmark of 5 per cent, an additional $267,300 will flow to net worth.

Companies usually publish their profit and loss statements monthly or quarterly. The seasonality of retail goods and services companies makes it difficult to compare quarterly statements that occur throughout the year, so the best approach is to compare balance sheets from the same point in time each year. Many retail companies with year-ends at December 31 or January 31 have to work their way through the first three quarters with little profit before the bulk of their profits are generated in the fourth quarter.

Although the balance sheet is important to the owners and lenders, the profit and loss statement is the most important document to the operating team. It can be thought of as a responsibility statement, because the efforts of each operating executive are reflected somewhere in the statement. The profit model in the Appendix show this well. The buyer, or merchant, is expected to produce an adequate gross margin from the cost of sales sufficient to cover all of the expenses of the business. Store management holds responsibility for the many store expenses. Because the retailer's greatest single cost is the cost of goods sold, the resulting gross margin from the sales is the cash remaining to run the rest of the business. Because so much of the retailer's sales income goes out to the supplier, gross margin is really the top line, from a cash management perspective.

The gross margin is the result of pricing, discounts and shrinkage. Increasingly, markdowns are controlled by the central merchant, with a small responsibility for store discounts delegated to the store manager. With this control in place, initial pricing and sale prices can be managed to respond to competitive and profit pressures. When Canadian retailers look for comparable operations to judge their performance, they are restricted because Canadian accounting rules do not require the divulgence of the gross margin amount as their U.S. counterparts do. The Canadian public companies can lump all their operating costs into one amount: "Cost of merchandise sold and all other operating expenses." This buries the real top line, gross margin. There are few exceptions in which the gross margin is shown. More retailers who rely on the public market for share capital should adopt this practice.

Most of the operating expenses occur at the retail outlet or service centre where the business is carried out. The rest of the expenses, although essential, are overhead. Think of the business, either goods or services, as having two distinct areas of operation: the store or service centre—or better still, the customer centre, where customers interact with the sales or service staff—and the support centre or "back office," the location of all the other activities that support the customer centre.

The customer centre is the business generator. This is where sales and relationships are made and lost, where customers are either satisfied or not satisfied. There is not much value in the support group if the customer centre is not successful, so smart retailers separate these distinct cost centres from each other. This subject is dealt with in detail in "Measuring Performance," on pages 224–235.

THE CASH FLOW STATEMENT

It is a mystery why few operators and even their advisers spend time understanding cash flow or analyzing the "statement of cash flows." HEI is typical: the cash flow statement is not there; perhaps it wasn't issued. Everyone seems to assume that cash flow is the job of the treasurer. But, although cash flow statements are not easy to read, to create wealth is to generate cash.

The reason the treasurer is most concerned with cash flow is because he or she is most closely connected to the bank. Cash flows to and from the bank daily. If sufficient funds are on deposit, all is well when the cash runs out; the bank provides what is needed until it flows in again from the revenue-generating activities. This arrangement is documented in a loan agreement with the financial institution. It is a simple, day-to-day transfer of funds and is of little interest to anyone other than the treasurer. But when things go wrong and the cash is depleted—and the banker says "Sorry"—that's when everyone needs to become involved with cash flow process. Table 5.1 illustrates simple cash flows into and out of the company.

Table 5.1: The company's cash flows

CASH IN	CASH OUT
Operating income	Operating losses
Sale of property or other assets	Purchase of property
Borrowed money	Purchase of assets
Sale of equity to investors	Paying down the bank loan
	Interest paid
	Taxes paid
	Dividends issued

Even without a formal cash flow statement, a careful study of the other two statements in the Appendix provides a good guide as to where the cash came from and went:

· There was no cash at the end of either year; the company has been borrowing from the bank.

· Although cash came in from net profits, it was diminished by a dividend payment.

· The rise in accounts receivable and inventory ($1,620,275 in 2005, compared with $2,312,184 in 2004) was a loss of cash of $691,907.

· The drop in trade payables (from $974,778 in 2004 to $935,540 in 2005) was a further cash decline, as the suppliers supported the inventory by $39,238.

· The property and equipment line increased, indicating that capital was spent on facilities or equipment. Whatever the reason, it resulted in a new mortgage ("mortgage payable" in the balance sheet) of almost the same amount to help finance the purchase.

· As a result of the flow of cash in and out for these and other changes to the balance sheet, the bank loan increased.

From the analysis above, it could be said that HEI is struggling with its growth plan throughout its operations except where it finally matters: the retention of earnings.

OPERATING STATEMENTS

Within each company, team members are responsible for managing different parts of the business. They may be responsible for drumming up the business (sales and marketing), supplying the business (warehousing and distribution), keeping track of the business (accounting and information technology) or financing the business (treasury). Small companies combine these functions, whereas larger ones divide them among a number of people.

The key word in the paragraph above is "responsible." The owner, president or CEO is ultimately responsible for the complete enterprise. This responsibility may be delegated, but it can't be relegated. When individuals are responsible for the financial success of a particular part of the business, they become accountable. Their area of responsibility needs a scoresheet so that their accountability can be measured. These scoresheets are known as operating statements. Taken together, the departmental operating statements add up to the overall results.

The job of the business leader and the head of accounting is to make sure that each operating statement summarizes the financial accountability of each department head. "Dumping" costs from one department or business unit (BU) to another, referred to as "overhead allocation," decreases the value of the statement and its significance to the BU managers. A typical dumping practice is to allocate the company's overhead costs to the operating division costs. Although it is fine to do this at the level of the company's profit and loss statement, it is unfair to do it at the department level, for two reasons:

- The bottom line of the operating department, better known as its contribution, is decreased by the arbitrary allocations beyond the control of the operating department head.

- Dumping eliminates the company's ability to determine whether or not the operating units are contributing enough or whether the overhead departments are too expensive.

HEI's profit and loss statement (see the Appendix) appears to be in two businesses: retail and contract. But down within the corporate overhead is the accounting for the new services department. A company of this size probably has a department head for each of the three business units. It is time for the members of the leadership team to look at their own contributions and to separate the company overhead so that they can see how their own business is doing within the growing company. Table 5.2 shows the departmental profit statement for HEI, which has been developed from the reworking of the company's profit and loss statement, separating the company overhead out of the operating statements.

HEI is profitable, but its potential is much greater. When the three business units are placed side by side in the table, it is obvious that the retail business is carrying the company. This is reasonable, because it was the original business, and the other two departments are just getting going. Using this statement, four detailed observations can be made about each business unit—a key activity that is not possible when looking at the normal profit and loss statement:

1. The breakout of the gross margins suggests that while the contract department has margins typical of a contract or wholesale business, the retail margins may be high, and lower prices might create higher sales and a higher gross margin dollar volume.

2. The services department exhibits a high gross margin, but this is typical of rental businesses because the inventory is rented, not sold,

Table 5.2: Household Extras Inc., departmental operating statement*

YEAR-END,
DECEMBER 31, 2005

	RETAIL		CONTRACT		SERVICES		TOTALS	
	($000)	(%)	($000)	(%)	($000)	(%)	($000)	(%)
RETAIL								
Sales	8,853	100.0	1,839	100.0	1,235	100.0	11,930	100.0
Cost of goods sold	4,802	54.2	1,563	85.0	320	25.9	6,687	56.0
Gross margin	4,051	45.8	276	15.0	915	74.1	5,243	44.0
EXPENSES								
Stores								
Labour	1,035	11.7	640	34.8	320	25.9	1,995	16.7
Occupancy	521	10.8	131	7.1		·	652	5.5
Advertising and promotion	72	0.8		0			72	0.6
Other store expenses	234	2.6	98	5.3	361	29.2	693	5.8
Total expenses	1,862	21.0	869	47.3	681	55.1	3,412	28.6
Total store contribution	2,189	24.7	(593)	-32.2	234	18.9	1,831	15.4
Corporate								
Distribution							349	2.9
Corporate overhead							1,058	8.9
Total corporate overhead						1,407	11.8	
NET PROFIT BEFORE TAXES							424	3.6

*There are slight differences between the Profit and Loss Statement and the profit model due to rounding and the business's big costs are labour. The statement suggests that the services department needs some advertising and promotion to raise its profile in the community.

3. The big drain on the company's profits is the contract division and its high labour rate. The management team appears to understand the metrics of retail but needs an education in how to make money at contracting.

The receivables of the two service departments shown on this profit statement are combined. Note that they have a significant effect on profitability and financing. These are the receivables of the contractor customer who does not use a credit card but instead takes advantage of the retailer's credit until its job is complete and it is paid. This high-risk practice demands that receivables be closely monitored and that strict rules be established for the collection of contractor debts. As receivables rise, as they did at HEI, bank loans climb to support the receivables. The closure of the contract business (referred to as a "loser") would increase profits and reduce the bank loan as the receivables are collected but customers would be lost.

4. Using this form of operating statement, it is easy to conclude that the company's overhead is excessive. A detailed review of each cost centre should reveal opportunities to decrease expenses or to prevent them from rising further when sales rise.

At the top end of retail performance, a few U.S.-based specialty retailers can report a net profit margin after taxes exceeding 10 per cent of sales. Although there are very few who perform at this level, clearly it is possible. The stronger and more appealing the retailer's offering, the higher the potential for high profits. Well-run retailers produce after-tax profits of 5 to 10 per cent, and this range is an ambitious but attainable goal for B2C companies.

MEASURING PERFORMANCE

"If you're not keeping score, you're only practising."

This familiar line has been attributed to two different people: Knute Rockne, the inspirational head coach of Notre Dame College, and John McEnroe, the great tennis player who dominated men's tennis from 1980 to 1984. It really doesn't matter who said it; both of them were winners in their time. The important point here is that this rule applies also to the details of retail from the top line to the bottom.

STATEMENT ANALYSIS

The importance of financial statements is understood only when they are analyzed and their key issues highlighted and trends noted. Earlier, this book described how technology is used to convert data into information that business leaders need to gain insight into the company's affairs. The same process applies in reviewing the financial statements. By themselves, they tell one story; but when compared in certain ways with past statements or different sources of information, they take on a new level of importance.

The balance sheet provides an opportunity to analyze the business in a number of ways. Using HEI as an example we see the significance of the following metrics:

1. *Cash/loans:* The first item, cash, is compared with the previous year's cash. Why is the company in debt at year-end?
2. *Current ratio:* This is the measure of current assets divided by current liabilities. The current ratio is the test used to determine if the company is solvent and can meet its debt obligations. The higher the ratio, the better. A ratio at or above 2:1 is preferable. HEI's ratio is negative—a warning signal.

3. *Debt-to–net worth ratio:* This ratio compares the financial amount of the creditors' interest in the business with the financial amount of the owners' (the shareholders') interest in the business. The more the owner holds, the better the ratio and the more secure the business. HEI's ratio is 1.12:1 in 2005, slightly worse than in 2004, when it was 1.08:1.

4. *Supplier support percentage:* This percentage compares trade or accounts payable with inventories. HEI's year-end inventory of $1,079,252 is supported by account and trade payables of $935,540, or 87 per cent. As long as the suppliers support this arrangement, all is well. The higher the percentage, the less needs to be borrowed to pay for the goods.

5. *Year over year:* Progress, or the lack of it, can be determined by studying the changes from year to year. Public companies usually have a profit and loss summary stretching back at least five years. This allows the investors or lenders to see the long-term effects of management's success over time. The two years of HEI's activity shown in its statements suggest that with the exception of its working capital, it is in reasonable shape. HEI's immediate goal should be to better manage the cash flow to bring down the bank loan.

Other important ratios are calculated by comparing elements of the profit and loss statement.

6. *Gross margin:* This is equal to gross profit dollars divided by net sales.

7. *Pre-tax profits (profit before taxes divided by net sales):* Many analysts refer to this as the "bottom line" because it is the end-result of the performance of the company before any taxes are paid.

HEI's after-tax profit of $424,000, or 4 per cent. This is below standard; management needs to extract profit improvements from every part of the business. Note that the HEI profit model is rounded to produce a pre-tax profit margin of 3.8 per cent.

8. EBITDA (*earnings before interest, taxes, depreciation and amortization*): This is often referred to as the operating profit, or cash from operations. It removes the non-cash items and the non-operating items from the ratio. HEI's EBITDA can be calculated by adding back to pre-tax profits $424,000 of the interest and depreciation ($48,000 + $202,000) to yield $674,000, or 6.3 per cent of $10,692,000. This is low for a specialty retailer, and half of what one would expect from this type of specialty store. If the contract division, shown as one of the three business units in Table 5.2, is eliminated, EBITDA might rise as much as $593,000, a significant EBITDA improvement. Another strategy worth investigating is the expansion of the services department. HEI has both rented space and owned space. This distorts the occupancy costs of carrying the owned space that does not include a rental factor. Analysts who encounter this anomaly remove the rent from the calculation of EBITDA and measure EBITDAR—this takes rental costs out of the cash flow calculation and allows the proper comparison of owned versus rented facilities.

9. *Revenue-to-profit CAGR (compound annual growth rate)*: High-performance retailers are able to grow their top line faster than their bottom line, year after year. Every retailer should strive to meet this standard of excellence. Those retailers that are attracting customers in greater numbers each year because of their brand equity, positioning and uniqueness are increasing their profits faster than their sales. HEI grew its total sales volume by 10.3 per cent while its services department grew 70 per cent.

Equally important performance ratios are provided by comparing elements of the profit and loss statement with elements of the balance sheet.

10. *Inventory turnover (cost of good sold divided by average inventory):* The trick with this ratio is determining the average inventory, as opposed to the year-end amount, as discussed earlier. Year-end inventories do not usually represent the average inventory because they are at their low point at that time.

    A better approach can be taken to get at average inventories. Take the previous year-end inventory, add the four quarterly amounts, and divide by five, or—better still—take the twelve monthly amounts plus the year-beginning amount and divide by thirteen.

    The turnover ratio is critical to many performance features, as discussed above and elsewhere in this book. It needs to be judged against those of other companies in the same business segment. Grocery stores may turn over their inventories as often as twenty-five times each year, whereas furniture retailers may turn over their inventories three to four times each year.

11. *Return on assets (ROA) (profit divided by net assets):* This measurement shows how productive the company's assets have been. Depending on the business, the higher the ratio the better. Companies that rent their premises instead of buying them will have more cash to spend on other essentials and a higher return on their assets. Using HEI's balance sheet, total assets are $4,525,378; its net income is $272,101; and its ROA is 6 per cent—another metric that yielded a below-standard result.

12. *Gross margin return on inventory (GMROI) (gross margin dollars divided by the average inventory for the full year at cost):* To the

merchant, this is probably the most important ratio. The formula was explained in Chapter 3. It describes the merchandise profits earned on the inventory, before any other costs are added.

PRODUCTIVITY ANALYSIS

Productivity is the output derived from the input. Some of the above examples are productivity ratios. A number of them focus on the gross margin revenues obtained from the inventory or the sales revenue obtained from the assets. Other productivity measurements are very valuable and deserve to be developed for different elements of the business. Here are a few favourites:

1. *Same-store sales (total annual sales divided by the number of sales units open for the full twelve months):* This measure requires the sales of stores open less than a year (because of new openings or closures) to be removed. It is the true measurement of growth.

2. *Sales per square foot (net sales divided by store square footage):* This measurement must include all of the floor space of the selling units, not just the selling space. The reason is simple: the cost of ownership or the cost of leased space applies to the total space. In the case of rented or leased space, this is referred to GLA (gross leasable area). HEI has five stores with 6,300 square feet per store, or 31,500 square feet in total. Dividing this amount into the total sales of all three departments that flow from these stores produces sales per square foot of $378. This is low for a high-margin business in the home furnishing sector.

   Sales per square foot should always be rising. This measure positively feeds the ratios of same-store sales and EBITDA and is the first and foremost indication of success. It is a measurement that can be compared with those of other retailers in the same business.

3. *Productivity of staff (total labour costs including ancillary benefits divided by net sales):* The fewer the labour hours expended to obtain the sales, the better the store contribution ratio. HEI's store staff of twenty-five produces $477,000 sales per staff member. A look at corporate expenses suggests that perhaps another ten people are employed outside the store group; this brings the company's employee productivity down to $340,000. For this ratio to be useful, the hours of work by part-time personnel must be converted to the equivalent of full-time personnel. This is known as FTE (full-time equivalent). Any company or industry group can develop this metric. A standard expectation is $300,000 per FTE. So HEI is in good shape here. As retail formats move from full-service modes to self-service modes, this key ratio improves.

PERFORMANCE METRICS

Beyond the measurements of financial and statistical data, other measurements allow the management of any retail business to monitor not only its efficiency and effectiveness, but also its ability to achieve its overall strategic goals. Following are a few examples of worthwhile performance metrics:

1. *Share of market (SOM):* This is not a readily obtainable measurement for most businesses. Yet it is an excellent yardstick for measuring success over time. If the business grows at a rate of 5 per cent per year but consumption of the product or service being offered is growing at 7 per cent each year, then the company is falling behind. Many industry statistics are published, and it is a challenge to relate any one business to them—but, over time, a consistent check on some benchmark will provide share-of-market comparisons.

One fairly simple approach is to collect customer names and postal codes (volunteered at the checkout) and compare these codes with population or household income statistics to provide a local SOM index. This also assists in understanding how large the market geography is and whether there are concentrations of customers that might support another store in the area.

2. *Average transactions per store:* This key measurement, monitored daily, helps with the setting of staff levels. Both the number of transactions and the size of the transactions are important to the store.

3. *Average inventory units per store:* Similar to the previous metric, this one concerns inventory control and possibly offers a reason sales are above or below those of other stores in the chain.

4. *Markdown percentages:* This measures the percentage of the potential gross margin lost through markdowns. The potential margin is the markup multiplied by all of the units in the shipment or sold in a specific time period. The final or "maintained margin" over the same period is subtracted from the potential margin to determine what has been lost. Three remedies are worth considering:

   · Reduce the amount purchased so that more of it can be sold before it needs to be cleared.

   · After clearance sales, raise the price again to test the demand for the product and to reduce markdowns.

   · Set guidelines for the dollar amount of markdowns as a percentage of potential full-margin sales. A reasonable benchmark is 20 per cent.

5. *Aged stock:* This measures the amount of inventory in excess of the average inventory, expressed as a percentage of total inventory— or, the percentage in excess of the budgeted inventory. Bankers look at the percentage of inventory older than sixty or ninety days

to judge the quality of the inventory for security purposes when lending funds to operators.

6. *Sales per FTE*: There are a number of metrics related to personnel costs. The most important is the sales unit or store payroll as a percentage of net sales. This is the largest—and the most controllable—variable cost.

SERVICE METRICS

Compared with retail goods firms, boosting the performance of service companies is more difficult. There may not be an inventory from which sales are generated, and the service-company staff may not be as homogeneous as that in a store. Furthermore, service-centre executives are prone to accept more variance across their sales units and to absorb excess costs that are difficult to find and reduce. However, these reasons are not an excuse for declining performance. Measuring and monitoring performance is fundamental to service success, both from a customer and a wealth point of view. Because service businesses are heavily dependent on personal service, a ratio is needed to relate customer support to staff levels. The services industry has a variety of published metrics, such as the percentage of seats occupied (airlines) and of beds or rooms occupied (hospitals and hotels).

The most important lesson here is to recognize that the best measurements will come from comparisons made within the business, not from without. There are too many variances in style and output among the various service companies. Comparing costs within comparative divisions or sales units is the first thing to do. Along with this study comes the comparison of individual output across the primary service staff.

Finally, it is important to talk to the customers. Most, if not all, of them are making comparisons with similar services every time they need help. They know best why they choose their particular service advisers. Key measurements are the quality and friendliness, along with the timeliness, of the service provider.

HEALTH METRICS

Not all the above performance metrics deal with financial performance. The soft-sided aspect of the business also deserves attention. Following are a few worthwhile health metrics:

1. *Employee retention (the turnover rate of store staff, both full time and part time):* Also consider the turnover of the FTE staff of the whole business. Too high a "churn rate" results in excessive recruiting and training costs, as well as possible lost sales through inexperience in dealing with customers. Too low a turnover might signal a lack of individual goals or too few reviews of staff performance, or it might signal an overall pay level better than that in the local market.

2. *Succession potential:* Often overlooked: what percentage of supervisory and management staff and specialists have identified a replacement who is ready to be promoted if necessary?

3. *"360" evaluations:* Each employee is given the opportunity to fill out a confidential questionnaire regarding his or her peers, superior and subordinates. Only the sum total of the ratings is made known, and only to individuals being measured—no one else. These highly confidential measurements are best made by outside professionals. The larger the divisional unit or company, the more meaningful will be the rating. When properly handled, these evaluations provide an incentive for self-improvement.

4. *Walk-out tallies:* Periodically, customers who leave without buying anything are intercepted and asked a few questions related to why they bought nothing. Summarized, the answers provide

powerful information for improving customer satisfaction, and all of the grim reapers of store failure are exposed: out of stock, wrong price, no help, too long a checkout lineup, couldn't find it, and so on.

5. *Advertisement success:* The costs of offering product or service program promotions are compared with the response to the program, as measured by the gross margin obtained.

6. *Long-term progress:* Choose the five most important metrics and chart their improvement or growth over time. Are they growing smoothly, or are they up and down? Find out why they behave the way they do.

BENCHMARKING

Benchmarking takes performance measurement out of the business unit to the wider world of competition and market leadership. It considers who is the "best in class" and asks: How do we compare? What do we need to match them? How long will it take? Good benchmarking requires a substantial expenditure of time and talent on statistical and market research. Accepting the challenge of benchmarking requires accepting the possibility that someone out there is handling a key metric better than the retailer who is asking the questions.

Not everyone believes in benchmarking. It is easy to suggest that whoever is best at some competitive metric will continue to look for even higher standards of excellence. So why work to catch up when it's a sure thing that the benchmark will rise even higher? But this attitude is an excuse; while benchmarking works best with major enterprises across broad markets, it can still be useful in small companies or for comparisons of sales units or departments.

The most efficient and effective approach to benchmarking is often taken by trade associations, who hire outside professional firms to survey their industry and return with the key benchmarks that are of common interest to the association members. Participants provide confidential information that is summarized and published as an industry-wide study. A helpful addition to these studies is the ranking technique. Each participating member receives a separate confidential report and a ranking of its metrics compared with those of all the others. These participants then work on their weaknesses and watch for an improved score when the next report is issued. Often the industry improves itself over time, and the customer is the beneficiary.

Take a simple benchmark: which women's apparel store is first in the mall to introduce the next season's styles and colours? The answer requires an understanding of seasonal planning and supply chain management to learn how different decisions influence the result. Benchmarking is not a number-crunching exercise; it is a collaborative study of a key process that has easily detectable results. This simple example brings into question many aspects of the seasonal planning process, including fashion show attendance, customer research, supplier co-operation, manufacturing, inbound freight scheduling, store distribution and clearance of end-of-season merchandise.

Another benchmark that concerns customers is the ease or difficulty of handling returns and exchanges. Here again, comparisons can be easily made and standards set. Competitors can be observed and "tested," just as customers can be queried and asked for suggestions. This benchmark is also a common subject of neighbourhood conversation. Far more people tell their friends about their store or service horror stories than about their successful shopping experiences.

Some operators are obsessed with metrics, benchmarking and performance measurements. They bog down their staff with constant introspection, unnecessary research and useless reports. But just as dangerous to the well-being of the business is the owner operator who runs it by "the seat of his pants," making decisions based on "the way we always did it." Finding a balanced approach to keeping score between these two extremes is not only instructive but essential. The challenge is to determine what needs to be measured, how often, how deeply and for what purpose.

MANAGING CASH FLOW

"Volume is vanity, profit is sanity, and cash flow is reality."

ROD McQUEEN

The slogan "Cash is king" is never more important than when it is applied to the consumer fulfillment businesses. Every B2C enterprise has countless customers and countless transactions. The irony is, they still need to be counted! It is the customers' transactions that create cash, and when they are frequent enough and large enough, the cash flow from these transactions pays all the bills, all the employees and all the regulatory authorities—and still provides something for the owner.

This wonderful process is referred to as liquidity. The key to creating wealth lies with the ability of the owner-operator to remain liquid. This chapter began by describing four sources of cash: operating income, sale of property or other assets, borrowed money and sale of equity to investors. This section will concentrate on how that cash can be maximized. But first, business operators must realize that cash always goes out before it comes in. The start-up process may take months before the cash register rings for the first time. All of the costs until that moment need to be financed by new equity or debt. But remember the cry of countless failed entrepreneurs as they went down: "Plan big. Start small. Don't borrow." As cash flows in from transactions, the need for more capital is reduced until the business can operate without dipping into capital.

It is possible to acquire sufficient business capital up front to avoid borrowing, but this is rare today. It will be assumed that a combination of equity, debt and cash from operations will keep the company fluid. Successful cash management not only reduces the need to borrow, but it also increases the chances that lenders will come forward when borrowing becomes necessary.

Service companies, unlike retail goods companies, need to watch their cash flow daily because it is heavily devoted to the company's payroll and customer receipts. These receipts may or may not be converted to cash with debit or credit cards. Services do not lie in inventory awaiting the sale. They flow out while the staff provides the services, and if all goes well, the cash comes in when the service has been provided. For example, at the end of a snowy day on which few visitors have entered the shop, the inventory is still available for sale but the staff costs are not recoverable. This is why so many service companies operate with an up-front membership of some kind. It provides a cushion of cash for the ongoing operation. It also provides an incentive to use the service on a continuing basis. The next section, "Financing the Business" (see pages 244–253), deals with the care and control of cash.

CASH IN

The most important step in good cash management is getting the cash in—getting paid for products and services supplied. Setting up the business to convert sales to cash by means of debit and credit cards is the first step. Depending upon the average size of each transaction, the amount of card use rises and falls. The greater the transaction size, the greater the use of credit cards. The big-ticket purchases tend to be made on a credit card—customers are thus borrowing from their bank instead of their store. Regardless, all three forms of payment have a cost attached that must be considered in the costs of running the business.

The latest and greatest initiative to encourage cash-in before cash-out is the gift card, otherwise known as the stored-value card. It has been used by the pay telephone industry for years but is now gaining importance in all retail sales promotion plans. At the time of the transaction, customers provide cash and take a "loaded" card in return. Later, they use their card to acquire goods and services, and the card is electronically decremented until it no longer has stored value.

The accounting treatment of this process is interesting. Cash is debited, and some form of payables, or deferred income—not sales—is credited. When a purchase is eventually made, payables are debited and sales are credited. Only at this point is the sale recorded and the inventory depleted. Stored-value cards are replacing cumbersome layaway plans, in which customers chose goods, arranged for them to be stored until a future date and made only a partial payment to secure them.

Stored-value cards distort the usual Christmas sales peak. Now, the cash comes in December, when the cards—rather than merchandise—are bought as gifts. This is a godsend for those who don't know what to buy or those who shop at the last minute. When the recipient of the card makes a purchase, the sale is recorded. Typically, December sales will drop because of this practice, and sales in January and February (or later months) will increase. It remains critically important that the provider of the card fulfill the obligation implied when the card was bought. And this obligation may not be met until some distant future date, unless the card has a time limit.

Retail store cash-register receipts are straightforward, but collecting cash is more difficult with service contracts. The best practice is to insist on signed agreements before the service begins, coupled with a down payment or commitment payment up front. Pre-authorized, post-dated cheques increase the likelihood of receiving timely payments.

Many contractors are unable to pay up front because they aren't paid for their work until the job is complete. But they need supplies to carry out their project. So they become an account receivable: cash out before cash in. Many retailers of goods also provide services like these as an extension of their offering. Sears, Roebuck and Co. began the practice long ago, with its famous motto, "We service what we sell." Receivables and inventory are both categorized as current assets, and both require similar controls to keep them from becoming too large and requiring discounting in order to collect on them. Slow-moving inventories are no different from slow-paying customers. Excess inventory can be cleared out at a low price while the provider of services can discontinue servicing a non-paying customer.

Retailers of goods are increasingly expanding their business by either wholesaling their merchandise to other geographic locations where they haven't opened a store yet or adding services that require a payment. This adds a significant level of complexity to the business—receivables control. There is no place for "softies" where receivables are properly managed: limits must be put on payment time and amount. Forgiveness slips into neglectfulness. Tough love is needed, even with favourite clients.

CASH OUT—START-UP

At the first stage in the creation of a retail business, it is all cash out: the up-front lease costs, the procurement of fixtures, hardware and soft-ware, the hiring of people to open and run the store, and then the big one—inventory. A 1,000-square-foot facility may cost over $100,000 to set up and prepare for opening day, when the cash register rings for the first time. Then, slowly, the cash coming in begins to cover the costs of the operation. But never forget that the greatest percentage of sales revenue is needed to pay for the goods sold or for the service agent's wages. A reasonable estimate of the time it takes a sales unit to break even from a cash point of view is sometime between the first and second anniversary of the opening.

Service companies have similar start-up costs, with one big exception: the cost of inventory for sale. Instead, they must provide cash for setting up the equipment and the infrastructure that supports the service. The required delivery vehicles, service centre equipment, real estate and offices, furniture and fixtures vary greatly, depending on what the service is. Renting and leasing can reduce the cash going out, but both of these choices raise the monthly fixed costs.

The service business's major cost equivalent to the original inventory costs of a typical goods retailer can be referred to "outreach." Somehow, the community or target customer base needs to hear about the new service and about how to become a customer. Outreach requires the front-line service staff to go out into the market much as a door-to-door salesperson does to raise awareness and interest. It also requires setting up an outbound call centre where the internal staff can handle call prospects and inquiries. Finally, it requires a website that introduces the business and sets out its reason for being. This website might include the technology to take orders and transact business.

It becomes obvious very early in the life of the business that the cash needed at start-up is usually beyond the resources of the founder. If he or she has no previous financial success to capitalize on, banks cannot be called on to help. The answer is capital support from investors who "buy in" to the concept and become part owners. This process is covered in the next section, "Financing the Business."

CASH OUT, AND GROWING

Most cash-out items can be set up to flow out regularly throughout the year: salaries and wages, rent, utilities, government payments, tax installments (including GST), technology and support rent, and so on. By far the largest swings in cash flows come from the seasonal impact of sales revenues and the receipt and payment of goods and purchased services. Although the sales volumes may be beyond the control of the business, the payment of goods and services can be controlled so as to smooth out the cash flow and avoid borrowing for short-term periods.

Table 5.3 demonstrates the impact of a single season's sale of a cash-out/cash-in item. In this example, $50,000 of merchandise was ordered by HEI and received for sale during the spring season. A great deal of information can be deduced from this table:

·   It demonstrates how retailers can go "cash negative" as they build inventories. If the goods had been scheduled to arrive on two occasions instead of one, the March shortfall of $35,000 might have been reduced to $10,000. Borrowed at 6 per cent for one month, this strategy would have saved the company $125. This may not seem like much, but it might cover the cost of a part-time staff member for a two-day weekend. Retail is detail!

·   The potential gross margin was $50,000, or 50 per cent; the final, or "maintained," gross margin, after the discounted prices were included and the goods were finally sold, was $36,000 or 42 per cent. If more sales and promotional effort or better display merchandising had resulted in a greater percentage of sales in the early months, the maintained gross margin might have been higher. This example demonstrates the importance of the controller taking an active role in merchandise and seasonal planning.

·   The last one hundred units sold at a loss, $15 below their unit purchase price. If they had been priced at break-even—that is, at

$50—an additional $1,500 would have flowed in. The impact of this type of pricing control flows directly to the bottom line. Starting the discounting earlier, with smaller increments of price reduction, might have produced a similar result. On the other hand, maybe a larger discount on the first clearance would have moved out more merchandise earlier in the season.

- Cash-out savings are also possible with good supply chain management. Good supplier relationships and contractual agreements can often stretch out the payments to smooth the cash flow.

Supplier support is now being provided throughout the retail industry for the final markdowns through SCM programs, especially in the area of seasonal apparel. "Share the wealth" is being coupled with "share the risk."

Table 5.3: Household Extras Inc., cash in and cash out

Unit cost = $50   Unit price = $100

		UNITS	UNIT PRICE	PURCHASE PRICE	SELLING PRICE	CASH IN	GROSS MARGIN	CASH OUT	NET CASH POSITION
JAN	Receive goods	1,000		$50,000					
FEB	Begin selling goods	150	$100			$15,000	$15,000		$15,000
	Initial gross margin						50%		
MAR	Pay for goods							$50,000	($35,000)
	Continue sales	300	$100			$30,000	$30,000		($5,000)
APR	Continue sales	200	$100			$20,000	$20,000		$15,000
MAY	Clearance sale	250	$70			$17,500	$17,500		$32,500
JUN	Season-end clearance	100	$36			$3,600	$3,500		$36,000
Totals		1,000				$86,000		$50,000	
Maintained gross margin							42%		

OUTSOURCING

The concept of outsourcing began with large companies that had sizable non-core business functions usually regarded as overhead. Organizations appeared that built their business on the premise that they could manage these overhead functions better as specialists than the large companies could as overhead. The key is the organizations' specialized expertise, the centre of their retail value proposition. The motive for outsourcing is reduced expenses and a better control of cash flow.

Small companies have the same problem that big companies have when it comes to overhead costs. For retailers of goods and services, some non-core activities that deserve outsourcing consideration are:

· Real estate: Although owning a premise may have long-term benefits in terms of value appreciation, turning the management and upkeep of the facility over to a specialist organization reduces the need for the company to hire staff to perform the specialized types of labour required.

· Technology: Today's outsourced technology services provide twenty-four-hour support, the latest in software, powerful backup support and rapid response times. The peace of mind these services provide, along with the "bang for the buck" they offer, makes this approach worth considering.

· Warehousing and distribution: This is another skill set that has become the focus of specialists. Sufficient facilities, equipment, staff and technology are often beyond the reach of most small retailers.

· Payroll and accounting: Now that they have the ability to electronically transfer information and store it securely, many small businesses are outsourcing these functions, reducing their payroll and technology costs and staying current with information such as statutory obligations regarding taxes and benefits contributions.

FREE CASH

Generally, "free cash" refers to the amount of cash available after all of the normal obligations of the company have been met. From net profit, the non-cash items are added back, as they were in the discussion of EBITDA (see page 226). Cash is further reduced when taxes are paid. Then funds must be set aside for capital expenditures such as lease-hold improvements or additions to the business. Perhaps it is time to spend extra funds to conduct some serious research into the customer base. Have the key people been rewarded by means of bonuses?

Having taken all these cash requirements into account, is there still some free cash? If so, is it time to reward the shareholders? In a private company, the payment of dividends may or may not follow a formula. Some entrepreneurs and family-owned companies take out a percentage of after-tax income each year, whereas others leave it in the business for growth and later rewards. An acceptable formula allows the owners to take an amount equal to the cash bonuses paid to the non-owner executives and employees.

After all the bills have been paid and cash has been set aside for future known obligations, is it time to take some out for personal rewards and the pursuit of happiness? Of course! That's what the business venture should be all about. But care has to be taken to make sure that cash is available to handle unforeseen contingencies or crises. Often the shareholders take out their dividends, and the operators are stuck with borrowing from the bank because an emergency—or better still, a sudden opportunity that deserves to be grabbed—arises.

The best approach is some sort of formula. Assume there is a bonus scheme for the top management tied to final results each year. A good way to reward these people is with a pool of funds equal to some percentage of the pre-tax profits. This pool can then be apportioned depending on the results of each team member. Now, declare a dividend to the shareholders of equal value. This balanced approach gets away from the annual debates about how much money should be allocated to whom. It sets up the owners and managers as partners. It doesn't make any difference if one or more of the owners is part of the management team. Each is rewarded for his or her contribution to the success of the business.

FINANCING THE BUSINESS

> *"Indeed, in a truly great company, profits and cash flow become like blood and water to the healthy body: They are absolutely essential to life, but they are not the very point of life."*   JIM COLLINS

LENDER AND BORROWER RELATIONSHIPS

It's review time again; the bank's account manager is sitting on one side of the table, and the retailer's financial officer is sitting on the other. Although they are discussing the retailer's financial needs over the next year, they are on different wavelengths.

The retailer is thinking: "If I could leverage my business with more financial support from my banker, I could get at a higher level of store refurbishing and take a larger receipt of goods into my inventory before the fall season opens up." The banker is thinking: "If I could reduce my exposure to this risky business, I'd feel better about its ability to service its debt payments more regularly, and I might begin to see some sort of paydown."

It is really quite simple. The banker holds the loan as an asset, whereas the retailer holds it as a liability. Yet they both have, or should have, the same objective: satisfying the customer while creating wealth for their respective businesses. To accomplish this, each must understand the other's goals, objectives and restraints.

What the retailer does not recognize is that the account manager has actually borrowed the money he or she has loaned the business from the bank. This money did not come for free. Certain costs are included in the bank's rate of interest charged to the account manager. First, the bank provides its funds to its lending units at a wholesale rate of interest. This rate recognizes the level of risk ascribed to the client and the "expected cost of loss" (ECL) that relates to the industry sector of the client as well as the way in which all of the bank's loans to this sector have behaved over the past few years. In times of economic trouble, when loans aren't paid and bankruptcies occur, this ECL will rise. Having established these costs of funds, the account manager will affix an interest rate that, if all goes well, will provide him or her with some profit for the undertaking.

What does a lender really need to know? It may seem like a mysterious art, but lending is based on sound business principles. Both sides must recognize that bank lending is a service business. Although the bank refers to its own "products" and "services," to the client it all comes down to the service provided. After all, if the loan agreement were a product, the client, the end-consumer, would be consuming the loan. Instead, the loan is literally loaned; it needs to be returned someday. As a service business, banking is all about relationships, not transactions.

Just as the borrower needs to understand the costing of a loan, the lender needs to understand the client's business. Time and again, when the question is asked of an owner-manager: "Why do you bank at XYZ?" the answer comes back: "Because they know my business." Developing this understanding takes time, but it makes a big difference, especially when there are money problems with cash flow or sudden needs that require a lender to take action. It is helpful for the business borrower to take a few key steps to establish a knowledgeable relationship:

- Provide a brief story of the business, its aims, its owners, its "reason for being."
- Describe the industry it is in—the size of it, the competition and the expected trends that will affect the business over the next few years.
- Explain what is unique about the products and services the business provides, especially the key attributes that will give this venture a leadership potential.
- Describe each member of the key management, their backgrounds, roles and responsibilities. This description should also introduce any board of advisers or directors who work with the owners and managers.
- Include the key points of the marketing plan: the seasonal emphasis, the target customer and the promotional plans.
- Describe the need for capital equipment, leasehold commitments, fixturing, vehicles and other key elements of support.
- Explain how the business works, who provides the customer's services, and how the inventory is acquired and controlled.
- Provide a financial plan, monthly for the next year, and annually for the next two to three years. A lender will recognize that the immediate future, that is, the next twelve months, is much easier to forecast than beyond, yet some sort of guess helps the lender determine the possibilities of success, based on the potential growth of the business. This is the time to demonstrate that loan costs and capital expenditures will not excessively burden the business.

·   Recognize the risks inherent in the venture, and spell them out to
    indicate what might be done to mitigate them, should they arise.
·   Avoid springing surprises. If the company's financial situation
    appears to be worsening, give the lender plenty of notice and
    maintain a dialogue by using progress reports.

The best time to approach a lender is before the loan is required.
This takes the urgency out of the picture and allows for a "get to
know you" phase before transacting business. An on-site visit allows
the lender to meet other principals and to see the operation first-hand.
A social get-together at the outset helps to solidify positive relationships. The borrower needs this time to get to know how a loan may
be structured, what choices are available and what the costs of borrowing might be. Never forget that everyone who places funds into
the business in the form of capital or debt fully expects to be paid
back at some future date and hopes for a worthwhile financial reward
of some kind. In line with the theme of this book, financiers enjoy
satisfying their customers while creating wealth!

Account managers do not lend money on their own. Analysts,
industry-sector experts, lending guidelines and risk-assessment frame-
works surround them. Risk advisers, often referred to as credit
managers, work closely with the account manager and act as members of the lending team to provide a check and balance.

SIZE MATTERS

Statistics Canada, in a 2000 report titled *Financing of Small and
Medium-Sized Enterprises,* published a study that dealt with borrowing and the size of the business. A supporting chart demonstrated
that small businesses have a more difficult time obtaining bank loans
than larger ones do. But this simple conclusion hides a more important truth: the longer a company can get along without borrowing

and the larger it grows, the easier it will be to obtain a loan. This leads to the first lesson in business financing: DYI–do it yourself.

INITIAL FUNDING

Time and again, the founder turns up at the lending institution to ask for a loan, and the loan officer states, in one way or another, "I'd be pleased to help you, but first, how much money have you put into the business?" Entrepreneurs need to demonstrate their passion for their bright idea by placing their money on the line. Not to do so is an indication of unease with the business concept or uncertainty of its success.

Normally the founder's funds come from savings, a house mortgage or a personal loan. This source is followed by financial help from family and friends. These are people close to the founder who aren't betting on a business plan—they are betting on an individual and his or her bright idea and team. These investors are often referred to as "angels." To expand on this group and acquire still more initial funds, the founder prepares a proposal for financing that is circulated among a larger circle of friends and acquaintances. This next input of funds, similar to the first inputs, is not being lent; the initial shareholders are acquiring shares. The founder holds on to "founder's shares" to ensure that he or she has a firm control of the enterprise, and then the others become shareholders with equal rights and obligations.

Pools of private equity are available for the right venture. These pools are usually under the management of venture capitalists who assess new opportunities and provide capital if the risk–reward equation looks favourable. Venture capitalists expect that for every winner there are up to three times as many losers, so they must take this risk into account when they "price" their input. Private capital is available at the start as seed capital. Later, when the venture looks like it may "fly," it is referred to as early-stage capital. Still later, when the successful venture needs funds to expand, the private funds are referred to as expansion capital. Getting to know who the venture capitalists are that specialize in consumer companies is a challenge, but it is worth the investigation and may pay off in the long run.

This initial receipt of cash flows directly to the early needs of the business. Some of it acts as a buffer between good and bad periods of customer sales. As it is consumed, and as the business shows signs of success, it is time to bring in another source of funds: loans. If a retail venture is not going to break even until well into its second year, all of the cash outlay needs to be financed from equity or personally guaranteed debt.

Most financial institutions recognize the importance of start-up and small businesses, and thus they have created complete divisions of trained specialists to handle entrepreneurs' needs. Banks provide these businesses, known as small and medium-sized enterprises (SMEs), with advisers and special products and services to meet their needs.

SMALL-BUSINESS LOANS

Canadians are fortunate to have available a financing product provided by the financial institutions and backed by the federal government program, Canadian Small Business Financing, which provides financing for up to a large percentage of the cost of:

· real estate and buildings;
· leasehold improvements; and
· new or used equipment.

This short list shows that these loans are start-up loans. They are not provided for the purpose of supporting the day-to-day operations or the acquisition of inventory. (The maximum amount of a Canadian Small Business Loan (CSBL) in 2006 was $250,000.) CSBLs are obtained from a bank, credit union or similar financial institution.

Before a small business can secure the loan, the bank will probably ask for certain security requirements. These may be required of either the company or the owners, depending on the circumstances.

Loan rates are controlled by the government regulations that support this program. They include administration fees and a registration fee. Like all loans, there are three requirements:

1. The business must operate as it said it would when the loan was acquired.
2. Interest and fees must be paid regularly.
3. The loan must be repaid someday.

This last requirement is usually taken care of by the later financing of a normal operating loan that replaces the CSBL as the business grows in size and profit.

OPERATING LOANS

Thanks to technology and online banking, it is possible to obtain an additional line of credit by acquiring a credit card–based loan. Usually the limit is set at $50,000, and the rates are in line with typical lending rates rather than personal credit card rates. This card is used for all types of purchases in support of the daily business needs.

Most operating loans act as revolving loans; that is, the funds flow from the bank to the client as required, rising and falling as needs change. Certain tests are made of the company's profit and loss statement and balance sheet. These tests allow the lender to study the risk and the probabilities of success with other members of the lender's institution. When the borrower agrees to these tests, they may become "covenants." The client can continue to borrow funds as long as it meets these tests. Four typical tests are taken:

1. *Cash flow:* This subject was dealt with earlier in this chapter. The lender is looking for a positive cash flow over time. Cash flow may

be negative for seasonal reasons, but otherwise it should remain positive. A ratio above 1:1 is desirable; the higher the ratio, the more liquid the business.

2. *Profitability:* This test, like the one above it, relates to the profit and loss statement. Although the business may be profitable at the operating level (EBITDA), it must also be profitable after meeting all of its obligations. Comparing it with other businesses in the same market provides the best test of this measurement.

3. *Liquidity:* This is the measurement of the relationship between the current assets and the current liabilities. It reflects the company's ability to meet its debts in a timely manner. These debts include the current portion of any of the outstanding loans.

4. *Debt-to-equity:* This measures all of the funded debt (not including supplier liabilities or other similar payables) compared with the equity, or net worth, of the business. Lenders are interested only in what they call "tangible net worth." This test asks, "If this company fails, will the net worth of the company cover the outstanding funded debt?"

There are many more tests, but these are sufficient to understand how the lender assesses the business on a continuing basis. The loan agreement will include a promise to maintain adequate financial records and to pass them to the lender periodically.

LEASING

There are number of advantages to leasing, and there are specialists who focus only on lease financing. Leasing provides fixed-rate financing. It reduces the expenditure of cash for equipment and facilities. As equipment and space needs climb, the lease can be adjusted upward. Technology has a habit of being replaced with better functionality as it becomes available; with lease financing, the hardware can be upgraded or replaced and the lease adjusted to the new cost base.

Even with these advantages, leasing isn't for everyone. The type of industry and type of equipment required need to be considered. There are tax implications to leasing that need to be understood. The key to leasing—its fixed rate and time period—can be detrimental to flexibility. Should a business suffer a downturn and it becomes necessary to cut back, leased goods are "locked in." The financing arrangements are usually inflexible. This hurts leased stores when it becomes necessary to close an unprofitable store.

A leased property, vehicle or machine belongs to someone else. Should its value increase, the increase flows to the lessor. Furthermore, it falls to the lessee to maintain the property or equipment in a manner acceptable to the lessor.

Banks and specialists offer two types of leases: operating leases and capital leases. The difference isn't tied to the lender's needs, but the two are treated differently on the borrower's balance sheet. Generally, if the lessee assumes the rights and obligations of ownership, even if it doesn't own the leased property, then the lease is treated as a capital lease. This usually applies to leases for computer equipment, where the lessee uses the asset for its entire life—which may be only a year or two. A similar treatment applies to store, office and warehouse fixtures. In these cases, it can be assumed that the lessee will not return the assets to the lessor when they are no longer needed.

Operating leases, on the other hand, apply to use and occupancy rather than to ownership. The best examples of operating leases are stores and vehicles. In both cases, these items will be returned to the lessor at the appropriate time. The cost of leasing them will be in the profit and loss statement, but the lease obligation will not be on the balance sheet.

ASSET-BASED LENDING

This type of lending allows the lender to provide a higher level of funding based on certain assets of the business. Typically, asset-based lending is used by retailers to finance their inventories and by service companies to finance their receivables.

Asset-based loans have fewer conditions attached to them in the form of covenants and tests for liquidity. Instead, the lender relies on a third party to monitor the assets being secured and to report to the lender periodically regarding the state of the assets. This monitoring includes a detailed review of aged stock or overdue receivables. Retail goods and services companies that understand the importance of their receivables and inventories and that are growing their businesses rapidly accept the monitoring discipline and costs because they can obtain a higher level of financing.

THE PARTNERS-IN-CASH

As entrepreneurs grow their business, they discover all too soon that they can't do it alone—they need helpers. They attract accounting firms, lawyers, research firms, advertising agencies, consultants and lenders. Entrepreneurs need to recognize that their relationship with lenders and service providers is an ongoing partnership, not a solicitation of outside service. They are all in the same game: providing customer satisfaction while creating wealth, over time. Owner-operators must set a place for them all at the family table and must include these partners in their continuing quest for ultimate success. The key to a successful partners-in-cash relationship is the constant sharing of information regarding the finances, problems and successes of the enterprise.

SIX | OWNERSHIP AND GOVERNANCE

BUSINESS OWNERSHIP

"Innovation is the specific instrument of entrepreneurship; the act that endows resources with a new capacity to create wealth."

PETER DRUCKER

THE STARTING POINT

A business usually grows and adds to its management team through four phases as it becomes more complex:

1. The single founder, with or without the involvement of the founder's family;
2. The founder and a team of like-minded friends;
3. A combination of the founder and externally recruited specialists;
4. A team of functional experts reporting to the founder.

Small businesses are often created when an experienced employee decides to start his or her own business. As senior employees contemplate retirement, many can't imagine not going to work each day. They may have acquired some financial resources and begin to dream about owning their own business. Most believe that is not too late to take the risk. They have a network of business associates to talk to, and day after day, they see others taking the plunge.

The most important question that an entrepreneur needs to ask is not "Am I capable?" but "What would I like to do?" This highlights the importance of good research into the products or services that are worthy of the entrepreneur's efforts and talent. The question that should be coupled to this is: "What can I see that customers need, and what do they want that I can provide?"

The majority of small and medium-sized enterprises (SME) employ fewer than ten people. But lumping small and medium-sized together in one category is inadvisable: the start-up company has yet to pass through the difficult start-up phase and move into a realm of predictability. Thus the leadership of small businesses is significantly different from that of medium-sized enterprises.

At the helm of most of small firms is either a single founder or a founding team or small group of aspirants who join together to accomplish something that alone they would be unable to achieve. As the firm grows, it adds professionals to augment the founders' skills. The faster the firm's growth, the sooner the experts are added. If added soon enough, they may bring equity capital that will allow them to participate in the firm's ownership as well as its growth potential.

Entrepreneurs are not necessarily outgoing, risk-taking workaholics. Their management style may range from despotic to caretaker. Anyone who wants to build a business needs only a vision and the will to succeed. A recent Yahoo! survey asked people around fifty years of age what kind of work would they prefer to do as they grow older. Almost 60 per cent replied that they wanted to own their own business. Almost 50 per cent also stated that it is never too late to start a business. (Two icons of the late-starter echelon are Ray Kroc, who founded McDonald's Restaurants at age 54, and Colonel Sanders, who started Kentucky Fried Chicken at age 67.) People who move into a new independent venture at this stage of life usually have a strong business background, some financial resources of their own and a passion for what they love to do and want to do.

There is plenty of evidence that women are playing a larger role in starting and growing small businesses, especially in the services industry. Many of these women are mothers; a favourite website for this special group of entrepreneurs is *www.mompreneursonline.com*, a site that draws more than seven million hits per month. Often, those who visit the site are considering turning their hobbies into a retail business. Or they may be mothers who are thinking of converting what they already do for others—caring for children—into a paying proposition, maybe as a personal service venture. Whatever the reason, these entrepreneurs usually start at home and grow towards acquiring a recognized business unit, staff, a lender and some type of real estate. Along the way, they usually learn that they need to be educated in the fundamentals of business.

Men and women start their own businesses to develop a bright idea or to provide something to an underserved market. Contrary to public opinion, they do not start their own business to avoid unemployment. If they do, they are starting on the wrong track. The word "entrepreneur" does not correctly describe this motivation. Women, especially, indicate that they have begun a new venture so that they can work for themselves. Many women have the ability to network and to share, and these attributes work well in a start-up situation.

There are no barriers to growth big enough to stop the creation of a great enterprise, but certain personal attributes are needed to take a bright idea to market and help it to become a leader in its field. Some of these attributes are soft-sided—others hard-edged:

- a devotion to excellence;
- an acceptance of the truth that achieving a balance between home and office is difficult;
- access to capital and cash, and maintaining the right balance between the two;
- a willingness to shun the limelight until the offering is recognized as superior;
- a refusal to accept the status quo;
- endless curiosity;
- an innate ability to attract and retain good people.

EARLY-STAGE GROWTH

With increasing size comes the need for more capital, more talent, more integrated systems and more business units. Those who provided the cash for capital and acquired shares may or may not be ready to contribute again at this early stage. Growth produces the need to satisfy the shareholders. If growth is developing as a result of customer satisfaction, then wealth can be created.

There are a number of sources of capital, and each has its own advantages and disadvantages. Usually, this need for new capital occurs long before public offering on a stock exchange, a process that requires investment counselling, underwriting and marketing. Early-stage growth needs access to capital from private-equity groups that specialize in financing new companies that they believe will prosper over time. Thus they can earn a good rate of return along the way or can be bought out by other investors later.

Here is where the company's advisory committee or board can play an essential role. If the committee includes some outside experts, the company will have the benefit of expertise in the field of financing and access to third party investors who are known to the advisers.

However, with outside financial help comes the obligation to give up some ownership of the firm. So shares are issued, capital is provided—and another place is set at the shareholders' table.

Smart owners know that ownership is more important than control. The more cash required for growth, the bigger the eventual business; the greater the wealth, the more it needs to be shared with those who invest. After all is said and done, owning a small piece of a huge company can be much more rewarding than owning a big piece of a small business that doesn't have the financial resources for growth.

GETTING GOOD ADVICE

Small-business ownership is not a work *or* a home activity. Throughout the day, home issues *and* office demands are dealt with as they arise, whether the owner is at home or in the workplace. Entrepreneurs seek advice from their spouses more often than from outsiders. Usually, their second-most-important resource is their accountant, and then their lawyer. Other advisers might be trusted business friends or professionals who bring to the table a wealth of business-related experience.

Like-minded business people can form formal associations that meet regularly to discuss matters of mutual concern and learn about good business practices from more experienced guests. One of the most successful groups of this type is The Executive Committee (TEC). The group leaders of TEC are usually retired executives who aren't ready for a life of leisure and who feel they have something to offer to the business leaders of emerging companies. Each TEC group meets monthly, and the TEC chairman visits each member for one to two hours at his or her office once a month. The monthly meeting always includes a guest speaker who discusses a topic chosen by the group.

FORMS OF OWNERSHIP

The type of the business's ownership can change as the firm becomes larger and more complex. The most common types of ownership, in order of increasing complexity, are sole proprietorship, partnership, private firm, and public company.

1. *Sole proprietorship:* At the outset, a single individual, the proprietor, owns the business. As long as this person can manage the business while acquiring the cash needed to grow it, refurbish the premises and buy the goods and equipment that are needed in a timely manner, this form of ownership is acceptable. The founder brings the vision and energy to the business; he or she has an idea regarding a new and unique way to satisfy customers. With this in mind, the proprietor sets out to create wealth.

2. *Partnership:* The simplest form of partnership is one in which two or more associates want to share in the ownership of the firm as well as its operations. Many service companies and most professional service firms are partnerships.

3. *Private firms:* A company that is not publicly listed on a stock exchange is a private company. Businesses that are moving to a larger scale and that need more money invite other people to become part-owners: they may be friends, business acquaintances or investors with capital and an interest in the firm and its prospects. Stock is issued to each investor, and the company becomes known as a "non-reporting issuer." Depending on the jurisdiction in which it is located, the company may include up to fifty shareholders. Like a publicly traded company, the private company has a board of directors, shareholder agreements, bylaws and shareholder reports.

   As the business grows larger, its leadership becomes more complex. Legal and accounting services need to be established to

meet the requirements of the provincial Business Corporations
Act or its equivalent. The business must issue reports regularly
and hold meetings at least once a year to review the results and
carry out certain governance and audit procedures. The owner-
operator, now a shareholder among other shareholders, leads the
firm to meet the financial-performance goals he or she has set so
that all the shareholders will reap the rewards of the risk they
have taken by acquiring shares.

From here on, the share-ownership business format is all that
is needed to achieve greatness and, hopefully, wealth. But as the
business adopts gradually more complex formats, this growth
also creates the requirement to share this wealth with others.
The proprietor trades off sole ownership control and restricted
growth potential for greater firm size and ultimate corporate
financial success. The firm's only limit to growth is the capacity
of its shareholders or partners to feed the business as needed.
This opens the possibility to offer shares to the public and thus to
migrate from a private company to a public one.

4. *Public company:* Libraries are full of texts on corporate ownership. Advisory firms that purport to have all the wisdom necessary
   to assist owners with corporate growth abound. Since this book
   is a "good ideas" text for private firms, the treatment of this subject will be kept to a minimum. But a few key issues deserve
   attention:

   · Liquidity: The two great assets of a business are people and
     cash. There must be enough cash at all times to run the busi-
     ness, meet unexpected challenges, compete with strength,
     attract the right people and acquire the physical and finan-
     cial resources needed for sales and services. The firm's ability
     to generate enough cash to succeed will determine whether

the shareholder ownership later expands to include public ownership.

- Value: As the business begins with one shareholder and grows to many, its owners need to see the value of their investment, and they need to see it grow while it provides them with some form of reward along the way. The distribution of ownership rewards in the form of periodic dividends becomes part of the culture of the company.

- Profile: The bigger the venture, the greater its profile. But moving from a private company to a public company raises the firm's profile greatly. The opportunity for free publicity comes from the public's curiosity about the price of the stock. But a high profile also has its drawbacks. Large companies seem to jump to the top of the news when they get into trouble. (The quotation introducing Chapter 7 says it all.)

- Control: With total control comes power; power to do what is both needed and wanted. Sharing ownership relates to sharing control. Here the hard-edged aspect of the proportion of shares individuals hold is balanced by the form of the control that is delegated to the leaders, either formally or informally. Every day in the business sections of the newspapers we read about corporate control being taken from key people and handed to others. Often this change is made without a plan, and the results can be disruptive, even fatal, to the business. It's the soft-sided aspect of business that needs to be managed here. Family-held companies, although private, are vulnerable to control problems. Often, one member of the family is in charge while other family shareholders are subordinate or not involved in the daily affairs. Balancing everyone's needs and wants in a business is a delicate process.

OWNERSHIP VERSUS MANAGEMENT

As the size of a business increases, owners begin to hire managers to run the day-to-day business while they put their minds to corporate financing, growth, strategy and governance. It is an oversimplification to say that the difference between ownership and management is the difference between thinking "beyond" and thinking "now." A better way to describe the difference is "heads up" compared with "heads down." In no way is this a comparison of unequal perspectives; both focuses are critical to the success of the business.

Managing a business with a daily routine requires a focus on the little things that create a successful day or week. Details of staffing and customer service are top priority. Meanwhile the market changes, new products and services emerge, and opportunities to expand surface. It is more work than one operator can master. Eventually a time comes to hire competent subordinates to oversee sales, purchasing and finance—time to appoint managers.

GOVERNANCE

"Management is doing things right; leadership is doing the right things."   PETER DRUCKER

The importance of governance cannot be overstated. The philosophy, principles and practices of governance apply as much to the owner-operator as they do to all private and publicly traded companies. Governance provides the business leader with a group of trusted advisers whose job is to provide oversight, support and scrutiny. They assist the leader in dealing with key issues such as long-term strategy, ownership obligations and fairness, and the business's obligations to its employees and the public.

As a business becomes more complex and the rules and regulations surrounding its risks and obligations become more arduous, its leaders need to associate themselves with people who can assist the owner or key executive with issues of ethics and compliance, priorities and contingencies, and conflicts and opportunities.

Some critics suggest that the owner-operator who holds 100 per cent of the shares needs no governance committee. But informally, each day, the leader probably needs help with matters that deserve the input of trusted advisers. Hardly an evening goes by when the key issues or problems arising from the day's work do not surface at the dinner table. Often the spouse holds equal shares, as do other family members. How many leaders are able to manage the challenges of a competitive venture, satisfy the customers each day, and create wealth at the same time?

Formalizing the governance process is a simple task of creating an advisory committee of some sort. Members of the committee may be paid or not. Boards of directors or advisory committees usually include insiders, who work closely with the head and management of the company, as well as outsiders, who bring special talents related to legal or accounting matters or to the industry in which the firm operates. Two forms of governance deserve consideration: the family council and the advisory council.

THE FAMILY COUNCIL

A high percentage of retail goods and services companies are owned by the family that created the business and continues to manage it. Often there are some shareholders who are active in the day-to-day operations and others who are not. This situation leads to a critical need to create a formal committee that will provide guidance to the president and his or her team and, at the same time, will conduct a periodic assessment of the business and its progress as well as of the key leader's effectiveness. This committee should include the non-active family shareholders to keep them up to date and involved in the business discussions.

The family council is the simplest advisory committee structure. Usually, five to seven people are appointed to serve the shareholders. The simplest committees often do not include any subordinates of the president. Outsiders who are not shareholders, such as an accountant or legal adviser, deserve to be paid for their time and advice, in the form of a meeting fee or an annual retainer.

In their early stages small businesses often do not have the funds to pay these experts, yet they need to rely on outside advice to help get the business going. A successful form of compensation for these advisers can be the provision of shares, with a special agreement allowing these shareholders to sell their shares back to the company after an agreed-to period at a price related to the value of the shares at that time.

THE ADVISORY COUNCIL

Larger family-owned businesses that have to deal with more complex external issues may opt for an interactive governance arrangement. As they grow, these businesses set up holding companies for a group of companies or for a group of shareholders, such as the family. Given their size, they may also have a group of shareholders who have invested significant funds into the company and want a role in its governance. Figure 6.1 illustrates how the advisory council meets these divergent needs.

Operating with this structure, each of the three groups shown at the top of the figure acts as a subcommittee to the council. Family issues can be dealt with privately at the subcommittee level, while the key industry, regulatory and advisory issues are dealt with at the

Figure 6.1: The role of the advisory council

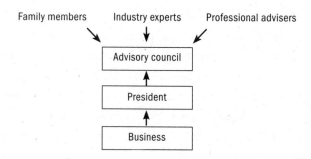

council level. Thus the meetings of the full council are more efficient and discussion of the extraneous details is kept to a minimum.

The bylaws of most organizations outline how the organization functions. Since the directors of an organization have the responsibility to represent the interests of the shareholders and often of the family members, the role of the directors or executive officers needs to be spelled out. The relationships between the directors, executive members and staff should also be defined and documented in a policy manual. This document will be an important source of information for both new and experienced directors and executives members. At a minimum, the manual should include:

- job descriptions of the directors, executive and staff;
- a list of the directors, executive and staff, including addresses and phone numbers;
- committee responsibilities, terms of reference and membership limits;
- procedures and policies;
- legal documents, such as executive and professional contracts, shareholders' agreements, and pension plan summaries;

- strategic plans;
- past and present financial statements and current budgets; and
- minutes of the meetings.

Being a director or officer involves a good deal of responsibility. It can be an exciting learning experience or a difficult burden. The right individuals in the right place can make an important contribution to the enterprise. Following are some ideas to help directors and executive directors become more knowledgeable about their roles and responsibilities while gaining personal satisfaction from their involvement as well:

- Know your responsibilities.
- Stay informed and aware of the company's progress and problems in order to objectively assess the chief executive.
- Be available to accept special tasks on behalf of the board.
- Ensure that you are aware of current bylaws, policies and procedures.
- Stay informed of all the organization's activities.
- Attend meetings regularly, and review minutes if you can't attend.
- Speak up early on issues in which you have a potential conflict of interest.
- Ensure that all positions have clear job descriptions.
- Ensure that there are correct procedures for financial management.
- Regularly review the insurance required to cover the risks inherent in the business.
- To the best of your ability, try to make unbiased, well-thought-out decisions.
- Keep in touch with the other board members.
- Ensure that regular evaluations of the organization's programs occur.
- Resign from the board or executive if you know you can't do the job.

There are two keys to successful boards: getting the best people to serve as members and making sure that clarity exists about what the board is supposed to do. Too many boards tend to be either "rubber stamps," which dutifully follow the lead of the organization's CEO or board chair, or "micromanagers," who become caught up in the day-to-day operations of the organization and can't delegate responsibility for making things happen.

TRANSITION

"You've got to love what you're doing. If you love it, you can overcome any handicap or the soreness or all the aches and pains, and continue to play for a long, long time.".   GORDIE HOWE

With the passage of time, businesses go through certain stages of life—as do people. Unlike people, though, business owners can change their company's shape at will, expand it or shrink it, sell it or close it. Each stage of a business's life cycle has its own strategies and demands for leadership, vision and talent and requires the business to deal sensibly with cash and financial support.

Figure 6.2: The stages of a business life cycle

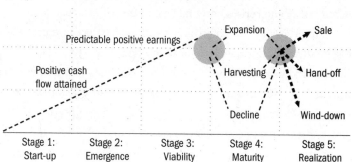

Figure 6.2 implies that each phase takes the same length of time. Nothing could be further from the truth. Moving from start-up to emergence often takes far longer than the owner and investors had planned. This figure attempts to portray the full life cycle of a business and organize it into meaningful components that have different needs and challenges.

Business growth involves the maturing of people, structures, systems and knowledge and an increase in complexity. Following is a brief description of the structural and monetary aspects of the five-stage business life cycle. The left column in the following set of tables is devoted to general comments on what must be done and what is happening. The right column focuses on the financial issues to be faced and the hurdles that must be overcome.

START-UP

The start-up phase is full of beginnings: new employees, new products, new customers, new bankers and possibly new shareholders (see Table 6.1). Covering continuing losses with fresh cash is probably the most difficult task the owner-operator must face. It can consume a great deal of time and take the founder's attention away from getting the business on its feet. Starting up a business is the most critical phase; many enterprises never make it to the next stage.

Many types of B2C companies have low barriers to entry. They essentially require capital for inventory and supporting equipment, fixtures and infrastructure. As a result, many men and women who want to be entrepreneurs and own a business think of stores, restaurants and personal service businesses as a desirable opportunity. This desire to own and operate a business is kept in the background while

Table 6.1: Business start-up

THE LIFE CYCLE	THE MONEY
· Settling on the mission, goals, positioning, features and needs.	· Moving cash from the originator's bank account to the business.
· Acquiring the minimum talent with the maximum potential.	· Putting together a "story" to obtain support from others.
· Creating products, services and channels of distribution.	· Attracting seed capital from family and supportive friends.
· Building premises.	· Finding lines of credit.
· Establishing a customer base.	· Developing financial controls, statements and plans.

marriage, raising children and saving money take top priority. As the kids grow older and the mortgage is paid off, self-employment begins to seem possible. Entrepreneurship and financial freedom become the dominant personal life-plan.

Not everyone can move from employment to self-employment. A thorough self-assessment is needed: What is your tolerance of risk? Do you have capital that can be used to get going? Do you have partners or investors who will support your venture? Will your family support you through thick and thin?

If the answers are positive, make a plan and begin to put it on paper. Make lists of questions. Find out which experts can help with the key elements, especially location and funding. Begin to make contact with people who can provide suggestions based on their related experience. Include also those who might assist with the initial funding of the business. Their financial input is known as "angel capital" or "safe harbour money" because it comes from supportive, patient, forgiving friends and relatives. Never forget that someday they will want their money back, plus a handsome increase in return.

Entrepreneurs, especially retailers, are full of enthusiasm as they start up their business. They have a vision and are anxious to get at it. Unfortunately, they face many potholes along the road:

· They overestimate the gross margin revenues that flow from their sales.

· They underestimate the capital needed at the start and all the way through this phase to establish and grow their business.

· They overbuy and build excessive inventories that need to be cleared but are forgotten in the crush of the start-up.

· They don't take the time to research the backgrounds of their first employees and often have to replace them early in the process.

· They are so busy with day-to-day activities that they do not stop to adequately plan ahead.

Next, begin to learn about the technology required. What functions can be automated? Will the system needs be bought or rented? Will payments be processed and bank relationships handled automatically? Any process that can be automated at the outset is one that won't burden the business with staff needs later.

Think through the selling process in great detail. The sale of goods in a retail environment is far different from the sale of services by call centres, salespeople or professional advisers: store salespeople close the sale, whereas service representatives should develop lasting relationships. These differences are important when recruiting begins. Using guidelines regarding the type of staff required and the experience needed, recruiting can be done to a standard rather than haphazardly.

EMERGENCE

Achieving ongoing positive cash flow is a great moment and worthy of celebration. At this point, the business has usually reached a level of certainty that demonstrates the viability of the strategy (see Table 6.2).

Table 6.2: Business emergence

THE LIFE CYCLE	THE MONEY
· Adding stores, territories, products and services.	· Recognizing that, more-or-less continually, the cash flowing in exceeds the cash flowing out.
· Building a competitive distinctiveness.	
· Setting up a board of directors or a family council to provide guidance to the CEO or president.	· Continuing to bring in cash for growth— each $1 of revenue growth may require up to $2 of capital.
	· Converting debt to equity to attract more of both.

VIABILITY

As the business grows, so must the capacity of the management group. Three recognizable steps match the financial issues shown in Table 6.3.
- *Basic*: There is always an entrepreneur at the start of a business. This individual is the owner and operator. He or she dominates all the business decisions and activities. As the tasks become too great, others are invited to join the business. Often the first one is the complement to the owner. If the leader is more comfortable performing the buying or sourcing role, a likely counterpart will be a customer-oriented person, happy with clients, marketing, public relations and service satisfaction. The next hiring will probably

Table 6.3: Business viability

THE LIFE CYCLE	THE MONEY
· Achieving a planned growth for the business and the share of market.	· Establishing that beyond the state of positive cash flow, the condition of profitability has arrived.
· Solidifying the management team with functional expertise and some form of profit-sharing incentives.	· Beginning to accumulate wealth.
· Adding IT, products and related services that emerge from professional research.	· Setting up leasing and letters of credit for IT, refurbishing, new equipment and importing.
· "Locking in" the preferred customers with retention rewards.	· Developing a rewards program for the the original investors and management.
· Establishing a governance structure including top management and knowledgeable independent advisers.	· Attracting new investors, depending on the strategy for the future.
	· Making the key decision: staying private or going public.

be of an accountant, bookkeeper, administrator and back-office person. With this individual on staff, the business begins to be able to plan, manage and control.

· *Intermediate:* With the arrival of trained people with specific responsibilities for certain functions or departments, the day is gone when decision making can be casual, around the coffee pot, or in the aisles; the numbers of people affected have risen. It is time for periodic reports, scheduled meetings with the owner and regular group meetings. These deserve an agenda so that everyone will know what might surface at the meeting and be prepared with input and support. By now, some of the team leaders will want to associate with their peers in trade associations that match their area of interest. Formal plans for the short term will guide the actions and hopefully control the expenditures related to this growth period. Care must be taken to ensure that there isn't an "overload" of bureaucracy created by the support functions and piled on top of the leaders' growing load.

· *Advanced*: The management team meets regularly and makes the key decisions. Priorities are set, trade-offs are made, and give and take prevails. At this point, the owner-operator realizes that he or she can't achieve the business goals without help and without listening to others, achieving consensus and practising a team approach. Responsibilities are delegated. Budgets are created, and performance is measured against pre-approved plans. Technology is acquired to get at control matters, payroll complexities and performance improvement. Commitments are made to conduct market research and do competitive tracking. Advisory help is formalized with the creation of a family council, advisory panel or board of directors. Staff members reporting to the key executives are organized into functions such as merchandising, operations, finance and control, distribution or supply chain management (scm) and marketing.

The expansion of the business may be handled with more capital or loans, or it may involve the process of franchising. Now that a successful model is in place, new entrants might buy the right to set up an equivalent business in another market area. The franchisor owns the concept and provides a brand, a business model and a start-up program. The franchisee provides the capital and the commitment to create the next unit and pays for the privilege to follow the concept. Then along comes another candidate to open the third unit, and so on.

As growth calls for capital, new shareholders join the company. Processes are put in place to keep them informed of the financial affairs of the business and the overall company progress.

MATURITY

Table 6.4: Business maturity

THE LIFE CYCLE	THE MONEY
· Constructing a long-range strategic plan.	· Researching and determining,
· Judging the opportunities and risks	periodically, whether to:
associated with new products, new	— expand;
services and new markets, with the aid	— re-engineer;
of extensive market and competitive and	— share the wealth;
internal research.	— hand it down;
· Reviewing management and staff in depth	— wind it down; or
to determine their interest in and capacity	— sell it.
for change.	
· Bringing together the owner(s), each owner's	
family and advisers, providing sage counsel.	

At this point in the transition of the enterprise, it is important to assess not only the wealth of the business but its health (see Table 6.4). Owner-operators and key executives may be aging and considering retirement. Health may be a key factor in their decision. Middle managers may see little opportunity to move up to the top jobs and may be quietly looking around for new opportunities. So the potential (and personal plans) of the next generation of family members must be considered:

· Are any family members ready (or expecting) to take over the business?

· Has their training been sufficient to ensure that they can be trusted to assume control?

· Are some of them "outside" the business and possibly wanting in?

· How will compensation, control and ownership issues be arranged equitably when the change is made?

REALIZATION

"Realization" means many things: to actualize, fulfill, complete, consummate or bring to pass. Moving from stage 4 to stage 5, "realization," can be either a planned or unplanned transition. Management, employees, family members who are involved, or the competition can spearhead it.

Table 6.5: Business realization

THE LIFE CYCLE	THE MONEY
· Getting ready to let go.	· Paying off debts and other obligations.
· Handing the enterprise to the next generation	· Setting up new share structures.
	· Arranging for appraisals.
· Overseeing a management buyout.	· Getting advice from investment counsellors.
· Finding a suitable buyer.	
· Liquidating it rapidly, or	· Obtaining an independent valuation of the business.
· Winding it down over time.	
	· Determining if shares or assets (in stages, or all at once) will be sold or transferred.
	· Turning all or part of it over to the right buyer or new owners.

Many companies reach a point in their life cycle when it becomes evident that growth is harder to accomplish and the possibility of decline is evident. This may come about as a result of changes in the economy, the death of a founder or key manager, competitive pressures, patent problems or perhaps just exhaustion. The challenge at this stage is to determine whether this is a permanent situation or a correctible one. The key to the dilemma can usually be found by studying the cash flow, from past trends and future forecasts.

· Does the business have the people to pull it through?
· What is the age of the founder(s)?
· How positive is their health and outlook?
· Has the competition made the road ahead too difficult to travel further?
· Can the firm offer a new product or service that will lift our results?
· Does it have the finacial resources to weather this downturn?
· Is this the time to exit?

LETTING GO

"It ain't over till it's over."   YOGI BERRA

For family businesses, letting go probably requires the delicate task of dealing with family priorities, ready and not-ready successors, and the biggest question of all: "When this is over and gone, what am I going to do?" Many entrepreneurs have their future all worked out because they took the "Freedom 55" advertisements seriously, but others have no idea what might be next. Those who successfully let go have learned, probably from their unhappy peers, that it is far better to retire to something than to retire from something.

Perhaps it's a question of age. There does not, however, seem to be a success formula related to age itself. A significant number of individuals over the age of sixty-five are still working—some because they want to, others because they have to. Leroy "Satchel" Paige, the legendary baseball pitcher who pitched three scoreless innings at age sixty, once opined, "How old would you be if you didn't know how old you are?" In support of letting go, he suggested: "Age is a question of mind over matter. If you don't mind, it doesn't matter."[13]

SUCCESSION

Financial institutions, consultants and lawyers have embraced a focus on "succession." But the word "succession" may be too narrow: it usually means handing down to the next generation. But realization is a much better term to describe this final chapter of a business owner's work life. While many owners think about it, few plan for their exit. In June 2005, the Canadian Federation of Independent Business published a research paper on the subject of succession.[14] Some meaningful statistics emerged in the report:

- Nearly 40 per cent of family-owned businesses expect a change in leadership within five years.
- Of those leaders who expect to make a change, 42 per cent have not yet chosen a successor.
- Only 33 per cent of Canadian family businesses believe it is important to keep the business in the family.
- Whereas 33 per cent of family businesses survive from the first generation into the second, only 15 per cent survive into the third generation.
- There is little evidence of business owners accepting the need to create a formal succession plan and the importance of establishing and sticking to a timetable.

Given the complexities of succession and the many choices concerning the direction to take, it would be a good idea to get advice from professionals. The most common useful professionals here are accountants, lawyers, valuators, estate planners and management consultant specialists. Each of these professionals' skill sets can be brought into the picture as the need arises. Often, a succession manager is hired to manage the process and advise the owners throughout the preparation of a formal plan and during each step of the process.

SELLING OUT

Tara Perkins, in an article published in the *Toronto Star*, "Business Exit Plan Is Needed," commented, "More than half of Canada's 2.5 million small business owners are expected to retire in the next 15 years, and experts caution that few are prepared."[15]

The process of "changing hands" is not a simple one, nor is it a short one. Exit strategies need to be developed with a two- to five-year time frame, especially if the successor is part of the family. The present business must be thoroughly assessed to determine its value, its positioning and who its new owners might be. Sometimes it is better to divest the business in pieces, perhaps by selling off non-core segments or losing divisions or stores. Often, the business's real estate is parcelled off to one buyer or retained by the owner while the operating business is sold to a new owner who obtains the right to acquire the real estate at a later date. Not only does this lower the purchase price of the business, but it also provides a continuing revenue stream to the seller.

Ellen Roseman, editor of the *Toronto Star*'s business section, published an article titled, "Ins and Outs of Selling a Business."[16] Within the article, she quoted Trevor Hood, a chartered business valuator: "A lot of owners are so entangled in operations that their businesses would be nothing without them. It's important to build an infrastructure." He goes on to say, "It takes a great deal of effort to prepare a business for sale. At the very least, you should plan on spending a year or two years on strengthening the business."

Often, the seller has no idea who the buyer might be. The seller's knowledge is limited to the current marketplace information about which competitor might be interested or which family member is ready and willing to take over. It would be best for the seller to retain the services of a business broker who understands the business segment and who has access to a possible compatible buyer or is aware of pools of capital where new owners and managers might be interested. These firms are specialists in the field of mergers and acquisitions.

At this point, the importance of the governance structure becomes very apparent. The founder or leader can gather the company's advisers together and obtain advice on the big issues or the options as to what direction to take. Letting go, like retailing itself, is a hard-edged issue as well as a soft-side one. The hard-edged issues are financial; the soft-sided issues are both personal and emotional. The advisers are now needed more than ever, because letting go is the point in the life cycle of the business where the wealth that has been created is either preserved or lost. A set of choices can be presented in an either–or chart, as illustrated in Figure 6.3.

Figure 6.3: Choices for letting go of the business

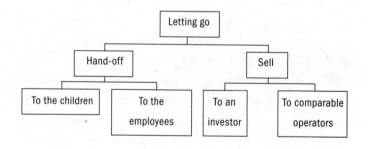

Selecting the right option is the task of succession planning. It may seem to be a simple decision, but it can be very complex. The one conclusion drawn by those who purport to be experts in the letting-go process is that it takes a lot longer than one expects. On the "hand-off" side of the argument is the process of preparing the successors to assume not only the leadership roles but also the ownership obligations of the business. Chances are, they have never thought about ownership; or, if they have, they have not been trained in the financial aspects of the operation, nor do they have funds available for investment in the business.

On the "sell" side of the argument the key question is usually, to whom? Qualified investment advisers should be brought in to help with this decision. The typical owner-operator has little experience with mergers, acquisitions, divestments and wind-downs. Investment advisers are trained in helping with the decisions, the process, the choices, the timing and the outcome.

Each of the many options is worthy of at least a manual or an extensive guidebook. Because this guide is meant to be an ideas book, each succession option deserves a brief description:

1. *The children:* Family businesses often include children who are fully occupied within the business as well as those who are shareholders but otherwise not involved. Those inside the business are usually in charge of different aspects, or functions, of the company such as operations, merchandising and finance. Choosing the right child to take over the leadership reins will lead to continuity and continued success. Once again, advisers should be brought into this decision. Family meetings are key, if only to keep everyone aware of the process and to assure them that their input is valued. A reasonable time frame for the ascension of one offspring to the leadership role is at least two years, probably three. This time is needed (after the decision has been made) to ensure that when the individual assumes control, he or she has an understanding of each function and support group.

2. *The employees:* This option may involve a management buyout
    (MBO) or a total employee buyout (EBO). It accepts the fact that
    the business is no longer a part of the founding family and recog-
    nizes that financial control will shift to a new entity. Since the
    wealth that has been built up over the years moves out of the busi-
    ness with the retiring owner, financing the new venture is the
    critical step. Those who have supported the business so far—bank-
    ers and suppliers—need to be assured that there will be continuing
    success. All of the employees who desire to become owners at this
    time will need to provide equity from their own resources.

    Many handovers involving the employees rely on an "earn-
    out" formula. Here, the buyers agree to provide a certain
    percentage of the purchase price at the outset, with the balance
    coming over a period of time from the earnings generated by
    the new owners. Their true ownership of their shares may be
    held in escrow until a certain percentage or the total purchase
    price has been paid.

3. *An investor:* This option allows the owner to remain as president
    and CEO while a new investor provides some or all of the capital.
    The original owner realizes his dream regarding wealth creation
    and still remains active in the business. Over time, the investor
    increases his or her involvement, making strategic changes involv-
    ing the size of the company, its offerings and possibly its new
    partners.

    Key to this investment option is the matter of continuity.
    Private investors may not be experienced in operating the ven-
    ture and may need time to put their own leadership group in
    place. They may also need to bring this new acquisition
    into another related enterprise. Investors often participate in EBOS,
    recognizing the opportunity to earn income from a successful

venture in which the employees are highly motivated to create wealth through their energy and talent.

4. *A strategic investor:* The buyer who adopts this option is selling to someone in a similar business that is often a competitor. The company being sold is then added to the buying company. The joining of the two businesses has the strategic potential of providing for incremental growth and has the added advantage of reduced combined overheads. The buyer sees this opportunity as the quickest and best way of growing his or her venture.

SUCCESSFUL WAYS OF SELLING OUT

The key to a successful sale lies in the "getting ready" phase. A few suggestions:

·   Always sell before it is necessary. The two greatest mistakes are waiting too long and acting too quickly. Do not leave the sale too late, when circumstances such as a death at the top or ill health demand that ownership change. Marketplace dynamics may also dictate the sale; this usually produces a compromised exit with a disappointing result.

·   Decide early on the reason for selling, and don't be swayed towards a compromise position. Retirement? Health? A new opportunity? A competitor's offer? An employee buyout? A personal need for cash? Consider all of these possibilities, and be aware of the ones that matter.

·   Take the time to prepare the business for the sale. Ensure that its physical assets are in top shape, and secure the important lines of supply.

·   Bring the key management in on the plan.

·   Take the necessary steps to demonstrate continuing profitability. This may require closing certain outlets, dropping certain lines, cutting out "nice-to-have" perquisites and laying off those who are not essential to the potential buyer.

FINDING A BUYER

The owner's idea of who might want to buy the business is usually very narrow. Consider these unknown players that might be waiting in the wings to acquire your business:

·   the company that needs badly what you have to round out its business;
·   the business that is fed up with your large share of its market;
·   the operator who craves size and market dominance.

Each of these players creates options that require you to call on an industry expert, who may be found within the major consulting firms or be employed by a financial institution, either acting with a few partners who have specialized industry expertise or acting on their own. Their essential motivation is financial. Typically, they charge a fee for preparing the company's marketing package, research into who the potential buyer might be and advice to the seller regarding preparation and choices. This fee is often a fixed price tied to a set of objectives and a timetable. They also charge a success fee, which will only be paid if and when the transaction is successfully completed. This fee is similar to the one charged by real estate brokers, but the success fee, like a commission, varies in its percentage of the gross proceeds of the transaction, depending on its size and complexity.

Count on the fact that when owners face the possibility of selling the business, they often firmly believe that the business is worth more than what the buyer may calculate. Far too many buy–sell negotiations break down because of this assumption. An important matter that separates the buyer from the seller regarding the offered price is the problem of financing. If the buyer does not have sufficient funds of its own and requires a loan to complete the transaction, the lender will insist that the costs of servicing the loan, when added to the expected profit of the combined company, be adequate. For this reason, a broker or adviser can help maintain objectivity. Furthermore, it is always wise for the seller to obtain a third-party evaluation of the business. These assessments tend to be more financial (hard-edged) and less emotional. This will better match the approach taken by the buyer.

STEPPING BACK

Now comes the big test: what to do when the succession deal is done. Hand-offs within the family or to the staff are relatively easy, and often there is a part-time advisory role for the retiring boss. But it may require the owner-operator to step back over time, to delegate more and more responsibilities. Special one-on-one training will help the chosen successor get ready. Bringing the chosen one into the governance group increases his or her understanding of strategy development, financing and people management. Stepping back is the lead-up to letting go. Here are a few suggestions to ease the process:

· stay at the top, but delegate more;
· read fewer reports, especially those regarding the day-to-day details of the business;
· avoid operating meetings, but attend planning meetings;
· avoid business meetings with suppliers—turn them into social get-togethers;
· continue to observe, but do not react to the observation;
· shift from directing to commenting and encouraging;
· take up a sport;
· join a charity;
· read travel brochures!

A NEW BEGINNING

Finally, it is time to adopt a new career, whether it is full retirement or something else. Many business leaders become involved volunteering for not-for-profit organizations and neighbourhood services and get great satisfaction from giving back to their community the wealth of knowledge they have accumulated in leadership and management. Others travel, not just for the leisure and pleasure, but to learn about the wider world. Still others go back to school and may even earn a post-graduate degree. Some actually look back at their life, their interests or their career and write a book! And yet, with all of these choices, many can't handle the freedom of choice and all that free time—they find a job where they can begin again, either as a part of someone else's bright idea or even a new one of their own.

SEVEN | THE RULES OF THE GAME DON'T CHANGE

"We can buy the back page of the morning paper for $25,000, but if we screw up we get the front page for free."   ALBERT C. PLANT

An additional personal note: I attended a strategic planning session in Boston in 1976. I remember only the first three of a number of "strategic truths." Since then, I have adopted a total of ten good rules that I refer to as "The Rules of the Game." Looking back over thirty-six years of retailing, I am satisfied that the rules of the game don't change. Here they are:

1. *Being in the right business at the right time is 80 per cent of the reasons for its success.* The other 20 per cent is good management and dumb luck.

2. *The law of the strongest is the best.* It's not bigness that wins; it's the market dominance of an idea, a product line or a needed service.

3. *All strategies eventually fail.* It's not the bright idea that lasts, it's the constant adaptation and reinvention of the idea that survives. This is the ultimate catalyst for innovation.

286

4. *If you're not keeping score, you're only practising.* It's not the top line that counts—it's all the lines. Measure everything that drives success, and then improve on the numbers.

5. *It's not the "what"; it's the "who."* It's not markets, technology, competition or products; it's one thing above all others: the ability to get and keep enough of the right people.

6. *Loyalty is caught, not bought.* It's not cards, points or miles; the deepest loyalty just forgives and comes back. Loyalty drives consumer equity and enterprise value.

7. *"Consumers are statistics; customers are people"* (Stanley Marcus). It's not statistical research that matters, it's listening to consumers and customers that counts.

8. *Location, location, location.* It's not about the store site, it's what you do to get people to come to you, whether you are selling from a store, a website, or a brochure or catalogue.

9. *The customer is always right.* It's not a detail of the shopping experience: customer respect is central to success.

10. *If the customer is wrong, return to Rule no. 9.*

APPENDIX | HOUSEHOLD EXTRAS INC. FINANCIAL STATEMENTS

HOUSEHOLD EXTRAS INC. BALANCE SHEET

Year-end, December 31, 2005

	2005	2004
ASSETS		
Current assets		
Cash		
Accounts receivable	$ 541,023	$ 1,380,778
Inventories	1,079,252	931,406
Prepaid expenses	71,553	27,886
Total current assets	1,691,828	1,340,070
Property and equipment	2,833,550	2,685,622
TOTAL ASSETS	$ 4,525,378	$ 4,025,692
LIABILITIES		
Current liabilities		
Bank loans	$ 804,786	$ 636,026
Account and trade payables	935,540	974,778
Income taxes payable	33,872	27,556
Current portion of mortgage payable	96,025	93,778
Total current liabilities	1,870,222	1,732,137
Mortgage payable	152,000	-
TOTAL LIABILITIES	$ 2,022,222	$ 1,732,137
SHAREHOLDER'S EQUITY		
Capital stock	$ 703,580	$ 703,580
Retained earnings		
Beginning of the year	1,589,975	1,381,309
Net income for the year	272,101	271,167
Dividends paid	(62,500)	(62,500)
Retained earnings, year-end	1,799,576	1,589,975
TOTAL LIABILITIES AND NET WORTH	$ 4,525,378	$ 4,025,692

HOUSEHOLD EXTRAS INC. PROFIT AND LOSS STATEMENT
Year-end, December 31, 2005

	2005 ($000)	2004 ($000)
RETAIL		
Sales	8,853	8,041
Cost of goods sold	4,802	4,136
Gross margin	4,051	3,906
CONTRACT		
Sales	1,839	2,191
Cost of goods sold	1,563	1,753
Gross margin	276	438
TOTAL SALES		
Total sales	10,692	10,233
Less total cost of goods sold	6,365	5,889
Total GM	**4,327**	**4,344**
EXPENSES		
Stores		
Labour		
Full-time	853	836
Part-time	604	609
Benefits	217	214
Total	1,674	1,659
Occupancy		
Utilities	125	114
Realty taxes	84	84
Insurance	28	28
Maintenance	174	205
Rent	242	225
Total	652	656
Advertising and promotion	72	63

Other store expenses		
Travel	10	39
Supplies, bags, etc.	80	72
Bad debts	7	9
Credit cards	104	92
Vehicles	55	47
Other miscellaneous	76	14
Total	332	272
Total store expenses	2,730	2,650
Total store contribution	**1,597**	**1,694**
Corporate		
Distribution labour	277	239
Distribution—other	72	64
Total distribution	349	302
Corporate expenses	260	247
Management salaries and benefits	547	469
Depreciation	202	206
Interest	48	56
Total corporate	1,058	978
Other income		
Party rental	872	586
Catering	275	142
Equipment rental	89	
Total other income	1,235	728
Less expenses	(1,002)	(719)
Total other income	234	9
Total corporate overhead	1,173	1,271
NET PROFIT BEFORE TAXES	424	424
Income taxes	152	152
NET INCOME AFTER TAXES	**272**	**272**

HOUSEHOLD EXTRAS INC. PROFIT MODEL

Year-end, December 31, 2005

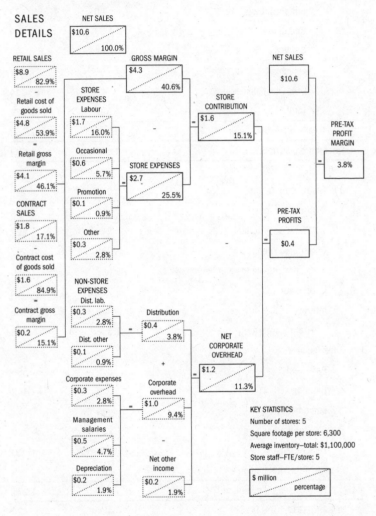

NOTES

1. Lawrence N. Stevenson, Michael R. Pearce and Joseph C. Shlesinger, *Power Retail: Winning Strategies from Chapters and other Leading Retailers in Canada* (Whitby, ON: McGraw-Hill Ryerson, 1999), p. 5.
2. Michael Treacy, *Double-Digit Growth* (New York: Penguin, 2003).
3. Statistics Canada, "Types of store retailers and surveys," http://www.statcan.ca/english/survey/business/storechain/types.htm. Accessed April 2, 2007.
4. John D. McKellar and Lisa Borsook, "Don't Go It Alone: The Top 10 Things to Know About Negotiating with Your Landlord," special presentation to the author (Toronto: WeirFoulds LLP, 2006).
5. Marina Strauss, Retailing Reporter—Toronto, "Indigo Eyeing More Toys to Boost Bottom Line" *Globe and Mail Report on Business*, September 20, 2006, p. B10.
6. Investorwords.com, "Optimization definition," http://www.investorwords.com/3474/optimization.html. Accessed April 2, 2007.
7. Thomas B. Wilson, *Rewards that Drive High Performance* (New York: AMACOM, 1999), p. 157.
8. Dana Flavelle, "One-Stop Shopping a Myth: Grocery Guru," *Toronto Star Business on Sunday*, October 22, 2006, p. A19.
9. TNS Retail Forward, *Retail Innovation: Ten Opportunities for 2010*, Retail Intelligence Conference, May 2005, Toronto, Ontario.
10. About: Retail Industry. "The Value of Interaction," http://retailindustry.about.com/od/crm_relationships/a/loyalty5actions.htm. Accessed April 2, 2007.
11. John Torella, *Whole-Being Retail Branding* (Toronto: J.C. Williams Group, 2003), pp. 14–15.

12. Sally Dibb, Lyndon P. Simkin, William M. Pride, and O.C. Ferrell, "Glossary," *Marketing*, fourth edition (Boston: Houghton Mifflin, 2000), http://users.wbs. warwick.ac.uk/dibb_simkin/student/glossary/ch09.html. Accessed April 2, 2007.

13. Answers.com, "Leroy 'Satchel' Paige," http://www.answers.com/topic/satchel-paige. Accessed April 2, 2007.

14. Doug Bruce and Derek Picard, "Succession Can Breed Success," *Canadian Federation of Independent Business Research*, June 2005.

15. Tara Perkins, "Business Exit Plan Is Needed," *Toronto Star*, February 12, 2006, p. A18.

16. Ellen Roseman, "Ins and Outs of Selling a Business," *Toronto Star*, March 4, 2007, p. A13.

INDEX

acquisitions and mergers, 22, 53, 278–79

advertising: costs, 151, 182–83, 209; outreach, 141–48; prices and, 57–58, 98, 100; successful, 122, 181, 233

advisers, 257–58, 262–67, 277–79, 283–84

airline industry, 51, 52

ambience, store, 18, 131–32, 169

assets, 214–15, 224, 227, 244–45, 253

associations, trade, 158, 233–34, 258, 272

attributes matrix, 47–48

automobile industry, 52, 144–45

baby boomers, 25, 51, 171, 183

banks, 173, 200, 214, 244–47, 249, 252

banners. *See* marketing

barriers to entry, 131, 151, 268–69

big box stores, 22–23, 51, 61, 66, 85

borrowing, 240, 244–48. *See also* debt

branding, 151, 205–11

budgets, 40, 130, 165, 273

businesses, small and medium-sized, 165–66, 249–50, 254–55

business life cycle, 267–76

business plan, 37–38, 269–70

business to business, 5–6, 143, 198, 207

business to consumer, 2, 5–7, 207, 235, 268

business to government, 6, 143

buyers, 83, 84, 186, 283–84

call centres, 116, 135, 142–43, 239

capital: equity, 255; expenditures, 133–34, 243; leases, 252; sources, 257–58; venture, 248–49; working, 26–27, 149, 157, 214–15, 217, 235–36. *See also* assets

cash, 214, 224, 226, 236–37, 243–44

cash flow, 2, 12, 13, 129, 218, 235–44, 250–51, 271, 276

cash registers, 12–17, 106, 201

catalogue retailers, 25, 82, 116, 129, 134, 137–38, 143, 184–85. *See also* Consumers Distributing

ALBERT C. PLANT, CMC, held executive positions with the T. Eaton Co. and Consumers Distributing Ltd. He then joined The Molson Companies as senior vice-president, a position that included the presidencies of companies such as Willson Office Specialty, Anthes Business Forms and Beaver Lumber. Following this he became CEO of the United Co-operatives of Ontario and later established his own management consulting business. Since 1995 he has been the retail industry advisor to RBC Royal Bank. Mr. Plant continues to advise new and established retailers regarding strategy and performance improvement. He was awarded an honorary life membership by the Canadian Association of Management Consultants in 2003.